New Governance for
Rural America

Rural America

Hal S. Barron
David L. Brown
Kathleen Neils Conzen
Carville Earle
Cornelia Butler Flora
Donald Worster

Series Editors

New Governance for Rural America

Creating Intergovernmental Partnerships

Beryl A. Radin
Robert Agranoff
Ann O'M. Bowman
C. Gregory Buntz
J. Steven Ott
Barbara S. Romzek
Robert H. Wilson

University Press of Kansas

Published by the University Press of Kansas (Lawrence, Kansas 66045),
which was organized by the Kansas Board of Regents and is operated
and funded by Emporia State University, Fort Hays State University,
Kansas State University, Pittsburg State University, the University of
Kansas, and Wichita State University

Library of Congress Cataloging-in-Publication Data

New governance for rural America : creating intergovernmental
    partnerships / Beryl A. Radin ... [et al.].
        p.   cm. — (Rural America)
    Includes bibliographical references (p.   ) and index.
    ISBN 978-0-7006-0770-9 (cloth : alk. paper)
    ISBN 978-0-7006-0771-6 (pbk. : alk. paper)
    1. National Rural Development Partnership (U.S.)   2. Rural
development—United States.   3. State-local relations—United
States.   4. Federal government—United States.   I. Radin, Beryl.
II. Series: Rural America (Lawrence, Kan.)
HN90.C6N477   1996
307.1'4'0973—dc20   95-46677

British Library Cataloguing in Publication Data is available.

Printed in the United States of America

10 9 8 7 6 5 4 3 2 1

The paper used in this publication meets the minimum requirements of the
American National Standard for Permanence of Paper for Printed Library
Materials Z39.48-1984.

Contents

Preface

This book was produced through a very unusual research process. Following the field network research strategy used elsewhere to track intergovernmental policy development, most of the authors were selected because their geographical location represented the states included in the original pilot effort. Only a few of the seven authors had worked together before the four-year research effort culminating in *New Governance for Rural America*.

It is not often that a group of seven senior researchers can put egos aside and write a book together! We were committed to practicing, not simply writing about, the art of collaborative work—the subject of our research. What started out as a group of individuals selected for the sake of convenience evolved into a cohesive collaborative team.

This transformation was achieved by means of two- to three-day meetings held twice a year, which provided us with the opportunity to work in a highly interactive fashion to develop detailed research designs, instruments, and formats for presenting data, and to share our findings and build comparisons. We worked hard, but also found time to socialize and explore restaurants (usually in Washington, D.C.). A set of warm personal relationships has resulted that we hope will lead to future collaborative work.

Acknowledgments

This volume was nurtured and supported over many years by several institutions and countless people. Dewitt John was responsible for generating the original research activity that provided the study with funds from the Ford Foundation through the Aspen Institute's program on state policy. W. Robert Lovan of the U.S. Department of Agriculture was a key figure in providing support for subsequent work through the Economic Research Service of USDA. Along the way, David Sears, Tom Rowley, and other federal officials gave us support.

We are most appreciative of the time and interest of individuals in government positions and private agencies, as well as others involved in the Rural Development Partnership around the United States, who gave us access to information and were willing to engage in dialogue about the Partnership's development.

Finally, we valued the insights of the review process within the University Press of Kansas, particularly the assistance of B. J. Reed for his comments on the manuscript.

Abbreviations

State Rural Development Councils

AKRDC	Alaska Rural Development Council
ARRDC	Arkansas Rural Development Council
CRDC	Colorado Rural Development Council
FSRDC	Florida State Rural Development Council
IARDC	Iowa Rural Development Council
INRDC	Indiana Rural Development Council
IRP	Illinois Rural Partners
IRDC	Idaho Rural Development Council
KRDC	Kansas Rural Development Council
KYRDC	Kentucky Rural Development Council
LARDC	Louisiana Rural Development Council
MARDC	Massachusetts Rural Development Council
MDRDC	Maryland Rural Development Council
MoROC	Missouri Rural Opportunities Council
MRDC	Maine Rural Development Council
MSRDC	Mississippi Rural Development Council
MTRDC	Montana Rural Development Council
NCRDC	North Carolina Rural Development Council
NDRDC	North Dakota Rural Development Council
NHRDC	New Hampshire Rural Development Council
NMRDRC	New Mexico Rural Development Response Council
NRDC	Nebraska Rural Development Commission
NYRDC	New York Rural Development Council
OHRDP	Ohio Rural Development Partnership
OKRDC	Oklahoma Rural Development Council
ORDC	Oregon Rural Development Council
PARDC	Pennsylvania Rural Development Council
RDCM	Rural Development Council of Michigan
SCRDC	South Carolina Rural Development Council
SDRDC	South Dakota Rural Development Council

TRDC	Texas Rural Development Council
URDC	Utah Rural Development Council
VCRD	Vermont Council on Rural Development
WSRDC	Washington State Rural Development Council
WRDC	Wisconsin Rural Development Council
WVRDC	West Virginia Rural Development Council
WYRDC	Wyoming Rural Development Council

Washington, D.C., Components

NRDP	National Rural Development Partnership (formerly National Rural Development Initiative)
NRDC	National Rural Development Council (formerly Monday Management Group)
PCG-WGRD	Policy Coordinating Group–Working Group on Rural Development

Other

CDBG	Community Development Block Grants
CGPA	Council of Governors' Policy Advisors
COG	Council of Governments
DOL	Department of Labor
DOC	Department of Commerce
EC	Enterprise Community
EDA	Economic Development Administration
EDD	Economic Development District
EPA	Environmental Protection Administration
ERS	Economic Research Service, USDA
EZ	Empowerment Zone
FAC	Food and Agriculture Councils, USDA
FEMA	Federal Emergency Management Administration
FHA	Federal Housing Administration
FmHA	Farmers Home Administration
HHS	Department of Health and Human Services
HUD	Department of Housing and Urban Development
ISTEA	Intermodal Surface Transportation Efficiency Act

JTPA	Jobs Training Partnership Act
MOU	Memorandum of Understanding
NAL	National Agriculture Library
NAPA	National Academy of Public Administration
NCARDP	National Commission on Agriculture and Rural Development Policy
NEA	National Endowment for the Arts
NRFDI	National Rural Economic Development Institute
NGA	National Governors' Association
PCRA	President's Council on Rural America
RC&D	Resource Conservation and Development Districts
RDA	Rural Development Administration
RDI	Rural Development Institute
RIC	Rural Information Center
REA	Rural Electrification Administrator
SBA	Small Business Administration
SCORE	Small Business Administration Service Corps of Retired Executives
SCS	Soil Conservation Service

Introduction

This book provides an analysis of an uncommon set of intergovernmental activities that took place in the four years between 1990 and 1994 (and continues today). It focuses on the development of an approach to intergovernmental decision making and change that, when put into place, had no popular name. Since then, however, it has been described as the "new governance."

This is a story of governmental problem solving by an unusual group of public and private officials, located in Washington, D.C., as well as across the states and communities, committed to improving the life chances of rural Americans. In early 1990, the Bush administration embarked on a rural development initiative that, on its face, looked much like past attempts to "do something" about rural America. In the past, policy changes had emerged from various administrations but disappeared as those administrations left office. According to several of its participants, the effort was an example "of what can be achieved through a modest investment, coupled with determined action to bring about a new way of conducting the public's business. . . . [It provides] the opportunity to usher in a significant, if gentle, revolution in the public sector" (Reid and Lovan, 1993, p. 1).

Among the efforts undertaken by the Bush administration was the creation of state-level Rural Development Councils that would coordinate rural development efforts among federal departments and agencies and establish collaborative relationships with states, local governments, and the private sector. The six elements within the Bush initiative included the creation of a President's Council on Rural America; establishment of a Working Group on Rural Development as a subgroup of the cabinet-level White House Economic Policy Council; creation of a Rural Development Technical Assistance Center and Hot Line; a rural development demonstration program; and an effort to target rural development programs on specific activities.

By the end of 1990, State Rural Development Councils (SRDCs) were established in eight states: Kansas, Maine, Mississippi, Oregon,

South Carolina, South Dakota, Texas, and Washington. By mid-1994, despite the change of administration that had occurred during the four years that had ensued, SRDCs were operating in twenty-nine states and in the process of organization in ten others. In addition, the Washington, D.C.–based interagency activity that also began in 1990—a group that was called the National Rural Development Council (NRDC)—continued with representatives from sixty agencies involved in the process.

Two Perspectives

In the process of analyzing this set of activities, we have highlighted two perspectives that help to understand its development: the intergovernmental perspective and the rural development policy perspective.

Intergovernmental Relationships

Federalism in the United States has been characterized by constantly changing expectations about the relationships between levels of government and accusations about the appropriateness of behaviors of federal, state, or local governments (Wright, 1988). The tension between federal level concerns for the creation of control systems and demands for autonomy (particularly by state governments) has surfaced on a regular—indeed predictable—basis. Depending on the political philosophy that is predominant, the pendulum has swung between bottom-up approaches (where the federal government defers to states or localities through mechanisms such as block grants) and top-down approaches (where the federal government emphasizes compliance with national requirements or standards).

By contrast, this policy initiative has attempted to reconcile the two sets of demands and established mechanisms that build on both Washington-based and state-based institutions and perspectives. While it does not avoid the natural tension between various participants in the intergovernmental process, it has attempted to devise mechanisms that manage that conflict along both vertical (federal, state, and local) and horizontal (interagency) dimensions.

Efforts to measure "success" in a variety of domestic policy areas are often stymied by the diverse perspectives and expectations of those involved in the venture (Berman, 1978). Diversity has many different elements. It relates to the heterogeneity of the United States itself and the variation across the country related to dramatically different demographic, geographic, and historical patterns. It relates to the different realities of federal, state, and local officials and of individuals who work at the community level. In addition, tribal, nonprofit, and for-profit representatives have different values and agendas. Diversity in this case also relates to the different time periods when the councils were organized. Although the study duration is less than five years, three different generations of councils appeared during this period and provide a sense of a life cycle of change efforts and diffusion of innovation.

Concern about the ability of the federal government to organize itself to make difficult choices has been heard in many corners in the 1990s (Osborne and Gaebler, 1992; Gore Report, 1993; Winter Commission Report, 1993). Over the past few years, expectations have changed dramatically about what governments should do and how they should do it. Whether as a result of economic shifts, technological development, or the globalization of our planet, there is clear dissatisfaction about past government solutions. This sentiment has been heard in many quarters: in the popular press, in the institutions of government, and in the offices and agencies where public employees are found. In many areas, it has become clear that the boundaries between the public and private sectors of society are much less clear than we once believed.

Some students of government have described this situation as a combination of "mismatches and fragmentation" (John, 1992). Fragmentation is viewed as a serious problem in a number of policy areas. For example, economic development, workforce training, and human services policy are hampered by the multiplicity of programs and institutional actors that must be involved in change. The search for new ways of doing the public's business has provoked a series of experiments across the country. While not originally defined as one of these experiments, the rural development initiative represented an approach that provided a sense of energy and possibility for constructive change before the reinvention concept and movement became the language of the day.

Several other elements that are associated with "new governance" are illustrated in the rural development activities. They emphasized efforts that cross traditional boundary lines (both in terms of level of government and in terms of public-private relationships), arguing that all major stakeholders in rural development must be participants in the process (Cigler, 1990). The initiative utilized what has been called a "network" approach that includes involvement of a wide array of participants (an open, inclusive approach to participation) and processes that emphasize collaboration and partnerships, giving all participants an opportunity to participate on equal terms. The effort also viewed the overall process as a "learning system" where feedback and information about performance are important elements.

Building on the work of Osborne and Gaebler, others have called for new approaches to make the needed changes. They emphasize four dimensions of change: Changing the participants in the process of providing public service or changing the ways that the parties interact (building alliances and collaboration instead of fragmentation, decentralizing decisions about decision and purposes); redefining the purposes of public action (focusing on mission not program, on results not inputs, on customers' perceptions of what they need rather than agency views); changing the means that agencies use to accomplish these purposes (focusing on investments not spending, providing more autonomy and collaboration for frontline workers, emphasizing quality not just efficiency, and calling for entrepreneurial management and experimentation); and changing the politics that guide public action (engaging and empowering citizens rather than announcing and directing initiatives) (John, 1992).

While the architects of the rural development initiative were not originally conscious of these broader concepts, they emphasized nine elements or principles in their work that reflect the new governance approach.

- All major stakeholders in rural development must be participants. These include, in addition to the Federal government, states, local governments, tribal governments, and especially the private and non-profit sectors.
- Participants are instructed to establish a process for dialogue among stakeholders. All must be able to participate on equal terms, with none dominating the process.
- Flexibility and local responsibility are by-words of the process. Each state council is free to establish its own organization, operating procedures, and goals, so long as they do not violate the basic principles of equality of participation.
- Collaborative partnerships among participating organizations are emphasized and encouraged. Significant attention is given to understanding the resources of other organizations and to establishing effective cohesion among them.

- The process is to continue only so long as it is effective. No permanent structures are created, and continuation of the initiative—as well as responsibility for funding it—is left in the hands of its participants.
- Empowering local problem-solving is emphasized. State councils are encouraged to tackle interagency problems on their own authority. Within the limits of their authority, Federal participants are expected to be entrepreneurial in meeting state and local needs. Only in the few cases that issues cannot be solved at the state level are they to be passed to the Federal level.
- A strategic approach to long-term development is essential. Councils are encouraged to lay the groundwork for long-term investments, and only undertake short-term projects that contribute to fundamental, long-term goals.
- Experimentation is viewed as essential to creativity. Because the initiative is seen as a new way of doing business, state councils were started on a pilot basis. Experimentation with new actions and methods is on-going.
- An environment that encourages information-based, learning-oriented action is critical to achieving both creativity and adaptability in the face of modern social challenges. Creating "learning organizations" is a watchword for the initiative. (Reid and Lovan, 1993, pp. 2–3)

The Rural Development Policy Issue

Since the Kennedy administration, there has been a series of initiatives undertaken by successive presidents to focus on the problems of citizens who live in rural America. Many of the problems that were confronted by rural America may have once been directly related to an agricultural economy and society. But by the second half of the twentieth century, the rapid increase in technology and distribution patterns severed much of that agricultural linkage. It was increasingly obvious that these communities required a different approach than that which emerged from the agricultural sector (Long 1987).

Until very recently, rural policy was defined in institutional and substantive terms that emerged from the New Deal era. Effectively, "rural" was synonymous with "agriculture"; it was assumed that interventions in agricultural production and distribution would lead to improved conditions for Americans who lived in rural areas.

By the 1970s it was clear that this strategy would not work. The proportion of rural workers employed in the natural resource industries fell steadily during this period and growing competition within the global marketplace also undercut attempts to bring industries to rural areas.

Some states took actions that had the effect of increasing their role in the delivery of public resources for rural development and governors and legislatures made the issue a part of their policy agenda (Roberts, 1990). Others, however, found it difficult to focus on issues that were defined narrowly as "rural" or, in the case of agricultural states, defined as more than agriculture.

A part of the federal strategy over these years was, thus, to create mechanisms to target rural development assistance outside of the U.S. Department of Agriculture (USDA). These mechanisms focused on community development, human resource development, and economic development. In the 1960s, programs included the Appalachian Regional Commission and the Economic Development Administration, as well as various efforts within the Office of Economic Opportunity. But another part of the strategy was targeted at USDA itself and approaches within the department that would support a shift from a purely agricultural agency to one with a broader rural focus. This focus, by definition, reached beyond the federal government to involve a range of other intergovernmental actors. The Rural Development Act of 1972 attempted such an effort as did activities during the Carter administration (including the creation of thirteen State Rural Development Councils). Carter initiated a study of rural development policy that concluded that the federal effort was not really a policy thrust but was, rather, a compilation of individual programs (Effland, 1993; Doherty, 1980). During the Reagan years, however, little was done to support these activities and budget stringencies provided the opportunity to eliminate efforts in this direction.

By 1990, despite disagreements about the form of an initiative, various elements could agree that something had to be done about rural America. Attention to these problems emerged from both Congress and the White House as a divided government sought to claim its attention to the problems of rural Americans. The 1990 Farm Bill largely crafted by Democratic members of Congress included provisions authorizing the creation of a separate Rural Development Administration in USDA. And in January 1990, President Bush announced the steps his administration would take "to strengthen the delivery of Federal support for rural development." The administration gave then-Secretary of Agriculture Clayton Yeutter instructions "to implement six proposals designed to improve the coordination of rural development programs and serve as a catalyst for future initiatives" (White House, Office of the Press Secretary, January 22, 1990).

According to one administration official, the Bush activity was conceptualized as a response to fundamental changes involving rural America. "It is well recognized that rural America has been going through some difficult times. While the national economy performed well over the last decade, rural employment and income growth lagged. Many rural citizens have moved away to the cities, leaving behind the aging and more poorly educated. These conditions . . . have resulted from basic and well-documented trends in the international marketplace that now put less value on what rural America has traditionally produced" (Hill, 1991).

After achieving the support of the governor, each of the councils was initially organized by the state Farmers Home Administration director and included a variety of federal officials located within the state (or in a regional office) as well as individuals from various segments of each of the states. Each council was expected to reflect membership from five partnership groups: federal officials, state officials, local government, tribal representatives, and the private sector.

Rural Development: A Working Definition

Given the diverse contexts in which policy change is placed, it would be erroneous—indeed foolhardy—to attempt to fit rural development into a single unified mold. It is clear that contextual differences create definitions and meanings that have very different constructions in the multifold settings across the United States. Beyond this, however, are further definitional traps. The array of voices that have been heard over the past few years expressing some level of interest in the rural development policy issue serves as the source for a greater understanding of the nature of the issue at hand.

It has become obvious that the boundaries for rural development are neither firm nor precise. While emphasizing the importance of providing new economic opportunities for their rural citizens, few participants in the process are sure about the means to achieve this goal. In some settings, the term "rural development" has become a subset of broader economic development activities and emphasizes issues of loans, grants, infrastructure issues, and forms of entrepreneurship development. Value-added approaches to existing agricultural production are also emphasized in this approach. In other settings, the term is closely linked to community development activities, particularly leadership development and efforts to mobilize hitherto disenfranchised citizens. Still other states focused on areas of human investment, particularly education.

Unlike some other policy issues, state policies involving rural development do not lend themselves to clear definition. Indeed, the closer one gets to rural issues, the more complex and variable one realizes that they are. In a nation as diverse as the United States, rural development questions confront variability by state and, in many instances, within states. It is challenging to find comparabilities between the frontier and mineral problems faced in the West and the plantation heritage of the old South. The rural populations of timber areas and southern small towns share little with the urban or suburban residents of their states. While some regional patterns can be identified, states that are contiguous to one another exhibit very different problems, responses, and programs. There are important differences between the economic and demographic conditions of the South, the Midwest and the far West. But even the seemingly similar agricultural background of the Midwest and current patterns of population decline produce states that define problems and solutions in very different ways.

As attention has been given to these issues over the past few years, some patterns have emerged. These patterns speak to increased attention to the problems of rural citizens in various settings: in state governments, local and community organizations and agencies, in the for-profit and nonprofit worlds. But while one can find these emerging outlines, state councils had to create definitions for themselves and determine relevance to specific programs and policies that address the needs of rural Americans. Indeed, given the variability of conditions and contexts around the country, it is not always clear whether one approach is better than any other.

This study employed a definition of rural development, listening to the approaches taken by the councils that included both economic development and community development strategies.

The Methodology and Study Approach

Since 1991, a team of academics has been engaged in the study of Rural Development Councils and associated Washington-based activities. Utilizing a variation on the field network methodology, (see Nathan,

1982; Agranoff and Radin, 1991), the team was organized to monitor the original eight pilot states during their initial period of activities. The original study of the eight pilot states was supported by the Ford Foundation through the State Policy Program of the Aspen Institute. The continuing study was funded by the Economic Research Service of the U.S. Department of Agriculture and the Aspen Institute. As the effort itself expanded, the study was enlarged to include eight additional states—sixteen states in total. The data collection for the study included extensive interviews with council participants, analysis of written materials, and observation at various meetings. In addition, data was collected on Washington-based activities, including in-depth interviews with participants in the interagency National Rural Development Council.

The data collection approach was devised to capture the multiple perspectives of the participants in the process, providing both a bottom-up (participants in the sixteen councils) as well as a top-down (Washington-based participants) vantage point.

The organization of the study itself emphasized a high degree of collaboration and interaction. Each member of the study team was responsible for at least one and up to four case studies of individual SRDCs. Regular team meetings provided the setting for the exchange of data (allowing a comparative analysis) as well as the formulation of conclusions and generalizations. This volume is itself an expression of a collaborative approach. Almost all of the chapters were jointly drafted by two team members; all members of the team had the opportunity to provide feedback on drafts.

Organization of the Book

The first two chapters of this book provide the context for the study and place the effort in a broader framework, emphasizing the literature and issues that inform the discussion. The first chapter focuses on intergovernmental relationships and behaviors while the second deals with the rural development policy issue. The third chapter focuses on the sixteen state councils that were included in the study and provides a picture of their demographic, economic, and political background, as well as their council organization. Chapter 4 analyzes the evolution of the initiative and the council concept. The SRDCs as intergovernmental networks are the subject of Chapter 5; Chapter 6 analyzes the activities that

were undertaken by the councils. Expectations and outcomes are discussed in Chapter 7. The final chapter revisits the perspectives from the
introduction and emphasizes an analysis of the initiative as an example
of "new governance."

Given the dynamic of constant change, the analysis that is provided
in this volume must be taken with a caveat. The situations that are
described at the point of completion of the research are likely to have
changed at the time of publication, reflecting the range of political,
social, and economic changes that constantly occur both within the
states and in the national government. However, while the details may
have shifted, the dynamic that is described continues.

References

Agranoff, Robert, and Beryl A. Radin. 1991. "The Comparative Case Study
    Approach in Public Administration." *Research in Public Administration*
    203–31, JAI Press.
Berman, Paul. 1978. "The Study of Macro- and Micro Implementation." *Public
    Policy* 26 (2), 157–83 (spring).
Cigler, Beverly A. 1990. "Public Administration and the Paradox of Professionali-
    zation." *Public Administration Review* (November / December), 637–53.
Doherty, J. C. 1980. "The countryside comes into its own." *Planning* (May),
    16–18.
Effland, Anne B. 1993. "Federal Rural Development Policy Since 1972." *Rural
    Development Prospectives* 9, 8–14.
Gore, Albert. 1993. *Creating a Government that Works Better and Costs Less: Report of
    the National Performance Review.* Washington, D.C.: U.S. Government Print-
    ing Office (September 7).
Hill, Walter E. 1991. "Making Rural Policy for the 1990s and Beyond: A Federal
    Government View." Paper presented at the Annual Agricultural Outlook
    Conference, Washington, D.C.
John, Dewitt, and Robert Lovan. 1992. New governance for rural development.
    Unpublished manuscript.
Long, Richard W. 1987. "Rural Development Policy: Rationale and Reality." *Pub-
    lius* 17 (fall), 15–31.
Nathan, Richard P., 1982. "The Methodology for Field Network Evaluation Stud-
    ies." In W. Williams, ed., *Studying Implementation.* Chatham, N.J.: Chatham
    House.
Osborne, David, and Ted Gaebler. 1992. *Reinventing Government.* Reading, Mass.:
    Addison-Wesley.

Reid, J. Norman, and W. Robert Lovan. 1993. "Reinventing Rural America: 'The New Governance.'" Presented at the Annual Conference of the American Planning Association, Chicago, Ill. (May 4).

Roberts, Brandon. 1990. *States: Catalysts for Development in Rural America.* Washington, D.C.: Council of State Community Affairs Agencies.

The White House, Office of the Press Secretary. January 22, 1990.

Winter, William. 1993. *Hard Truths/Tough Choices: An Agenda for State and Local Reform.* Albany, N.Y.: Rockefeller Institute.

Wright, Deil S. 1988. *Understanding Intergovernmental Relations.* 3rd ed. Pacific Grove, Calif.: Brooks/Cole.

Additional Readings

Radin, Beryl A. 1995. *Intergovernmental Partnerships and Rural Development: Profiles of Twenty-Nine State Rural Development Councils.* National Rural Development Partnership, Washington, D.C. (May).

Radin, Beryl A., Robert Agranoff, Ann O'M. Bowman, C. Gregory Buntz, J. Steven Ott, Barbara S. Romzek, and Robert Wilson. 1995. *Intergovernmental Partnerships and Rural Development: An Overview Assessment of the National Rural Development Partnership.* Economic Research Service Staff Paper, Number 95508 (April).

Radin, Beryl A., Robert Agranoff, Ann O'M. Bowman, C. Gregory Buntz, J. Steven Ott, Barbara S. Romzek, Thomas Sykes, and Robert Wilson. 1995. *Intergovernmental Partnerships and Rural Development: State Rural Development Councils in Sixteen States.* National Rural Development Partnership, Washington, D.C. (May).

1 | Intergovernmental Relationships
Tensions and the Search for Solutions

INTERGOVERNMENTAL RELATIONSHIPS and federalism are rarely the subject of press headlines in the United States. Yet the issues and problems that concern relationships between levels of government underpin much of what has been debated in American domestic policy during most of the twentieth century. While American political leaders conduct their debates around specific policy issues (such as welfare, education, or rural development), they are constantly grappling with broader dimensions of the institutional roles of federal, state or local governments.

It is obvious that federalism is an essential part of the American political culture; it is embedded in the structure of the U.S. political system and institutions, codified in its Constitution and legal framework, and integrated into its basic decision-making processes. But despite its close association with core American values, the concept of federalism is often unclear, cloaked with conflicting perspectives, and constantly changing. It is characterized by accusations about the appropriateness of roles of actors within the system. It is often a captive of the political philosophy that is predominant and, tied to changes in political power, swings back and forth between approaches that emphasize values of flexibility and autonomy of state or local actors and those that emphasize values of accountability for expenditure of federal dollars.

This chapter focuses on a variety of issues that stem from the relationships and behaviors between levels of governments and other actors in the American political system. It highlights the intergovernmental lens as an approach to understanding federalism in action; it reviews the legacy of problems that surround the relationships among these actors; it discusses an array of possible instrumentalities to deal with these problems; and it reviews developments in the current intergovernmental environment, particularly those around the new governance or reinventing government movement of the Clinton administration. Finally, the general patterns in intergovernmental relationships are illustrated by focusing on the rural policy sector.

The Intergovernmental Lens

For many years, scholars of federalism emphasized two conceptual approaches to their study of relationships between levels of government: the legal or structural approach and the study of fiscal relationships between jurisdictions. The legal or structural approach concentrated on the constitutional system of shared and separate powers defined by type of institution as well as level of government and the allocation of formal responsibilities and authorities within that system. The study of fiscal relationships focused on the allocation of taxing responsibilities and the patterns of transferring funds from one level of government to another.

As Deil Wright has noted, from the New Deal on, public officials and scholars have used the term *intergovernmental relations* to describe another conceptual approach to the study of relationships between governments. This approach focuses on the activities or interactions between governmental units of all types and levels within the United States (Wright, 1988, p. 12). Several elements emerge from this approach: an inclusive approach to define governmental units, an assessment of the actions and attitudes of officials, the modes of regular interaction among officials, and the relationship between policy issues and these relationships. Wright comments that this approach "makes visible the varied colors, terrain, and patterns on the political landscape that were previously obscured" (Wright, 1988, p. 39). Robert Agranoff has argued that it is now common for scholars and practitioners to focus on intergovernmental relationships because nations are increasingly managing the interdependencies between their units of government (Agranoff, 1992).

But despite the widespread use of this term, there is not agreement within the field nor conceptual clarity about what it means. The term is frequently used interchangeably with others; Wright notes that many authors do not feel the need to define it or to distinguish it from federalism, new federalism, cooperative federalism, and similar terms. (Wright, 1988, p. 13; Stewart, 1982).

There are several reasons for this conceptual messiness. Although most students of federalism in the United States will agree that fragmented powers are a point of departure for understanding the American system, they differ in the conceptual model that may be used to "map" the relationships between the national (usually called federal), state, and local levels of government. Deil Wright (1988) has noted that there are at least three models that have been used to describe these relationships (see Figure 1.1). The *inclusive authority* model assumes that the national government plays the superior role and will control dealings with other levels of government. The *coordinate authority* model emphasizes the autonomy of states; local governments are viewed as total creatures of the state and the national government's dealings with the state assumes that both parties are separate and distinct. The *overlapping authority* model, by contrast, conveys several messages: many areas of policy require national, state, and local involvement; the areas of autonomy and discretion for any single jurisdiction are limited; and levels of governments require bargaining and negotiation to obtain adequate power and influence to carry out programs (Hanf, 1978; Agranoff, 1990).

Some have argued that use of these models changes over time; that is, that one or another more accurately defines relationships between levels of government during a particular era. Others have noted that the choice of one of these models represents a particular set of policy or political interests. For example, it is most common for the National Governors' Association (NGA) to approach issues from the perspective of the coordinate authority model because that model protects the autonomy of state governments. Others seeking national responsibility for a

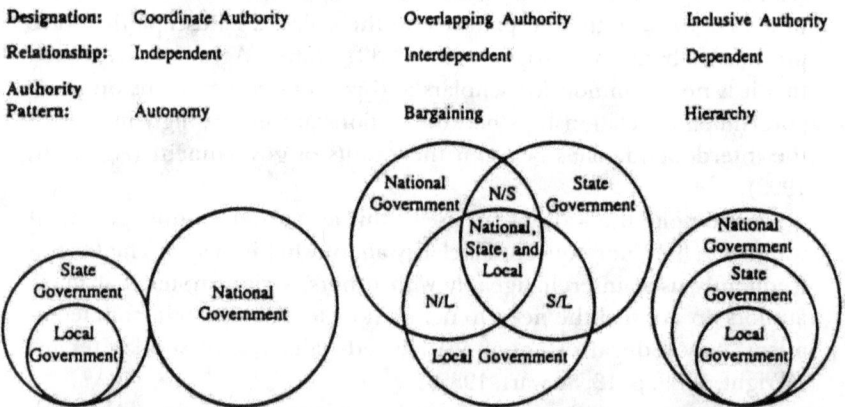

Designation:	Coordinate Authority	Overlapping Authority	Inclusive Authority
Relationship:	Independent	Interdependent	Dependent
Authority Pattern:	Autonomy	Bargaining	Hierarchy

Figure 1.1. Models of National, State, and Local Relationships (Wright, 1988, p. 40).

policy issue (such as Social Security) would argue for a variation on the inclusive authority model.

Similarly, there are different substantive approaches to the study of relationships between governments that contribute to the lack of conceptual clarity in this field. A structural approach to the topic would emphasize the formal lines of authority that separate or relate one level of government to another. This approach might concentrate on formal methods of delegation of power, hierarchical lines of authority, and methods of defining and stipulating specific prerogatives of particular jurisdictions. Those who lead with this approach often argue for clarity in relationships between governments, searching for neat definition of roles and responsibilities. If conflict occurred between governments, then a mechanism would be put into operation (such as the Supreme Court) to determine who would be the clear winner or loser in the situation.

By contrast, a behavioral approach to intergovernmental relationships would emphasize the processes of decision making and the relationships that develop between participants in the process. This approach would deemphasize the "hat" that a particular player would wear and, instead, would concentrate on the imperative of coming to a decision. This approach tends to accentuate mechanisms such as coordination to facilitate decision making.

The third substantive approach focuses on the development of relationships between government in terms of specific policy issues. It does not search for consistency across policy areas but, instead, conducts the search for solutions in terms that engage only the specialized interests and concerns related to the issue at hand. This approach results in what is often called "picket fence" federalism (a term coined by former North Carolina governor Terry Sanford), defined by Wright as a set of separate alliances "between like-minded program specialists or professionals, regardless of the level of government in which they serve" (Wright, 1988, p. 83). These alliances cross institutional lines as well as levels of government; at the national level, they have produced what have been called "iron triangles"—relationships between three sets of actors around a particular program or policy area: interest groups, congressional committees and subcommittees, and career bureaucrats (see Figure 1.2).

Actors within the intergovernmental system tend to choose an approach that best reflects their particular interests. Interest groups that

Congressional
Committees
and
Subcommittees

Interest Groups

Bureaucracies

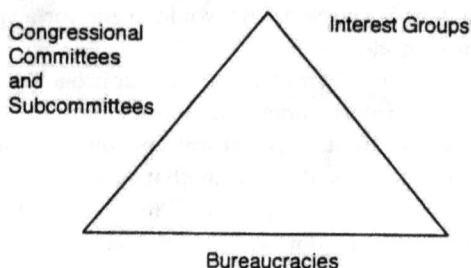

Figure 1.2. Iron Triangle Relationships.

represent particular jurisdictions (such as the National Governors' Association, the National League of Cities, the National Association of Counties) might emphasize the structural approach because of their interest in protecting their authority and autonomy. And differences are often found between actors that operate at the state and local levels. Politicians who attempt to reach a decision or address a problem are likely to be open to information and participation by actors if they are able to provide useful information or speak for constituent interests. Policy specialists emphasize professional values and are most likely to engage in the debate in technical terms and speak to those who share their worldview.

Given this cacophony of interests and approaches, it is not surprising that the debate around intergovernmental relations has been both unstable and conflictual. The instrumentalities that have been used to develop relationships between levels of government reflect social expectations that produce diverse and often conflicting goals. The strategies that have been employed have had difficulty addressing interdependencies between issues and actors. Rather than providing a way for federalism to function as a mediating institution within a diverse society with multiple and conflicting interests (Elazar, 1987, pp. 195–96), these approaches to federalism have produced what the founding fathers intended. They tend to exacerbate the fragmentation of the American political system, to exclude rather than include interested parties, and to minimize opportunities for cooperation or collaboration across jurisdictions or policy systems.

Over the past decade, however, another approach has developed around intergovernmental relations that emphasizes the importance of bargaining, negotiation, and networking as essential processes of decision making rather than traditional hierarchical command and control approaches or formal structures as venues for decision making. This approach flows from the overlapping authority model and highlights a movement away from a "sorting-out" of intergovernmental roles to an interdependent approach. It focuses on the development of interorganizational networks that include both governmental and nongovernmental actors and proceeds along a path that includes the acceptance of the independent and separate character of the various members, avoidance of superior–subordinate relationships, interfacing of political and career actors, inclusion of appropriate specialists when needed to focus on technical issues, and agreement to abide by tasks and goals (Agranoff, 1986).

This approach includes both the process and substantive nature of contemporary issues. It suggests that different processes must be used to reach decisions. But it also draws on the policy notion of issue networks. This concept, developed by Hugh Heclo, is viewed as a "web" of largely autonomous participants with variable degrees of mutual commitment or dependence on each other. Heclo focuses on the hybrid interests which provoke such alliances. He notes:

> With more public policies, more groups are being mobilized and there are more complex relationships among them. Since very few policies seem to drop off the public agenda as more are added, congestion among those interested in various issues grows, the chances for accidental collisions increase, and the interaction tends to take on a distinctive group-life of its own in the Washington community. (Heclo, 1979, p. 102)

The networks, according to Heclo,

> comprise a large number of participants, with quite variable degrees of mutual commitment or of independence on others in their environment; in fact, it is almost impossible to say where a network leaves off and the environment begins. . . . Participants move in and out of the network constantly. Rather than groups united in dominance over a program, no one, as far as one can tell, is in control of the policies and issues. . . . Network members reinforce each other's sense of issues as their interests, rather than (as standard political or economic models would have it) interests defining positions on issues. (p. 102)

The issue network approach provides a way to include various interests in a process, cutting both horizontally (across multiple issues) as well as vertically (down the intergovernmental chain). It also establishes a framework that is responsive to the transient nature of policy coalitions, with various networks established for a particular situation but dissolved when that situation changes. Unlike the changes that have been unsuccessfully attempted through structural solutions, the issue network appears attractive as an alternative path.

While this approach has intrigued intergovernmental scholars, it has not been used extensively in the world of practice. Intergovernmental dialogue continues to be characterized by a focus on separate programs, policies, or organizations and a search for clarity and simplicity in the delineation of roles and responsibilities. The debate around intergovernmental issues has been waged at two often contradictory levels: a general, macro and sometimes symbolic approach and, sometimes at the same time, a specific policy approach. Both, however, reflect the high political stakes that are frequently involved in the determination of lines of authority as well as allocation of resources. As a result, the intergovernmental terrain has been subject to constant uprooting that reflects the ideology and political agenda of the party and officials in power.

The Nature of Intergovernmental Problems

During the past three decades there have been two major issues in the intergovernmental debate in the United States: autonomy versus control and collaboration versus competition. These areas of debate have occurred at various levels of government; they have affected the relationships between the federal government and states, states and localities, and the federal government and localities.

Each of these two areas has sparked predictable questions. The autonomy versus control debate asks two main questions that involve the vertical relationships between levels of government: to what extent should higher levels of government empower lower levels then get out of the way so that they can get their jobs done? And to what extent should the payer of the piper call the tune? There is no simple answer to these questions. Over time federal and state legislators and executive branch officials have found it more workable to maintain the tether of financial and programmatic constraints than to let it go. Likewise, it isn't easy to answer the question about the relationship between funding and requirements.

The answer to this query depends on where one sits and which political philosophy is predominant. A federal official might be expected to say, "Use federal funds to implement federally created programs and expect to be accountable to us about the way funds are spent." By contrast, a state-level counterpart might say, "Just give us the money and we'll respond to the needs of our citizens, not to the perceptions that are popular inside the beltway." The problem is one of degree: how much autonomy and how much control? That there must be some level of control (some might call it accountability) of states receiving federal funds or cities or counties receiving state funds is not in dispute. But there is dispute about the extent to which that accountability gives the higher level of government the right to tell those at lower levels what to do in every instance. In recent times, the issue has been defined as a problem of unfunded mandates; state and local officials argue that they have been required by the federal government to adopt particular policy and program directions without federal resources. The angst about this conflict is felt in Washington as well as in statehouses, county courthouses, and city halls throughout the country.

The second element of the debate is focused on behavioral rather than structural questions. It also centers on the horizontal dimension of intergovernmental relations. Is interagency coordination more than a rhetorical device? Is it really possible to devise effective working relationships among agencies? Can agencies in the same business, but that compete for budget dollars and legislative and executive attention, engage in collaborative problem solving? Can they find ways to effectively manage their differences and produce wise agreements that advance the interests of the constituencies they are intended to serve? Intragovernmental collaboration is as vexing a problem as is the payer-tune issue. Taken together, empowering pipers, and expecting them to play together seems contradictory, but without true empowerment the intergovernmental tune will continue to be discordant and much too piercing.

A Historical Analysis

Prior to the Civil War, as Walker (1981; 1995) observes, the states were much more active than the federal government in areas such as economic development. The federal approach was "hands-off," thus the pendulum was virtually at rest on the autonomy side of the ledger. Dual federalism, connoting a distinct separation among the functions and responsibilities of the levels of government, was the operative model through the early 1930s. The assumption was that the powers of federal, state, and local officials were mutually exclusive. Moreover, as Wright argues (1988), the search for the boundaries of these powers was played out in an environment of competition and conflict. The federalism metaphor for this era was "layer cake federalism." The term signified the separations among the institutions and functions of the three levels of government. The functional role of the national government grew in the latter part of this dual federalism period. Most significantly, the federal government moved away from its laissez-faire role in economic development to a much more active role as regulator of the economic system. Concurrently, the state and local governments retained important functions such as education, public welfare, and public hospitals.

The growth of federal grants to state and local government also signaled a change in intergovernmental relationships. By 1930, fifteen federal grant programs were in place, indicating the transition to a more cooperative period. According to Wright (1988), it was during this time (the 1930s, 1940s, and early 1950s) that "complementary and supportive relationships [among intergovernmental actors] were most prominent and had high political significance" (p. 71).

Shared functions were characteristic of this phase, described by Morton Grodzins's popular "marble cake" metaphor. Grodzins (1961) argued that "no important function of government was the exclusive province of one of the levels, not even what may be regarded the most national of national functions, such as foreign relations; not even the most local of local functions, such as police protection and park maintenance" (p. 8).

The influence of the federal government expanded considerably during this period as it took on new roles of regulator, reformer, and promoter of the economy. The states, however, were not wholly dominated by the federal government, even given the substantial strings attached to conditional federal grants-in-aid. Indeed, as Wright (1988) points out, there is much evidence to support the notion that this period saw a strengthening of the capacity of state governments to respond more effectively to the needs of their citizens. The state role was not simply that of compliant recipient of federal funds. States emerged as partners with the federal government in the American system of governance. Collaboration, cooperation, and mutual assistance characterized the behavior of participants in the intergovernmental arena during this time.

Due to the continued growth of federal grants to states and localities, the intergovernmental field witnessed a functional concentration of interests that began in the 1940s and continues today. For example, public administrators and policymakers concentrate on the separate dimensions of program areas such as housing, health, education, and welfare. To be sure, these are broad policy areas in their own right, but the connections among them began to become blurred. Collaboration and cooperation gave way to competition and duplication in both the vertical and horizontal dimensions of intergovernmental relations. Administrative rules and regulations grew exponentially. Control became much more important than autonomy to those granting the funds—at both the state and federal levels. Concern with reporting requirements and compliance with regulations began to drive programs and color intergovernmental relationships. Professionalization and the growth in size of the federal bureaucracy with a programmatic and functional emphasis corresponded to the grant fields. More importantly, it resulted in the establishment of vertical functional autocracies—concentration of interests—at all levels of government advocating for programs and the special interests the program supported. Wright (1988) uses the "water tap" metaphor to describe this concentrated phase of intergovernmental relations. Federal funds, he says, flowed in narrow streams to the state and local level and "the interconnectedness and interdependency of national/state/local relations were confirmed and solidified" (p. 74). In some cases, funds actually bypass states and go directly from the federal level to local agencies.

As in the immediately preceding phase of intergovernmental relations, states were partners, not simply conduits for federal funds. They retained their own functions and made their own grants to local entities. The fact is, however, that the state role vis-à-vis the federal government was weakened by the programmatic approach characteristic of this period. According to Walker (1981), the effects of the expansion and activism of federal government activities resulted in a concentration of political forces in support of specific grant programs and put relatively more power in the hands of those who turned on the spigots than those who drank from the trough. The same can be said of the relationship between local and state governments.

President Lyndon Johnson himself used the term "Creative Federalism" to illustrate his administration's approach to intergovernmental relations—an approach that included new intergovernmental tools such as planning requirements attached to federal grants, project grants, and citizen participation requirements. It was during the Johnson administration that the trend toward the functional concentration of interests solidified. The federal government began to require the submission and approval of plans by state agencies prior to the receipt of grant funds. Many states complained that these requirements were far from creative and were instead unnecessarily burdensome. Grant recipients argued that they resulted in the submission of bureaucratic compliance documents rather than meaningful plans. Project grants also required the submission of extensive documents—proposals that had to be approved prior to the awarding of funds. Project grants, according to Wright (1988), "place far greater discretion in the hands of grant administrators than do formula grants, in which statutory or administrative formulas determine recipient entitlements" (p. 78). The citizen participation requirements also limited the discretion of grant recipients to act without consulting clients about such matters as operational and administrative decisions.

Project grants gave recipients the opportunity to design programs that met their own needs within the bounds of federal guidelines. However, many cities and states found themselves chasing federal dollars and playing grantsmanship games simply because the money was there. National goals related to the Great Society's war on poverty took ascendancy as more and more federal funds were targeted to the urban disadvantaged. Private sector actors continued to be key players in the intergovernmental arena and, in some areas, complicated relationships between the federal government and the states. The activist role of the federal government flowered and its power relative to the states grew as both states and localities became more dependent on federal funds.

During the 1960s and 1970s there was also a renewal of antagonistic and adversarial intergovernmental relationships. Participants perceived the period to be one of disagreement, tension, and rivalry. This was also the period characterized by the "picket fence" metaphor. In the early part of this period, vertical programmatic linkages strengthened and resulted in increasing competition among functional areas. The players in this competition included public policymakers and administrators as well as representatives of major public interest groups. Each programmatic picket in the intergovernmental fence (such as highways, welfare, health, and agriculture) represents an interest based alliance in competition with others. While the pickets represent vertical functional alliances, they do not represent a hierarchical dominance of the federal government over the states. Indeed, tension heightened over federal strings attached to grant-in-aid monies. In addition, different forms of horizontal linkages have occurred in the picket fence relationships; many have bypassed general-purpose elected officials and have, instead, created linkages between federal, state, and local specialists that fan conflict between those individuals and general-purpose elected officials.

In addition, the tension was accompanied by a strengthening of the states' resolve not to become fiscal wards of the federal government. Bargaining and negotiation over grant terms and conditions became the norm. States found that they had more latitude in the implementation of federal programs than many thought they did. As Wright (1988) explains, "National administrators of grant programs rarely control or 'order' their like-minded state counterparts to make (or not make) a specific decision. The more likely course of action is to debate, discuss, deliberate, and negotiate a course of action" (p. 84). Devolution and decentralization were the order of the day under President Nixon with a resulting shift, albeit a slight one, of intergovernmental power back to the state level. This in turn increased state-local tensions as localities found themselves caught in a double bind. Cities—which in fact are creatures of the states—became dependent upon federal grants-in-aid. This dependency created political tension between state and local governments, heightened by state-to-local mandates; mandates not accompanied by resources.

The phase of intergovernmental relations of the 1970s and 1980s is described as the Calculative Phase by Wright (1988). It, too, was a confrontational period described by Walker (1981) as overloaded and dysfunctional. The states continued to bargain and negotiate over grant terms and conditions, but the rules of the game were specified by the federal government. The states were still seen as partners in the intergovernmental process, but often as unwilling partners. Wright (1988) offers "facade federalism" as the metaphor to picture the period chiefly because in some circumstances "power has gravitated so heavily toward national officials that federalism, in its historic and legal sense, is nonexistent" (p. 98). One could say essentially the same with respect to state-local relationships.

It is against this backdrop that the intergovernmental dilemma is played out. On the one hand, the state concern is about federal mandates and programs that do not fit the nature of problems in particular states. On the other hand, the federal concern is about accountability and performance. Federal officials are understandably uncomfortable with a no-strings-attached "dole" to the states. Each set of concerns is reasonable, given the realities of the two actors. The challenge to public officials at both levels is how to balance the two. This challenge is intensified by the diversity among the states.

The National Government and the States

State Diversity. To say that there is great variety among the fifty states is to state the obvious. All too often, however, "one size fits all" programs or policies are made in Washington and thrust upon the states. While there are legitimate pressures that push the federal government to this approach, the result often appears to be ludicrous. Too often, the federal expectation is what works in one state will work in another.

The differences between states relate to many elements—history, geography, topography, and demographics. As Glendening and Reeves note, intergovernmental relations reflect "historical, cultural, legal, organizatinal, financial, political, and geographical settings. They may occur on both horizontal and vertical planes. Not only are the federal relationships of the national government and the states included, but so are the interstate, state-local, interlocal, and national-local relations" (1984, p. 13). But the diversity across states that relates to intergovernmental relationships involving rural issues can be seen in variations in factors such as governmental structure, political culture, and capacity to identify and deal with the problems of citizens.

Governmental Structure. Governors' offices (and executive branch agencies) in the states are vehicles for the debate about many domestic issues. These formal institutions of government are constrained by a number of factors, the most important of which is the state legislature. States vary in terms of these relationships. Iowa, for example, has a structure characterized by a strong governor and a weaker legislature. North Carolina's legislature, by contrast, is clearly the stronger of the two institutions. A tradition of shared power between the governor and the legislature is found in a number of states. Other states have relatively weak governors and, concurrently, legislatures that historically have been less than active.

Political Culture. Institutional conflict between the legislature and the governor in a number of states has been exacerbated by political conflict. Divided government has become the reality in many states and one-party control of state government is fast becoming a relic of the past. In some states, it has been possible to develop bipartisan agreements involving issues. Others have partisan conflict related to racial politics. During the past decade, many states have experienced budget crises, which have led to an increase in the role of the legislature and significant budget battles between the governor and the legislature.

Capacity. States vary in their ability to develop programs, policies and strategies in many policy areas. Depending on the issue, there may be complex policy and political responses. Many issues are imbedded in larger discussions of economic or community development and involve debates about the appropriate strategy for change (e.g., whether interventions should be targeted on the state as a whole, on specific sectors, or characterized as a responsibility of the state government or local communities). Many issues are debated not in their substantive form but in the guise of tax and fiscal policies. The capacity of states to respond to the problems of their citizens is a function of technical expertise and knowledge, but in large part it is also a function of political will. Administrative capacity to attend to the problems of citizens also varies across the nation. Many states are faced with institutional systems characterized by fragmented authority. Few states have a single agency with all the authority necessary to meet the development needs of their citizens.

Instruments of Intergovernmental Relations

The interdependence among levels of government in the American system and the persistence of the control/autonomy and collaboration/competition dilemmas means that it is increasingly necessary to focus attention on the instruments or tools of intergovernmental relations. Given the complexity of these linkages it is essential that an array of instruments be used to fashion the most effective working relationships among intergovernmental actors. Four broad categories of instruments are of particular interest: structural, programmatic, research and capacity building, and behavioral. None of these categories of intergovernmental tools or instruments is a panacea. Intergovernmental actors must look at issues from a number of different perspectives simultaneously. Structural, programmatic, educational, and behavioral approaches each are appropriate under the right set of circumstances.

Structural Instruments

Structural matters focus on the ways that bureaucracies operate and have to do with formal roles and relationships; patterns of authority and leadership; rules, policies, and regulations; and mechanisms for differentiation and integration of formal roles, tasks, and relationships.

Reorganization. Formal roles and relationships are shaped and reshaped in the design and redesign of organizations. Patterns of authority and leadership are disrupted and reestablished. Redesign, or reorganization, is a tool frequently employed in government as a means of responding to changing needs and priorities. Reorganizations can bring together programs that seem to be related, thus affecting horizontal intergovernmental relationships. However, reorganizations cannot settle issues related to conflict between levels of government. Reorganization can be approached on a grand scale (as was the case with President Nixon's Ash Commission, charged with studying the organization of the federal government) or on a more incremental base (as was the case with President Carter's Reorganization Project in the Office of Management and Budget). As Radin and Hawley (1988) point out, the Ash proposals sought to create mega-departments, assuming that these centralized bodies would improve the efficiency of government operations and service delivery. These proposals never had the support of Congress and were not adopted. By contrast, President Carter was more successful in his reorganization attempts, particularly the effort to create the Department of Education. Among other things, Carter's reorganization was undertaken to achieve better coordination of federal education programs that had been scattered across the federal government.

Some state-level reorganizations have been spawned by federal incentives. In the 1970s, several states created departments of behavioral health or departments of substance abuse, believing that they would be in a better position to take advantage of federal grant funds targeted at comprehensive approaches to those issues. Similar reorganization efforts were undertaken by local governments.

Coordination. Coordination and efficiency are the bywords of the structural approach. Coordinating mechanisms are tools for structural integration; the integration of units differentiated by function or level or geography. Implicit in attempts at reorganization, in fact, is the assumption that increased coordination and efficiency will make it easier to manage both horizontal and vertical intergovernmental relationships. While it is disputed whether this actually occurs, proponents of this approach make such an argument.

In practice, coordination is often transparent. It is easy to say it is being done, but its tangible products are illusive. While interagency coordination has costs, it does not necessarily require new appropriations, or identifiable budgetary line items. Unlike reorganization, coordination doesn't run the risk of alienating political constituencies, and it is difficult for one to argue that coordination is unnecessary or seriously detrimental to major interests. Applied properly as intergovernmental tools, formal mechanisms of interagency coordination can strengthen horizontal relationships. At the same time they can both strengthen a higher level of government's capacity to hold lower levels responsible for program performance and empower actors at those lower levels so that they can improve performance.

Deregulation. Rules, policies, and regulations are instruments for controlling intergovernmental relationships by increasing control and decreasing autonomy. Consequently, deregulation swings the pendulum in the other direction. Mandates are impediments imposed on lower intergovernmental actors from above through regulatory mechanisms. Mandates are removed through deregulation and are relaxed or removed through ad hoc experiments such as waiver procedures or regulatory negotiation.

Devolution and Decentralization. These are structural tools with which the federal government may delegate power to the states or states may delegate power to local governments. When used, then, devolution and/or decentralization has the ability to shift the pendulum toward autonomy. President Nixon's New Federalism was an attempt at devolution and a reaction to many of the centralizing tenets of Johnson's Creative Federalism. According to Walker (1981), it supported

> greater decentralization within the federal departments to their field units; a devolution of more power and greater discretion to recipient units; a

streamlining of the service delivery system generally; a definite preferring of general governments and their elected officials; and some sorting out of some servicing responsibilities by governmental levels. (p. 105)

Devolution took the form of general and special revenue sharing and attempts by President Nixon to impound federal funds as a way to eliminate program resources. Proponents of devolution are quite willing to trade control by the federal government for discretion on the part of state and local officials.

Decentralization has been employed in much the same manner by some states in an effort to manage intergovernmental relationships. Use of this tool involves passing authority (some would say, "the buck") to local units of government. In some instances, when states are given federal mandates without resources, they simply pass the mandates on to local government. This coping mechanism shifts the burden of the intergovernmental dilemma but it clearly doesn't solve it.

Regulation and Oversight. Regulation is itself a structural intergovernmental tool, even though the degree to which the federal government exercises oversight with respect to its state and local grantees is, in part, a political/ideological matter. In the Nixon, Reagan, and Bush years, for example, the operative ideology was minimal federal involvement and maximum state and local responsibility. Block grants and revenue sharing carry fewer strings than conditional grants. In addition, they do not tend to build the type of strong political constituencies found in categorical programs.

Oversight can occur at the input, process, or output side of programs. Input requirements generally specify the form and elements of the program design, leaving little discretion for the program implementor. Process requirements include elements such as citizen participation or planning requirements that are built in to ensure accountability. Output (or impact or performance) requirements tend to rely on evaluation as an accountability tool.

Evaluation requirements are either imposed by legislative or administrative mandate. Depending on where one sits, evaluation can be looked at as a management tool necessary for intelligent decision making or as an unwarranted intrusion on management discretion. Evaluation requirements are often used to assure that grant recipients are able to justify the expenditure of funds. Not only are these requirements built into programs, recipients are often required to pay for them with grant funds. However, evaluation can also facilitate additional autonomy on the part of state and local grantees. If evaluation is related to performance rather than input or process (that is, focuses on outcomes and program impacts), grantees may be given more discretion as to the way they produce those outcomes and impacts.

Process requirements can include citizen participation and planning approaches. Citizen participation requirements provide an opportunity for a form of accountability that is imposed early in the life of a program. While some may view them as a constraint, others view them as an opportunity to improve programs and avoid unnecessary conflict in their implementation. The idea of consulting with parties who will be affected by decisions is consistent with the general notion of empowerment; it empowers program clients as well as program operators.

Planning requirements can also be used as a form of process accountability. Like other requirements, they can be viewed as a set of constraints or as an effective instrument for intergovernmental management. Planning processes allow a jurisdiction to identify its current status, its goals, and its strategy for change. This requirement might stipulate that the process occur openly, with ample opportunity for input from those affected by plan implementation.

Programmatic Instruments

This second category of instrumentalities employed to deal with the intergovernmental dilemma involves the application of resources and redesign of programs and grant types. From the federal perspective, the intention has been to make it easier for states and localities to attack social and economic problems by providing them the resources to do so. In many instances, these resources have emerged as a result of lobbying by states and localities. While this approach was the most common response to newly identified problems, limited resources make it less commonly used today. Various grant forms—such as competitive project grants, formula grants, matching grants, and block grants—continue to be used.

The Shift toward Broader Purpose Grants. Highly specific categorical grants are the most restrictive but also the most targeted type of federal funding. These grant forms — particularly project grants — require potential eligible recipients to submit applications under guidelines specified by federal grantor agencies. Depending on the area, states continue to have discretion in this process. In some cases, applications from local units of government (or the private sector) must be reviewed and receive favorable recommendations from state agencies prior to submission to the federal grantor. As a general matter, however, categorical grants are heavily weighted toward the federal control approach.

In the late 1960s and 1970s, efforts to reform federal aid resulted in the creation of general revenue sharing and several special revenue sharing or block grant programs. Block grants in law enforcement, employment and training, community development, and social services were enacted that strengthened the hand of state and local officials in their dealing with federal grantors. While these approaches appear to be fairly radical approaches to intergovernmental management, many observers believe that they resulted in rather incremental changes in the system.

Partnerships. As intergovernmental tools, partnerships generally involve setting priorities and providing incentives at higher levels of government and letting others take action to achieve them. It means less reliance on service delivery through public bureaucracies and more utilization of public-public or public-private partnerships. Partnerships involve federal, state, and local governments and the private sector in a variety of activities. While states and localities have traditionally been partners in the intergovernmental arena, this approach focuses on the creation of specific partnership forms in response to the tensions inherent in the intergovernmental arena. Osborne and Gaebler (1992) point out that under partnership schemes governments share or trade services or contract with one another for specific services. Additionally, information, ideas and other resources may be shared in partnerships. Creating partnerships involves reframing the intergovernmental dilemma at the federal level. Rather than focusing on the trade-off between control and autonomy, this approach attempts to assure some measure of control and, at the same time, do more to empower states and localities so that they can be full partners in the federal system.

Collaborations. Collaborations may involve the granting of federal funds in large awards to a set of state or local agencies conditioned upon their ability to work together and share resources. The Clinton administration's Pulling America's Communities Together (PACT) is an effort that attempts to link community-based strategic planning and collaborative processes to address youth violence, using funds from several federal cabinet departments. Another example is a bid by the U.S. Department of Health and Human Services to promote state interagency efforts to reduce the impact of perinatal alcohol and other drug use on families. As noted by Jones and Hutchins (1993) this call for collaboration is based on a recognition that no single agency or system of services can effectively respond to the myriad needs presented by those in or at risk for alcohol and other drug dependency. They go on to say that the interagency collaboration envisioned "requires partners to relinquish total control of resources in favor of the group process. Resources are pooled while consortia members jointly plan, implement, and evaluate new services and procedures" (p. 26). This programmatic approach overlaps with structural instruments in that it indicates a recognition by federal, state, and local officials that old structures must give way to new ones if intergovernmental problems are to be solved.

Research and Capacity Building Instruments

The third category of intergovernmental instruments involves, in today's jargon, "empowerment." Implicit in this empowerment notion is the idea that steps may have to be taken to build increased management capacity at all levels if empowering is to have a chance of succeeding. So empowerment is an empty exercise if it does not also include the tools the newly-empowered need to get the job done. Specific tools in this category include research, the collection, storage, and dissemination of information, and training and other forms of capacity building.

Research. Research is an indirect tool of intergovernmental management aimed at helping people understand problems and issues, options, and consequences. To the extent that public policy research is cross-cutting it can aid those promoting interagency coordination. To the extent that research produces useful knowledge which is in turn utilized below the federal level, it can increase the negotiating power, thus the autonomy, of state and local intergovernmental actors.

The Provision of Information. Federal and state governments often serve as clearinghouses for those seeking information on just about anything. The federal government operates numerous information clearinghouses and some are accessible from personal computers. The precise impact of the opening of the information superhighway on intergovernmental relations is yet to be determined. It seems a safe bet, however, that more and better information will both improve interagency coordination and strengthen state and local discretion.

Capacity Building. This is one of the most widely used tools of intergovernmental management. Generally, it involves efforts by the federal or state governments to strengthen the capabilities of state or local officials to manage programs on their own. As Honadle (1981) notes, in the debate over mandates without money the fact that central governments provide substantial technical assistance to officials at lower levels, and that they have been doing so for some time is often overlooked. This assistance can be in the form of grants or contracts that provide for training and skill-building in the areas of program design, planning, and evaluation, to name just three. As a result of their emphasis on increased discretion for state and local government, the Nixon and Reagan brands of new federalism gave rise to serious concerns about management capacity at those levels.

There are two ways in which capacity building and the strengthening of state and local expertise in specific program areas are intergovernmental management tools. First, it makes sense for the grantor to ensure that grantees who are provided additional discretion have the skills and abilities necessary to manage the grants. Second, development of management skills facilitates compliance with federal grant requirements.

Behavioral Instruments of Intergovernmental Relations

The traditional view of the federal official's dilemma is whether to allow more or less autonomy or to impose more or less control. Control can be framed in a narrow fashion, holding grantees accountable for inputs and processes. However, looking at the situation through a wider lens suggests that the federal government should concentrate on performance, and autonomy means that grantees are empowered and given the tools they need to accomplish that performance. This broader view requires attention to individual and group processes of communication, organizational development, strategic planning, and processes of conflict management (Cigler, 1990).

Conflict Management. No matter what metaphor is used to describe the intergovernmental system, there is evidence of conflict. The issue, then, is not to attempt to avoid or suppress conflict but, rather, to prevent unnecessary conflict and to manage conflict that does occur toward productive ends (Buntz and Radin, 1983).

Conflict prevention in an intergovernmental context calls for attention to building consensus among actors in particular programmatic or policy areas. Actors are urged to identify and overcome barriers such as the language and jargon of different program cultures and resistance to change among agency staff.

Conflict management might involve taking a negotiated approach to the promulgation of rules and regulations, as opposed to a "decide, announce, and defend" approach. For more than ten years, the Environmental Protection Agency has engaged in a process of negotiated rule making referred to as "reg-neg." Regulatory negotiation involves affected parties and the agency in an orderly process of debate and discussion over proposed regulations. This consultative approach has produced environmental regulations acceptable to all. It has also enabled the EPA to move away from the decide, announce, and defend approach, which landed it in court more often than not.

Individual Communication. Closely connected to the consensus building/conflict management notion is the idea of improving communications between levels of government as a way to manage the control/autonomy dilemma. Effective intergovernmental relationships in an environment of resource scarcity and political uncertainty demand openness in interactions across governments. They demand federal officials who can listen, delegate, manage conflict, and build consensus. Barking out orders in a "command and control" method of communicating from federal to state and local levels is not viewed as an adequate way to manage intergovernmental relations.

Group Communication. Hearings are among the time-honored and formal means of group communication in policy development. Hearings provide a forum for representatives of groups in and outside of government to take positions and express their views. They also provide a means for governmental actors to collect information and shape ideas that later become policy. Hearings can be traditional and formal or of the town meeting type. If one reframes the intergovernmental dilemma and looks at it as an opportunity rather than a problem, hearings can be another way to build consensus. If one looks at these issues in a narrow sense, hearings can be viewed as a way to exert federal influence. Federal officials come to town with trumpets blaring and flags unfurled; pomp and circumstance could replace substantive communications.

Organizational Development. Organizational development (OD) interventions such as team building, quality-of-work-life programs, total quality management, and the like are generally seen as intraorganizational tools. These and other OD interventions are employed as instruments of planned change by organizations seeking to strengthen management teams and improve organizational performance.

Organizational development interventions can also be employed, however, to strengthen intergovernmental management. Partnership efforts can be themselves instruments of planned change when they are intended to help federal and state actors sort out their roles and approaches. Intergovernmental management programs can also help strengthen the capacity of state and local governments to pursue their own interests while recognizing and integrating national concerns. In this way, intergovernmental relationships are improved and producing policy change. This set of instruments tends to fine-tune rather than fundamentally change interorganizational and intergovernmental systems.

Strategic Planning. Strategic planning is a way to clarify goals and priorities; it can be used across organizations as well as within them. It is a systematic way of relating an organization (or an organizational system) to its external environment. As such, strategic planning cuts across other behavioral instruments. Rainey and Wechsler (1989, p. 509) point out that conflict resolution, consensus building, and group decision and individual communication techniques are integral parts of strategic planning and strategic management activities.

Strategic planning involves a process of scanning the environment for threats and opportunities and then matching an organization's distinctive competencies with those threats and opportunities. As with OD interventions, strategic planning can be undertaken within organizations or cooperatively by more than one organization. It is a cross-cutting instrument that can draw together other instruments and enable actors to establish a vision for the future.

As an instrumentality of intergovernmental management, strategic planning can be used as a tool by intergovernmental actors to identify conflicts likely to arise, clarify the processes by which those conflicts will be managed, identify other issues facing the intergovernmental system, and formulate strategies for managing those issues. It can be used to drive improvements in working relationships among actors.

The Current Intergovernmental Environment

Given the relationship between intergovernmental issues and broader social and domestic policy concerns, it is not surprising that one finds a shift in approach and strategy to these items when governments change. Over the years, Democratic administrations have been more likely to emphasize the redistributive role played by the federal government and to assume a relatively activist approach to the role of government. They have been less likely to trust the good graces of state and local officials and to emphasize oversight and control. Republicans, particularly over the decade of the 1980s, sought to diminish the role of the federal government and to assume that most problems were best solved by private rather than public institutions. This approach is evident in the emergence of the Republican majorities in the 1994 Congressional election and the Contract with America. In addition, the anger in some of the western states at the federal government over public lands also illustrates this mind-set.

Presidential leadership in domestic policy since 1976 illustrates these differences. Jimmy Carter, a former governor, sought to maintain an activist role of the federal government (particularly involving civil rights issues) even though he gave rhetorical attention to the concerns of governors. The pendulum swung dramatically in 1980, however, with the Reagan administration's attempt to dismantle the domestic policy role of the federal government and, instead, to turn authority back to states with greatly diminished federal resources. Congressional opposition to many of these measures stopped the White House from achieving its dismantling goals. This pattern continued during the Bush administration, although the ideological edge to the debate between the two ends of Pennsylvania Avenue was largely avoided.

To some degree, Bill Clinton approaches intergovernmental relationships somewhat similarly to Carter. A former governor, past NGA chairman, and longtime advocate of the ability of states to solve problems, Clinton appears to be comfortable with policies that allow states to put their own imprint on the implementation of national policies. While he accepts a more activist federal government than his immediate predecessors, his administration has been receptive (some would say encouraging) to proposals by governors and states to implement policies in their own way. Much of this has been done through waiver authority in a number of policy areas (particularly in welfare and Medicaid).

Clinton has also embraced the notion of change and "reinventing government," articulated by David Osborne and Ted Gaebler in their 1992 best-seller (Galston and Tibbetts, 1994). While arguing that they believe in government and seek to address the citizen disillusionment that they see around them, Osborne and Gaebler draw on examples of what they view as success that draw heavily on private-sector models and minimize adherence to traditional accountability devices within government. The Clinton administration "spin" on these issues (best exemplified by the Gore National Performance Review) contains a similar critique of traditional ways of doing the government's business.

Several patterns can be detected in the first two years of the Clinton administration. Perhaps the most visible approach was found in the overall Gore report, *Creating a Government That Works Better and Costs Less: The Report of the National Performance Review*, particularly as it commented on the overall dimensions of the intergovernmental system.

> Virtually every expert with whom we spoke agreed that this system is fundamentally broken. No one argued for marginal or incremental change. Everyone wants dramatic change—state and local officials, federal managers, congressional staff. As it manages its own affairs, the federal government must shift the basic paradigm it uses in managing state and local affairs. It must stop holding programs accountable for process and begin holding them accountable for results. (1993, p. 47)

This approach focuses on the intergovernmental dilemma by adjusting degrees of control, changing the way that federal officials look at their relationships with state and local governments, and focusing their attention on performance rather than input. It appears that the Clinton administration is making conscious efforts to deal differently with officials at other levels of government. "Giving Customers a Voice—and a Choice" and "Empowering Employees to Get Results" are strategies within the report that involve elements of improving communication. The Gore Report's six-step approach to cutting red tape includes empowering state and local governments. It argues that to "reinvent government" it is necessary to address intergovernmental relationships by giving state and local governments more control over programs and their own ability to produce results.

The supplemental report issued by the National Performance Review (NPR), "Strengthening the Partnership in Intergovernmental Service Delivery," further defines this approach. It notes that the NPR's broad goals—cutting red tape, putting customers first, empowering employees to get results, and cutting back to basics—cannot be achieved "without a new approach to intergovernmental partnership in delivery services to the public." It also argues that a well-functioning intergovernmental system "is central to Americans' quality of life and Washington's ability to pursue a domestic policy agenda." The recommendations included in this report continue some of the agenda items of earlier presidents—regulatory and mandate relief, grant consolidation, and elimination of paperwork and procurement requirements.

At the same time, however, the report calls for active facilitation of interdepartmental and intergovernmental collaboration. It notes:

> Partnership should be the hallmark of the proposal — between the federal and lower levels of government, and among and between the public, private, and private non-profit sectors at the service delivery level. . . . At the same time, legitimate federal interests must be protected and compliance with broad cross-cutting regulations (equal employment opportunity, worker health and safety, for example) ensured.

Among the mechanisms proposed to achieve these goals is the Clinton administration's cabinet-level Community Enterprise Board, chaired by the vice president and established to oversee new initiatives in community empowerment. According to the NPR report, "The Board would lead the federal government in a new effort to improve the coordination and integration of major domestic program service delivery initiatives. This board will be committed to solutions based on 'bottom-up' initiatives."

Both of these reports reflect Clinton's own personal commitment to inclusion of multiple players in a policy debate and an aversion to the norms and practices of traditional political conflict. This personal style appears to encourage an approach that can be viewed as a subtext of the "reinventing government" agenda—the need for systems and strategies that encourage collaboration beyond the same old players. This style is reinforced by Clinton's intellectual approach to issues and his conceptual challenge to reach for comprehensive policy changes.

Other Clinton predilections are found in policy issues such as the 1993 Forest Conference (often called the Timber Summit). This meeting pulled together the various actors concerned about the Pacific Northwest and northern California forests and, perhaps for the first time, sought to find ways to reconcile the competing adversaries. Three working groups were established immediately after the meeting to focus on forest management and economic development, and to focus on how federal government agencies could work together. The comprehensive strategy broadened the cast of participants as well as the dimensions of the issue and sought to establish venues that legitimated the involvement of business, labor, environmentalists, tribes, community groups, and members of Congress.

Clinton's actions involving the 1993 Midwest flood relief also illustrate his strategy. The president, vice president, and members of the cabinet met with the affected governors in a face-to-face, televised meeting. That session allowed the cabinet to respond directly and publicly to governors' concerns, report ongoing activity, and make promises about future action. To the governors' surprise, one of the cabinet officials had checks ready to hand them for a significant portion of the flood relief monies for which they were eligible.

Both the health reform and welfare reform strategies are another illustration of Clinton's game plan. Before either proposal was crafted, government task forces (drawn from a range of agencies) held meetings and hearings across the country, providing an opportunity for individuals who had relevant experience to make their views known. In some cases, these meetings provided a way for government officials to see as well as hear problems firsthand; in other instances individuals had an opportunity to submit proposals to address problems. In both instances, the process had both inclusion and collaborative aspects.

However, the changes that occurred in Washington in January 1995 suggest that Clinton's national policy agenda will be subject to very different pressures than were experienced during the previous period. For some observers, the pendulum swing to the right moves the intergovernmental agenda away from Wright's overlapping authority model to a set of relationships that is more like the coordinate authority approach.

Rural Policy through the Intergovernmental Lens

Intergovernmental relationships involving rural policy illustrate the importance of both vertical and horizontal dimensions. Vertical relationships involve a range of configurations of federal, state, and local authority. But unlike a number of other domestic policy areas, until quite recently the traditional tension in the system has not been between federal and state governments, largely because federal efforts involving agriculture, natural resources, and some aspects of rural community development have bypassed general purpose state and local governments. Rather, the conflict has been between those who serve as advocates for agricultural interests and those who argue for a broader and more inclusive definition of "rural." Creation of horizontal relationships—relationships between separate programs and structures—has been of concern to federal policymakers, particularly since the Eisenhower era.

The history of rural policy in the United States parallels the development of agriculture policy through much of the nation's history. This story is tied to a number of specific areas, among them roads, research and development, and redistribution and equity.

Roads. Early in the nineteenth century, the rapid development of the frontier and the South created a need for new transportation facilities to link agricultural areas with existing markets (Osbourn, 1988a, p. 9). Initially the debate over the creation of a federally subsidized network of roads and canals was waged on constitutional grounds, with opponents arguing that the national government did not have the authority to develop such a system. While modest federal activity did take place (for example, the building of the Cumberland Road), until the end of the century roads in rural America were predominantly local institutions (Barron, 1992, p. 82). Rural opposition to moving beyond a local approach to the issues did not subside until the turn of the century, when eastern states assumed responsibility for this area. Rural commitment to local control of roads was most pronounced in the Midwest (Barron, 1992, p. 91.) After World War I, the widespread adoption of the automobile and the limitations of county and state administration led road reformers to appeal to the federal government (Barron, 1992, p. 93). While farmers focused on construction of less expensive roads, called "farm to market" routes, others argued for a federally financed system of highways that linked urban areas and followed scenic routes across the country (Barron, 1992, pp. 94–95). Under pressure from their rural constituents, states were often unable to respond to their demands; this prompted increased pressure for a greater federal role (Barron, 1992, p. 97). The 1921 Federal Highway Act tried to accommodate the farmers' demands as well as those from urban groups.

Research and Development. Three major pieces of legislation were adopted following the Civil War that set into place a federal presence in agriculture accentuating its research and development role. The "agriculture reform" package of 1882 included the Homestead Act, the establishment of the U.S. Department of Agriculture, and the Morrill Act (Osbourn, 1988a, p. 13). This package of legislation reflected the federal government's role as a major player in pushing for change in agriculture. According to Sandra Osbourn, "The establishment of the Department of Agriculture and the enactment of the Morrill Act were the opening moves in a continuing national strategy of supporting the application of science and technology to the practice of agriculture" (p. 14).

The Morrill Land Grant Act provided assistance to states by making public lands available to them for specific kinds of education: agricultural and mechanical colleges. Its development essentially bypassed general-purpose state government (Bonnen, 1992, pp. 190–201). Soon after, the Hatch Act of 1887 authorized agricultural experiment stations in each state and established grants to states for testing, research and publication, and dissemination of scientific information. (Osbourn, 1989, p. 15). This early grants-in-aid approach was extended through the Smith-Lever Extension Act of 1914 (which called for dissemination of research information produced in the agricultural colleges to farmers) and the Smith-Hughes Act of 1917 (which provided for federal grants to be matched by state contributions for instruction in agriculture and the trades). During this period, a State Relations Office was established within USDA to act as the coordinating agency for relationships between the federal department and the agricultural colleges and experiment stations (Baker et al., 1963, p. 81). The Agriculture Experiment Stations, which relied almost entirely on federal funds in their early years, received increases in state appropriations as commercial farmers accentuated the value of discoveries made by station investigators (Kerr, 1987, p. 199).

The Land Grant system (and the Cooperative Extension Service which runs within it) operated as a very independent program, with a classic iron triangle of interest group, bureaucratic, and congressional support. It is described as a partnership of the land-grant universities and USDA (Rasmussen, 1989, p. 4). Indeed, many programs focused on rural areas were either administered locally by independent and special agencies (such as farmer committees, cooperatives, and regional planning and development organizations) or directly by federal bureaucracies (Sokolow, 1987, p. 2). However, at the same time, state budgets contribute extensively to the running of these programs; the federal contribution is approximately 30 percent of the system with state funds providing the dominant share of the remaining funds (Rasmussen, 1989, p. vii). These programs used various forms of capacity development and strategies building on the research and development approach devised early in the century.

Redistribution and Equity. By the early twentieth century, there was increasing concern about the economic health of the rural sector. Growing urbanization suggested that Americans did not appreciate the importance of the rural sector. Theodore Roosevelt appointed a Country Life Commission, whose report has been called "the first nationwide study of rural living" (Osbourn, 1988a, p. 18). It argued, "The farming interest is not, as a whole, receiving the full rewards to which it is entitled, nor has country life attained to anywhere near its possibilities of attractiveness and comfort" (Baker et al., 1963, p. 22). The commission called for action from multiple sources: the federal government, states and communities, voluntary organizations, and individuals acting alone (Baker et al., 1963, pp. 15-16).

Congressional action expanded in the succeeding years but did so in a way that provided support to individual farmers and did not involve state and local general-purpose governments. The Federal Farm Loan Act of 1916 provided long-term credit for farmers; the Warehouse Act gave farmers loans for storage of some crops. The Agriculture Marketing Act of 1929 established mechanisms to attempt to control prices by buying and selling farm commodities (Osbourn, 1988a, p. 22). By the New Deal, increasing concern about the economic health of rural America culminated in the emergency programs of the Roosevelt administration (especially those for poor farmers under the Resettlement Administration and its successor, the Farm Security Administration). The activity undertaken through the Agricultural Adjustment Act of 1933 created concern over direct administration of some programs from Washington and possible duplication and overlap between these programs and those administered through the state extension services. An agreement was reached between representatives of the land grant colleges and top department officials to "give the problem of Federal-State relationships, as affected by the new policies and programs, 'full, unhurried, and careful examination.'" (Baker et al., 1963, p. 255). The agreement that was eventually reached gave state extension services the role of initiator in setting up county land use planning committees to deal with the perceived overlap and duplication (Baker et al., 1963, p. 259).

Concern about low-income farmers continued in the post–World War II period. Eisenhower called for a program for low-income farmers that focused on individual farms and farm families (Osbourn, 1988a, pp. 31–32). With the Cooperative Extension Service in the lead, rural development committees were organized to include representatives of local agencies, USDA and other federal agencies, and community leaders (Rasmussen, 1985, p. 3). The Kennedy administration created the Rural Area Development program that focused federal attention on rural issues beyond those attached to agriculture, emphasizing interdepartmental and interagency coordination efforts. This was a key shift in federal policy.

The Johnson administration's efforts accentuated the link between rural poverty and urban disorders (Osbourn, 1988a, p. 38) and the importance of working across multiple federal agencies to address the problems of rural Americans. An executive order was signed in 1966 establishing a Rural Development Committee to coordinate and provide a forum for consideration of rural problems (Osbourn, 1988a, p. 42).

Efforts to focus on poor and small farmers as well as nonfarm rural residents were frequently stymied by the political power of the "big four" interest groups: the American Farm Bureau Federation, the National Grange, the National Farmers Union and the National Farmers Organization. Although these groups were often in conflict with one another over specific policies, all of them emphasized their constituencies who were farmers not rural residents (Salamon, 1987, p. 3).

Intergovernmental Relationships in Rural Policy since 1968: Federal Experience.
By the Nixon administration, intergovernmental rural policy reflected
the Republican administration's general approach to domestic policy.
He proposed a block grant that would allow states the opportunity to
decide where to spend money allocated for rural development, replacing eleven categorical grant programs (Salamon, 1987, p. 8). General
revenue sharing funds provided resources for rural communities.

In addition, in an effort to reduce government spending, Nixon
called for an increased role for the private sector in rural areas: tax credits to private businesses that invested in nonmetropolitan areas (Salamon, 1987, p. 9). Nixon also sought a major reorganization of the
federal government, putting most of the USDA programs in a superde-
partment called the Department of Community Development (Salamon, 1987, pp. 9–10). Congress refused to support many of Nixon's
proposals; however, they were to resurface in subsequent Republican
administrations. The attention to rural development did survive in a
symbolic way in the 1972 Farm Bill, which contained provisions to create
an assistant secretary for rural development in USDA.

Unlike Nixon, who sought to minimize differences between urban
and rural settings, the Carter administration focused on specific needs
of small communities and rural development. Legislation was enacted
that focused on improving the effectiveness of existing resources, rather
than increasing the resources available or making major structural
changes in the delivery system (Osbourn, 1988a, p. 53). Carter's Georgia roots and those of a number of his staff were particularly attuned to
the problems of rural citizens.

An interdepartmental Assistant Secretaries Working Group for Rural
Development was formed that, among other issues, emphasized the lack
of capacity at both the state and local levels for managing rural development (Osbourn, 1988a, p. 54). It also targeted on the problems of disadvantaged groups in rural America. The Working Group identified a
number of areas that needed attention, including the appropriate roles
of the three levels of government in the planning and implementation
process of rural development (Osbourn, 1988a, p. 56). The Carter
administration, while considering a structural solution not dissimilar to
that proposed by Nixon, instead decided to accentuate a coordination
strategy that involved working with the existing rural development structure, rationalizing funding cycles, and simplifying application and planning requirements (Osbourn, 1988b, p. 24).

At the end of the Carter administration in 1980, the Rural Development Policy Act created a new undersecretary of agriculture for small community and rural development. Proposals to create a permanent interagency Working Group for Rural Development were not adopted. The act directed the secretary of agriculture to increase the coordination of federal programs with the development needs, objectives, and resources of local communities, substate areas, states, and multistate regions and to improve state and local government management capabilities, institutions, and programs related to rural development (Osbourn, 1988b, pp. 61-63).

Despite the provisions of the 1980 Act, the Reagan administration chose another course. Budget cuts were proposed for most of the rural nonfarm programs (Salamon, 1987, p. 25). The administration believed that the federal government should not be involved in this policy area, that it "violates correct relationships within the Federal system and between the public and private sectors" (Osbourn, 1988b, p. 67). It argued that state and local governments and the private sector were the appropriate agents for developing and carrying out rural development policy. This was consistent with a general domestic policy thrust and there was no attempt to focus on special problems of rural (as opposed to urban) settings.

Consolidation of categorical grants to state and local governments was proposed, along with the budget cuts. While some interdepartmental activity took place, particularly during the second Reagan term, the rural development strategy that was employed "reiterates the Administration's commitment to encourage growth in that sector through tax relief, regulatory reform, more aggressive trading practices, control of inflation, reduction of interest rates, and the improvement of productivity through basic research and development" (Osbourn, 1988b, p. 75).

A part of the federal strategy during Democratic administrations over these years was thus to broaden the scope of the policy issue and create mechanisms to target rural development assistance outside of the U.S. Department of Agriculture (USDA), particularly to the underserved. These mechanisms focused on community and human resource development, as well as economic development. In the 1960s, programs included the Appalachian Regional Commission and the Economic Development Administration, as well as various efforts within the Office of Economic Opportunity. States were also given an increased role, particularly with their ability to control allocation of Small Cities Community Development Block Grant funds.

But another part of the strategy was targeted at USDA itself and approaches within the department that would support a shift from a purely agricultural agency to one with a broader rural focus. However, the Department of Agriculture had little ability to exert pressure on the land grant system to give increased attention to rural development issues (Cornman and Kinkaid, 1984, p. 45). By contrast, Republican administrations sought to decrease the federal role through block grants and budget decreases and, at the same time, improve the coordination of remaining programs.

Rural Intergovernmental Relationships since 1968: State and Local Experience. Since the Kennedy administration there have been efforts to involve rural and small-town governments as instrumentalities of federal policy. During the late 1960s and early 1970s, multi-county, substate planning and development regions were viewed as the vehicle for developing, coordinating, and implementing efforts to assist declining rural areas throughout the nation (Bender, Browne, and Zolly, 1987, p. 161). More recently there has been attention to the role of general-purpose state governments in developing and implementing rural policy. By 1988, the rural assistance issue began to emerge on the gubernatorial issue agenda. Erik Herzik's analysis of agenda items mentioned by governors from 1970 to 1988 shows the rural issue appearing for the first time in 1988; during that year it showed up as the eighth most frequently mentioned item (Herzik, 1991, p. 33). By that point, states took a number of actions that had the effect of increasing their role in the delivery of public resources for rural development (Roberts, 1990). By 1988, the National Governors' Association (NGA) proposed a new alliance between the federal government and the states in rural development. In this scheme, the states would take over more of the delivery and local coordination of programs, but at the same time, the NGA emphasized the importance of many of the federal delivery mechanisms and, of course, federal funding. According to one observer, "In reality, much of the NGA strategy was an attempt to restore federal funding for rural programs, while allowing a broader state role in allocating those federal funds. By the mid-1980s the combination of an economic downturn and a reduction in federal support had left state governments under great pressure to fill the role the federal government had abdicated" (Freshwater, 1991, p. 7).

The Rural Legacy: A Backdrop for New Governance. Since the middle of the nineteenth century, farm policy and farmer organizations focused on relatively narrow economic interests; since the New Deal and the creation of commodity price supports, farm interest groups developed a national presence in Washington, participating in policy formation (Bonnen, 1992, p. 193). But as the number of farmers decreased, there began to be an acknowledgment that the narrow economic interests of farmers did not address all of the problems of rural Americans. Effectively, "rural" was synonymous with "agriculture"; federal program elements were clustered in USDA and it was assumed that interventions in agricultural production and distribution would lead to improved conditions for Americans who lived in rural areas. This definition led to a set of intergovernmental relationships that were limited in both their horizontal and vertical dimensions. Few federal rural programs were found outside USDA despite concern about health, education, and job training problems of rural citizens. Similarly, few federal rural initiatives involved state governments; most dealt directly with local governments, farmers, and other businesspeople (NGA, 1988, p. iii).

This focus, by definition, reached beyond the federal government to involve a range of other intergovernmental actors. The Rural Development Act of 1972 attempted such an effort, as did activities during the Carter administration. During the Reagan years, however, little was done to support these activities and budget stringencies provided the opportunity to eliminate efforts in this direction.

Bonnen has argued that one important barrier to an effective rural development policy is the lack of vertical linkages among levels of government. He notes that although rural problems are location-specific, "underdeveloped or lagging rural areas ultimately have an impact on the economic welfare of citizens beyond the boundaries of any local government. . . . Given the many national, state, and local governmental jurisdictions that are affected by rural public services, the benefits of any rural development policy (or, conversely, the costs of continued rural underdevelopment) will be widely shared throughout American society" (Bonnen, 1992, p. 197). Bonnen notes that the need to develop a coordinated national, state, and local rural development policy will confront the opposition of more narrowly focused farm commodity interest groups. He also notes that the effort requires a coordinated system for sharing the costs of a rural development policy.

By 1990, despite disagreements about the form of an initiative, it was clear that various elements could agree that something had to be done about rural America. Attention to these problems emerged from both Congress and the White House as a divided government sought to claim its attention to the problems of rural Americans. The 1990 Farm Bill largely crafted by Democratic members of Congress included provisions authorizing the creation of a separate Rural Development Administration in USDA. And in January 1990, President Bush announced the steps his administration would take "to strengthen the delivery of Federal support for rural development."

Conclusions

The policy landscape that confronted the State Rural Development Councils thus demanded an approach that could deal with an extremely complex governmental system. The boundaries of the policy issue were not clear. Because rural residents have multiple problems, one could imagine that a federal policy initiative could reach across the federal domestic landscape. Most of the problems facing rural residents called for resources that were beyond the control of a single actor; in many cases, the problems demanded action from government at all levels as well as nongovernmental entities. Yet the role of state governments in this area was variable across the country. No single actor was responsible for creating the problems and no single actor could solve them. However, many participants could respond to some aspect of these issues. This reality set the framework for the 1990 Rural Development Initiative.

References

Agranoff, Robert. 1986. *Intergovernmental Management: Human Services Problem-Solving in Six Metropolitan Areas.* Albany: State University of New York Press.

————. 1990. "Frameworks for Comparative Analysis of Intergovernmental Relations." Occasional Paper #26, School of Public and Environmental Affairs, Indiana University (August).

Baker, Gladys L. et al., U.S. Department of Agriculture, Centennial Committee. 1963. *Century of Service: The First 100 Years of The United States Department of Agriculture.* Washington, D.C.: Government Printing Office.

Barron, Hal S., 1992. "And the Crooked Shall Be Made Straight: Public Road Administration and the Decline of Localism in the Rural North, 1970–1930." *Journal of Social History* 26 (1) (fall), 81–103.

Bender, Lewis G., William P. Browne, and Thaddeus C. Zolty. 1987. "The New Federalism and Substate Regionalism: Changing Perceptions of Rural Officials." *Publius* 17 (fall), 161–74.

Bonnen, James T., 1992. "Why is There No Coherent U.S. Rural Policy?" *Policy Studies Journal* 20 (2), 190–201.

Buntz, C. Gregory, and Beryl A. Radin. 1983. "Managing Intergovernmental Conflict: The Case of Human Services." *Public Administration Review* 131(5), 403–10.

Cigler, Beverly A. 1990. "Public Administration and the Paradox of Professionalization." *Public Administration Review* (November/December), 637–53.

Cornman, John N., and Barbara K. Kincaid. 1984. *Lessons from Rural America.* Washington, D.C.: Seven Locks Press.

Elazar, Daniel J. 1987. *Exploring Federalism.* Tuscaloosa: University of Alabama Press.

Freshwater, David. 1991. "The Historical Context of Federal Rural Development Policy." *Western Wire* (spring), 2–14.

Galston, William A., and Geoffrey I. Tibbetts. 1994. "Reinventing Federalism: The Clinton/Gore Program for a New Partnership Among the Federal, State, Local and Tribal Governments." *Publius* 24(3) (Summer).

Glendening, Parris N., and Mavis Mann Reeves. 1984. *Pragmatic Federalism: An Intergovernmental View of American Government.* 2nd ed. Pacific Palisades, Calif.: Palisades Publishers.

Gore, Albert. 1993. *Creating a Government That Works Better and Costs Less: Report of the National Performance Review.* Washington, D.C.: U.S. Government Printing Office (September 7).

Grodzins, Morton. 1961. *The American System: A New View of Government in the United States.* Chicago: Rand McNally.

Hanf, Kenneth. 1978. "Introduction." In Kenneth Hanf and Fritz W. Scharpf, *Interorganizational Policy Making: Limits to Coordination and Central Control.* Beverley Hills: Sage Publications.

Heclo, Hugh. 1979. "Issue Networks and the Executive Establishment." In Anthony King, ed., *The New American Political System.* Washington, D.C.: American Enterprise Institute for Public Policy Research, 87–124.

Herzik, Eric B. 1991. "Policy Agendas and Gubernatorial Leadership." In Eric B. Herzik and Brent W. Brown, *Gubernatorial Leadership and State Policy.* New York: Greenwood Press, 25–37.

Honadle, Beth W. 1981. *Perspectives on Management Capacity Building.* Albany, N.Y.: SUNY Press.

Jones, Virginia H., and Ellen Hutchins. 1993. *Finding Common Ground; A Call for*

Collaboration. Arlington, VA.: National Center for Education in Maternal and Child Health.

Kerr, Norwood Allen. 1987. *The Legacy; A Centennial History of the State Agricultural Experiment Stations, 1887–1987.* Columbia, Mo.: Missouri Agricultural Experiment Station, University of Missouri–Columbia.

Osborne, David, and Ted Gaebler. 1992. *Reinventing Government.* Reading, Mass.: Addison-Wesley.

Osbourn, Sandra S. 1988a. "Rural Policy in an Era of Change and Diversity." Washington, D.C.: Congressional Resarch Service, Library of Congress (July 13).

Osbourn, Sandra S. 1988b. "Rural Policy in the United States: A History." Washington, D.C.: Congressional Research Service, Library of Congress (July 13).

Radin, Beryl A., and Willis D. Hawley. 1988. *The Politics of Federal Reorganization: Creating the U.S. Department of Education.* New York: Pergamon.

Rainey, Hal G., and Barton Wechsler. 1989. "Managing Governmental Corporations and Enterprises." In James L. Perry, ed., *Handbook of Public Administration.* San Francisco: Jossey-Bass, 499–512.

Rasmussen, Wayne D. 1985. "90 Years of Rural Development Programs." *Rural Development Perspectives* (October), 2–9.

Rasmussen, Wayne D. 1989. *Taking the University to the People: Seventy-five Years of Cooperative Extension.* Ames: Iowa State University Press.

Roberts, Brandon, 1990. *States: Catalysts for Development in Rural America.* Washington, D.C.: Council of State Community Affairs Agencies.

Salamon, Aaron, 1987. "The Politics of Federal Rural Development Policy: Factors Affecting Program Organization." U.S. Department of Agriculture, Economic Research Service (August).

Sokolow, Alvin D. 1987. "Introduction: Small Governments as Newcomers to American Federalism." *Publius* 17 (fall), 1–13.

Stewart, William H. 1982. "Metaphors, Models and the Development of Federal Theory." *Publius* 12 (spring), 5–24.

Walker, David B. 1981. *Toward a Functioning Federalism.* Cambridge, Mass.: Winthrop Publishers.

Walker, David B. 1995. *The Rebirth of Federalism: Slouching Toward Washington.* Chatham, N.J.: Chatham House Publishers.

Wright, Deil S. 1988. *Understanding Intergovernmental Relations.* 3d ed. Pacific Grove, Calif.: Brooks/Cole.

Additional Readings

Agranoff, Robert. 1992. "Intergovernmental Policy-making: Transitions and New Paradigms." Paper prepared for Conference on Transitions in Public Administration, Orebro University–Indiana University–SPEA (May).

Crane, Steven. 1975. "Rural Depopulation and the Political Process of Federal Rural Development." Ph.D. thesis, University of Iowa.

Effland, Anne B. 1993. "Federal Rural Development Policy Since 1972." *Rural Development Prospectives* 9(1), 8–14.

Elazar, Daniel J. 1994. *The American Mosaic: The Impact of Space, Time and Culture on American Politics.* Boulder, Colo.: Westview Press.

Flora, Cornelia B., and James A. Christenson. 1991. "Critical Times for Rural America." In Cornelia B. Flora and James A. Christenson, eds., *Rural Policies for the 1990s.* Boulder, Colo.: Westview Press.

Long, Richard W. 1987. "Rural Development Policy: Rationale and Reality." *Publius* 17 (fall), 15–31.

National Governors' Association. 1988. *New Alliances for Rural America: Report of the Task Force on Rural Development.* Washington, D.C.: National Governors' Association.

U.S. Congress, Senate. 1909. *Report of the Country Life Commission,* 60th Congress, 2d Sess., S. Doc. 705.

2 | The Rural Development Policy Issue

Challenges Facing Rural America

RURAL AMERICA FACES a number of significant challenges at the end of the twentieth century. Many of the nationwide economic trends place severe pressure on rural areas. Traditional economic sectors, especially those tied to agriculture and natural resource extraction, are unable to generate the employment and income levels of the past. In addition, the rural sector in many regions has benefited from the decentralization of manufacturing from the old industrial heartland and cities, but now rural manufacturing must compete in a world economy. The low wage levels in rural manufacturing, particularly in the South, no longer represent a comparative advantage. The advanced technology manufacturing sectors, because of their requirements for skilled, well-educated labor, have tended not to locate in rural America.

A further challenge is found in the infrastructure arena. Deregulation in the 1980s in transportation, banking, and other areas did not "unleash" competition in rural areas. In fact, the removal of service obligations from companies, which occurs with deregulation, may mean the loss of services for rural areas. The history of infrastructure provision to rural areas has generally been one of innovative and effective public policy. Whether this will be the case for the critical new infrastructure—telecommunications—remains to be seen.

There are some bright spots for rural America. Rural areas with natural amenities have been able to attract the country's aging population to retirement communities, and to take advantage of the demand for leisure and recreational activities. In addition, there have been some innovative uses of telecommunications, particularly in terms of overcoming remoteness, in economic development.

Diversity among rural areas also places a challenge before communities and public policy. There is great variation in economic structure and conditions around the United States that requires diverse community action and public policy response. Agricultural policy shifts will not necessarily affect large segments of rural America, as agricultural and farm income has become less of the driving force. Communities adjacent to metropolitan areas are much better positioned than distant communities. Some rural areas have very good human capital resources but limited employment prospects. Infrastructure and financial capital remain important concerns in virtually all rural regions of the country. But one message is clear. The old way of doing things no longer works; change and innovation must be central concerns.

Chapter two explores the challenges facing rural America. To understand the magnitude of the challenges and the rural development setting, contextual information is provided in the first part of the chapter. This material includes a discussion of the meaning of rural development and related terms, an analysis of the structural changes in the national economy, and an exploration of state government policy. In the second part of the chapter, the focus shifts to the rural economy and rural development policy.

Rural Development: What's It All About?

"Rural" has both positive and negative connotations. The duality is captured in the comment by a journalist: "Rural America, with its enticing vistas of fields, forests, buttes and mountains and its unenticing economy of failing farms, depleted mines and low-wage factories . . . " (Barringer, 1993, A6). Connotations aside, the word "rural" eludes easy definition. In fact, according to two leading observers of the rural scene, "no universally accepted definition exists" (Reid and Sears, 1992, p. 215). In their work, these observers have used a practical designation: sparsely populated areas. Even the federal government is of more than one mind on what is rural. The United States Bureau of the Census designates as rural those areas outside places with populations of 2,500 or more. Alternatively, other agencies classify county areas beyond the borders of Metropolitan Statistical Areas as rural.

A recent attempt at resolving the definitional impasse differentiates rural from urban (Deavers, 1992). Rural areas are characterized by small-scale, low-density development, as is the case with small towns and open country; their distance from large urban centers (physical distance, and remoteness due to geographic barriers, as well as social and cultural isolation); and the specialization of their economies. In sum, rural areas tend to be somewhat peripheral to the rest of society.

"Development" is another problematic word. Long associated with progress and modernization, the word has generally carried positive connotations. More recently, however, the development process is no longer automatically seen in a positive or neutral light. The rethinking of development has come, in large measure, as a result of the environmental costs associated with the process. Thus development, which had traditionally been measured in terms of economic growth, is increasingly being thought of more broadly with some attention to "natural capital" and resource management (Porter and Brown, 1992). Sustainable development, one of the watchwords of the 1990s, grew out of this rethinking of development. ("Sustainable development" also suffers from definitional confusion. John (1994) reports that one expert stopped counting various definitions of the term when the count reached sixty.)

Understanding rural development requires an untangling of several other phrases: economic development, community development, and agricultural development. Economic development is frequently equated with economic growth and is measured by indicators such as income levels or number of jobs. However, economic development is more than simple growth. It implies a change in the character or structure of the economy of an area. "It refers to a qualitative shift in resource use, labor force skills, production methods, marketing measures, income distribution, and financial capital arrangements" (Kane and Sand, 1988, p. 10). One of the broadest definitions of economic development is this: "Economic development could be seen as an ongoing process of building and maintaining local and regional institutions which not only generates an acceptable quality of life today but promotes continued and/or enhanced viability into the future" (Sears et al., 1992, p. 13). The more developed the community, the greater its ability to adjust to demographic trends and economic shifts. In other words, economic development creates resilience.

Community development and agricultural development are specific, but not necessarily unrelated types of economic development. Community development focuses upon the economic and social conditions of particular places, large and small. In terms of government programs, those associated with community development have tended to be "bricks and mortar" programs that provide funds for activities such as infrastructure installation and housing rehabilitation. An argument could be made, however, that more people-oriented government programs such as welfare assistance, job training, and public education are also forms of community development. In fact, greater attention to the "human infrastructure" increasingly characterizes community development. An example makes an interesting point. In Michigan, a county-based development organization initially included the word "community" in its title. It eventually dropped "community" because leaders believed that the organization's purpose was mainstream economic development. To them, "community" implied more of a leadership training and institution building process (Cigler et al., 1994).

Agricultural development focuses on a sector of the national economy and has traditionally been equated with farming. (Fishing, timber, and mining are commonly included in the designation "agricultural.") And that brings us back to rural development. Rural development differs from agricultural development because of its nonsectoral nature. It has moved beyond agricultural improvement to include other economic sectors such as manufacturing and services. Yet rural development is distinctive in that it focuses on less populated areas and attendant conditions.

Structural Change in the National Economy

By the late 1970s, the dramatic effects of technological change and intense international competition had transformed the structure of the United States economy. The change originated in the 1960s but became particularly visible in the 1980s. A broad range of new technological products and processes affected economic structure and labor markets. This process was occurring on a worldwide basis, facilitating international trade and integrating the world economy.

The most striking manifestation of structural change occurred in dramatic employment shifts in the manufacturing sector. Traditional durable manufacturing sectors, ranging from metallurgy, machinery, and automotive to nondurable sectors such as food processing and textiles declined in terms of their shares of national employment and of gross national product (Wilson, 1993). The traditional industrial heartland of the country, particularly the old industrial cities, suffered most from these declines in manufacturing. Even though the traditional manufacturing sectors were losing their share of national employment, certain regions with historically low levels of manufacturing employment were able to attract these firms. The highest shares of manufacturing employment in the late 1980s were found in southern states (the Carolinas, Georgia, etc.). Many rural areas benefited from this decentralization of manufacturing. Other manufacturing sectors, frequently called advanced technology manufacturing (computers and the like) expanded but tended not to locate in the old industrial heartland or in rural areas.

The second major shift associated with structural economic change occurred in the service sectors, where very substantial increases in employment share and less dramatic increases in shares of gross national product occurred (Wilson, 1993). The service sectors are quite diverse, demonstrating different employment growth rates and responding to different types of demand. Some service subsectors, such as transportation and utilities, grew slowly; others, particularly the producer services and health and education, grew quite substantially. The shift from manufacturing employment to service-sector employment, coupled with the longer-term trend of relative decline in primary natural resource and raw material production, reflects a fundamental change in the economy. Some have used this shift as evidence of the emergence of a postindustrial society.

The recent period of dramatic economic change has brought to the forefront a new infrastructure. As the importance of information in the economy grows (that is, the producing, storing, and processing of information) the transport of information has become a critical element (Wilson, 1993). Telecommunications serves this function and it has evolved into an increasingly important infrastructure. The integration of computers and telephone systems in modern telecommunication systems has allowed for enormous increases in productivity in the sector and by businesses using the technology. The telecommunications revolution allows for the spatial dispersal of economic activities. Some so-called back office operations, such as credit card operations, can be decentralized. Also, for firms that process or produce information, location distant from clients is possible. This sector, as will be seen below, has important implications for rural America.

The structural changes in the national economy have had quite distinct effects on the various regions of the country. As a result, state governments have reoriented and redesigned their development policies.

State Development Policy

The term "state development policy" refers to the package of goals, strategies, policies, and programs that state governments employ in their effort to promote economic growth and development. Efforts can be targeted to a specific sector such as agriculture, to particular enterprises as in the case of small businesses, and to specific areas such as distressed communities. Development policy tends to be a consensus issue enjoying widespread support; however, there is much disagreement over how best to "do" it. The national economic upheaval described in the preceding section along with increased foreign competition and Reagan-era "new federalism" have complicated the policymaking environment (Fosler, 1988).

States as Forums for Development Policy

Economic growth and development are central to states. As Jones (1990, p. 219) notes, "the public agendas of state and local governments are, and historically have been, dominated by policies intended to promote growth." For example, in its 1993 session, the Arizona legislature adopted several new tools designed to attract business. These included an increase in research and development tax credits, tax concessions for manufacturers using recycled products in their processes, a foreign shipment tax exemption, and an exemption from highway taxes for motion picture industry vehicles ("Economic Development Potpourri," 1993). Arizona's actions are not unusual; economic development policy is a legislative priority across the states. In 1994, North Dakota legislators met in a special session to formulate and adopt a series of tax exemptions designed to make the state more attractive to a relocating corn processing plant (Mahtesian, 1994).

The intentions of the development-promoting policies are clear, but the outcomes are far from conclusive. Because states are open economies, the effects of policy actions are difficult to measure. Brace (1989; 1993) examined state economic performance at three different periods: a time when the national economy was flourishing, a period in which the economy was undergoing a transition, and an era in which the federal government decreased its support for states and localities. Several explanations of state economic performance were tested: state policy characteristics, national economic conditions, and other exogenous forces such as energy cycles and federal expenditures. Although states themselves were important determinants of economic growth in most periods, national economic trends were also statistically significant explanations in many states. Overall, states with the fastest growing economies tended to be states that were the most sensitive to external economic influences.

Despite the attention to economic development and the dollars spent in its pursuit, much of what has been advocated has been advanced without much empirical evidence about effectiveness of different approaches. Yet the characteristic that distinguishes state and local economic development activity—its competitiveness—forces jurisdictions to keep economic development at the top of the agenda (Beaumont and Hovey, 1985).

Nonnational governments compete for economic development because of the decentralized nature of the federal system. Governmental jurisdictions cover specific territories, but capital is mobile, so business firms can move from one location to another. Because these firms are so important to the economy, governments offer incentives to influence their location decisions. As noted above, the impact of these incentives on firms' decisions is not clear, but most jurisdictions believe that they cannot afford not to offer them (Ledebur and Hamilton, 1986). Interjurisdictional competition for capital investment is most intense when the stakes are high, that is, when the location decision will mean a substantial number of jobs. An example makes the point. The 1992 announcement that the German automobile firm, Mercedes-Benz, was seeking a site for its first United States manufacturing facility unleashed no-holds-barred interstate competition. Over 100 sites in thirty-five states were considered initially, with the field narrowed to sites in Alabama, Iowa, Nebraska, North Carolina, and South Carolina by the spring of 1993. Each state offered a substantial package of tax breaks and low-cost land in an effort to attract Mercedes. The finalists included rural sites in the three southern states. In late September, Mercedes announced that Vance, Alabama, population 450, had been selected as the location for the $300 million plant.

But the price that Alabama will pay is a dear one. The state is providing $92.2 million in land and facility construction costs, $77.5 million in infrastructure development, $60 million in training, and a twenty-five-year tax abatement. Estimates put the state cost at approximately $200,000 per job. The extravagant bidding for the Mercedes plant raised some eyebrows, but in the words of one Alabama economist, "the symbolism (of winning the Mercedes facility) may be as important as the direct economic impact" (Holmes, 1993, A10). Indeed. As reported in *The Economist*, the mayor of Vance now sports a Mercedes hood ornament on his GM pickup truck ("The Invaders Are Welcome," 1994). The Mercedes-Benz case reflects what influential local development officials have labeled a "very competitive" economic development process (Bowman, 1988).

To some degree, government incentives and concessions amount to a giveaway to business. Critics claim that competition for economic development results in the relocation of a given amount of economic activity from one community to another, with no overall increase in national productivity (Goodman, 1979). These critics would like to see increased interjurisdictional cooperation. However, while the rhetoric of cooperation is strong, state behavior is quite different. For example, efforts to establish a "no pirating" pact among states in the Great Lakes region have been unsuccessful (Carlson, 1983). Local governments have found cooperation elusive as well. According to the National Association of Counties, only 5 percent of counties frequently coordinated their economic development activities with other counties (NACO, n.d.). Only slightly more (19 percent) have engaged in frequent coordination with their constituent cities. On balance, economic development has tended to be a singular proposition, with each jurisdiction pursuing its own destiny.

Although competition is the dominant and, some would argue, natural condition, there are examples of interstate cooperation. Those same Great Lakes states, where governors could not agree on industrial pirating, formed a Great Lakes protection fund and launched a $750,000 international marketing campaign to promote "North America's Fresh Coast" (Bacas, 1990). In the Mid-South Trade Council, a loose confederation of six states centered in Memphis, each member state leads a trip or coordinates an initiative (such as a foreign buying trip) for the other states. The rationale is simple: if my state cannot "win," it is preferable to have a neighboring state do so rather than one outside the region. Thus far, member states have found joint efforts to be sufficiently productive to maintain their involvement. These illustrations underscore the new, albeit modest, trend toward multistate and regional cooperation. And it may continue. State development officials, according to a recent survey, actually favor a "state-local cooperative" model as a way to pursue economic development (Ambrosius and Maynard-Moody, 1991). However, models are one thing, actions are quite another. In the same survey, a significant proportion of the respondents defended competition because, they contend, competition enhances the generation of effective solutions to economic problems. Still, most agree that interstate competition has gotten out of hand. Concern about "bidding wars" led the National Governors' Association at its 1993 summer meeting to endorse a proposal intended to limit competition by focusing on workforce preparation and infrastructure quality instead of company-specific incentives.

Policy Approaches to Economic Development

Although community efforts to spur economic development have a long history, it was not until the depression that the first statewide program of industrial recruitment was established. Mississippi, through its Balance Agriculture with Industry program, made it possible for local governments to issue bonds to finance the construction or purchase of facilities for relocating industry. Other southern states emulated Mississippi's program, tempting out-of-state businesses with tax breaks, public subsidies, and low wages (Herbers, 1990). Aggressive industrial recruitment, dubbed "smokestack chasing," had spread beyond the South by the 1970s.

Yet even as states raided other states for industry, statistics were beginning to show that between 80 percent and 90 percent of new jobs came from existing firm expansions and start-up businesses, not relocating businesses. About the same time, pressure from foreign competition intensified. It became increasingly clear that the old days of industrial recruitment would not be sufficient to spawn new businesses and keep state economies strong. State policymakers embarked on a new era or "second wave" in economic development. States established venture capital pools, created small business incubators, and initiated workforce training programs in an attempt to support "homegrown" enterprise. It would be misleading, however, to conclude that the second wave replaced the first. Even with these new initiatives, states continued to chase out-of-state smokestacks (Bowman and Kearney, 1993).

Organizations such as the Council of Governors' Policy Advisors (formerly called the Council of State Planning Agencies) and the Committee for Economic Development began to talk about a second wave of strategies in the mid-1980s but it was Osborne's (1988) book, *Laboratories of Democracy*, that popularized the notion. His analysis of innovative strategies for economic revitalization in Massachusetts, Michigan, and Pennsylvania, which accentuated the role of the state governor, captured the attention of policymakers and the public alike. Another volume of case studies appearing that year echoed the argument: "state economic development efforts have moved far beyond conventional 'smokestack-chasing'—heavy industry recruitment strategies—to include the creation and expansion of new industries by providing capital, promoting exports, and encouraging entrepreneurship" (Fosler, 1988, p. i). Eisinger (1988) labeled second-wave approaches as "demand-side," to differentiate them from the more traditional first-wave or "supply-side" approach. A supply-side approach attempts to stimulate investment by lowering costs associated with production. Smokestack chasing, with its offerings of tax concessions and other incentives to a relocating firm, is a prime example of supply-side behavior. A demand-side approach, on the other hand, is more market sensitive and thrusts state governments into a more entrepreneurial role. In designing a demand-side strategy, a state might target industries serving growing markets, especially those that export beyond local borders. Rather than offering industrial revenue bonds to a relocating low-wage textile manufacturer as a supply-side approach would dictate, a demand-side focused state would "initiate the formation of a public-private consortium to explore and develop agricultural applications of new biotechnological research" (Eisinger, 1988, p. 228).

In the 1990s, some observers of the economic development scene began to detect what they are calling a "third wave," to keep the watery metaphors afloat (Ross and Friedman, 1991). This newest wave represents "a rethinking of what government can do and cannot do, and how it can do it more effectively" (Fosler, 1991, 34). Second-wave programs, well-intentioned perhaps, simply did not have adequate scale or focus to transform state economies. Third-wave efforts seek to correct those deficiencies. One of the keys to the third wave is getting economic development programs out of state agencies and into private organizations. Rather than directly supplying the program or the service as government has in the first and second waves, government would provide seed capital. Some states already have third-wave programs in action. North Carolina's Rural Economic Development Center, a private nonprofit organization, receives $2 million annually in legislative appropriations. The center has raised $2.5 million from the private sector and offers information, technical assistance, and capital in needy rural communities. In Michigan, six Business and Industrial Corporations (BIDCO) created by the state use small amounts of public money to leverage private investment. The combined funds are invested in moderately risky ventures that commercial banks will not touch. As part of the investment, the BIDCOs acquire some of the equity in the enterprise. When a

BIDCO-assisted firm is successful, BIDCO shares in the profits, thus providing even more money to invest (Herbers, 1990).

In a general sense, the third-wave theme pervades Osborne and Gaebler's (1992) book, *Reinventing Government*. This prescriptive volume is a call for the public sector to become more entrepreneurial in almost all of its endeavors. It compares the types of policy instruments typically used by traditionally-oriented governments to those adopted by more entrepreneurial governments. Included among the traditional tools are tax policy, grants, subsidies, and loans. Among the nontraditional, which Osborne and Gaebler further categorize as innovative or avant-garde, are technical assistance, vouchers, seed money, equity investments, and property exchanges, all of which can become part of the economic development function. The fundamental argument is that entrepreneurial governments enjoy more success than those that cling to traditional modes of operation.

The "wave" terminology offers a means of capturing some of the shifts in emphasis in state development policy. The waves do not represent irreversible phases or even distinct stages. Traditional, first-wave approaches remain popular (and garner the lion's share of resources) in many states (Mahtesian, 1994). Hanson's (1993) analysis of state development policy as of the mid-1980s showed that few states engaged in widely differentiated development-promoting activities. State governments seek what works. Ideally, a state government should be internally united for its economic development effort, but several natural cleavages such as partisan politics, legislative-executive disputes, and agency turf battle make cohesion difficult. Evidence from statistical studies suggests that the greater a state's institutional capacity, the more successful its economic development strategies (Brace, 1993).

As a state's top elected official and chief executive, the governor commonly takes the lead in economic development, creating task forces and blue-ribbon panels (Clarke, 1986). Most states use advisory boards to refine and adjust their economic strategies as changing conditions dictate. These committees vary in responsibility and authority and their primary function is to provide input from a variety of perspectives. Once an economic development strategy is in place, the next challenge is implementation. "First-wave" economic development strategies were the province of state agencies. Adherents to the "third wave," however, argue that state agencies have not responded creatively and effectively to the challenges confronting them. Third wavers advocate getting government agencies out of the economic development business and replacing them with more flexible, public-private hybrids or private sector organizations. The legislatures of Illinois, Iowa, Kansas, and North Carolina seemed to be riding the third wave in 1991 when they cut the budgets of their economic development agencies. The Illinois Department of Commerce and Community Affairs was the hardest hit, cut by 40 percent, from $90 million to $51 million (Pilcher, 1991).

State governments, aware that their economic development activities have appeared incoherent and even counterproductive to the outside world, have attempted to clarify their role. In doing so, many states have engaged in strategic planning. There are four major components to the strategic planning process: mission or goal identification, review of external and internal environments, setting of priority strategies and action steps, and implementation and evaluation (Blair and Reed, 1995). Strategic planning can be useful for several reasons, according to the National Association of State Development Agencies (1987). First, it produces an understanding of the state's economic bedrock. Second, it provides a venue in which public- and private-sector leaders can exchange perspectives and develop a consensus about the state's economic future. In addition, strategic planning moves the economic development issue from goal setting to implementation. Finally, it provides a mechanism for adjusting and correcting the state's actions in reaction to emerging economic trends.

The Rural Economy

The discussions of economic change and state development policy beg the question: what has this meant for rural America? More specifically, how have the transformation of the national economy and the shifts in state development policy affected rural areas? Changes relate to shifts in the agriculture, natural resource, and manufacturing sectors; demographic characteristics; and rural diversity.

The Agriculture, Natural Resource, and Manufacturing Sectors

The role of the agricultural and mining sectors of the United States economy between 1967 and 1988 demonstrated an irregular pattern, with sharp increases from 1973 through 1975 and 1978 through 1981 and a sharp decline from 1982 through 1986. In 1967, agriculture and mining accounted for about 5 percent of GDP and in 1988 they accounted for about 3.8 percent (see Figure 2.1).

The volatility of the agriculture and natural resource sector is associated to a significant extent with the prices for commodities in the international market. The sharp increases in share of GDP are associated with the increases in the international price of oil. In addition, the devaluation of the dollar in the 1970s reduced the relative price of U.S. com-

Percent

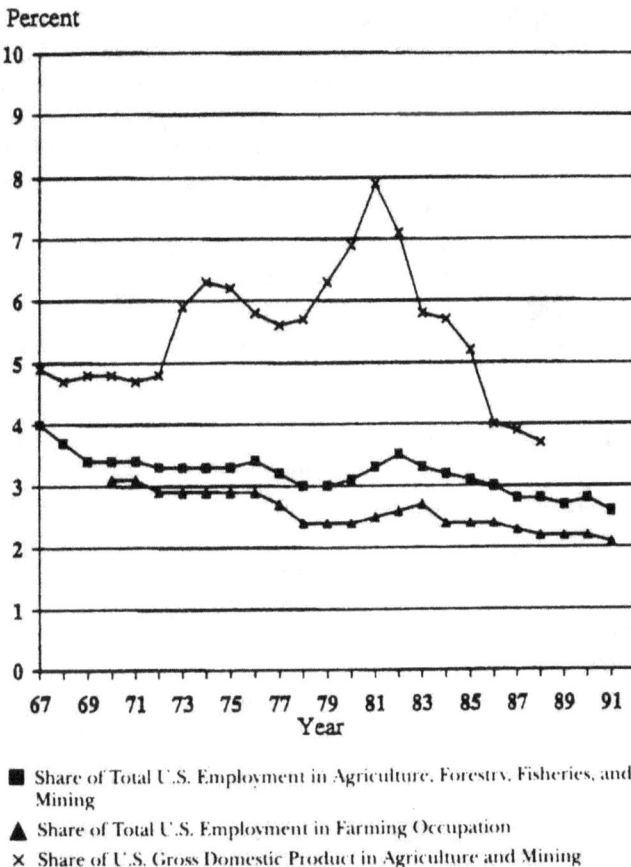

■ Share of Total U.S. Employment in Agriculture, Forestry, Fisheries, and Mining

▲ Share of Total U.S. Employment in Farming Occupation

× Share of U.S. Gross Domestic Product in Agriculture and Mining

Figure 2.1. Agriculture and extractive sectors' share of the U.S. gross domestic product and employment, 1967–91 (adapted from Wilson, 1993, Tables 2.2, 2.3, and 2.5).

modities, producing an increased demand for U.S. natural resource commodities on the international market (Flora and Christenson, 1991). The decline in the share of the GDP in the early 1980s coincides with a step recession in the United States, an overvalued U.S. dollar and the decline in world oil prices. The world recession later in the 1980s generated weak demand for U.S. commodities. Energy prices were broadly lower in the 1980s and this hurt mining and energy communities in the United States (Deavers, 1992). The volatility of prices for agricultural and mining commodities obviously creates volatility in the communities dependent upon these products, especially communities that are specialized in a product faring poorly in international markets. For example, many of the energy-oriented boomtowns of the 1970s went bust in the 1990s.

The share of total national employment accounted for by agricultural and mining employment has been much less volatile. However, the pattern has been largely one of long-term, relative decline; the share was around 4 percent in 1967 and a little less than 3 percent in 1988, with modest peaks in 1976 and 1982. Between 1979 and 1986, the farming sector lost 330,000 jobs (Hady and Ross, 1990). In 1988 employment in farming occupations had declined to just over 2 percent of total employment in the country. Mining employment has also declined, by 14 percent between 1979 and 1986 (Hady and Ross, 1990).

The employment shares in these sectors are substantially less than their share of GDP, reflecting the fact that these sectors are capital intensive, especially mining, and thus require relatively little labor. While this result reflects a long-term trend, dating at least from the early part of this century when modernization of agriculture was initiated, it nevertheless indicates that the rural economy of the country is depending less on direct employment in the agriculture and mining sectors.

The manufacturing sector has been substantially affected by economic change. However, a disaggregation of the manufacturing sector shows significant variation, some with unique implications for rural areas. Traditional manufacturing has decentralized from the industrial heartland. The region now most specialized in manufacturing is the east south-central region, consisting of Georgia, Mississippi, and Alabama (Wilson, 1993). Many types of firms, ranging from low-wage textile and food processing companies to capital intensive automobile manufacturing plants, locate in rural areas. The Economic Research Service classifies nonmetropolitan counties by degree of specialization in their economies and found that in 1986, 516 of the 2,300 nonmetropolitan counties had a specialization in manufacturing (Hady and Ross, 1990). The attractiveness of rural areas to manufacturing, especially in the South, was in part the result of relative low-wage rates found in rural areas. However, rural manufacturing has taken on characteristics of the national manufacturing sector. Between 1979 and 1986, nonmetropolitan counties lost 400,000 manufacturing jobs (Hady and Ross, 1990).

The sector most responsible for employment growth in rural areas is the service sector. As noted above, services include a range of subsectors, each with different growth prospects. The most rapidly growing subsector, at the national level, is producer and business services, and these tend to have an urban location pattern rather than rural (Wilson, 1993). Rural areas have significant increases in the share of employment in health and education, government, and consumer services employment.

The impact of the dynamic telecommunications sector on rural America is uncertain. One critical element of this uncertainty is whether the technology will have a centralizing or decentralizing effect on the location of economic activity. Empirical evidence of both centralizing and decentralizing tendencies exists, but at present it is not clear which will dominate. While the general impact is not yet clear, access to advanced systems and innovative uses of the technology have produced significant development in a number of rural areas (Schmandt et al., 1991). The great success of Wal-Mart is in part related to a satellite-based inventory and communications system. In these instances the telecommunications system has had the effect of reducing the cost of remoteness for rural areas. The telecommunications opportunities available in education, health care, and other services hold the potential for making their delivery to rural areas substantially less costly.

Demographic Characteristics and Economic Well-Being

Some changes in the demographic composition of rural America have followed old trends. Outmigration from rural areas, as the agriculture sector becomes more capital intensive, dates from the 1930s. After a period of rural renaissance in the 1970s with more rapid population growth in the country's nonmetropolitan areas than in metropolitan areas, the long-term pattern returned in the 1980s. During the middle of the 1980s, 500,000 individuals left rural areas every year, matching historic highs in rural outmigration, although toward the end of the decade the rate declined significantly (Galston, 1992; Beale and Fuguitt, 1990). Nearly half of all rural counties actually lost population in the 1980s (National Commission on Agriculture and Rural Development Policy, 1990).

Further complicating the problems of the rural population are shifts in the age composition. The rural population has aged more rapidly than the population as a whole, especially as the younger working-age population migrates from rural areas. The educational requirements of employment in the changing economy place a premium on high levels of education and the young and the relatively well-educated are more than proportionally represented among the outmigrants. This undermines the labor force that remains in rural areas and limits the type of economic enterprise that can be attracted.

One other dimension of this aging process is that the increasing number of retired Americans are settling in rural areas and small towns. A number of small towns, particularly in the South and Southwest, are retirement communities (Economic Research Service, 1995). The economy of some rural areas is increasingly dependent on servicing retired populations. Retirement income, such as Social Security, can become a major source of economic activity in such areas.

The pattern of outmigration and changes in the economic structure in rural areas generates a number of significant differences between urban and rural indices of economic well-being. The average earnings differential between nonmetropolitan and metropolitan areas increased from $5,000 in 1979 to $6,200 in 1987 (in inflation-adjusted dollars) (Barabcik, 1990). Secondary income, especially through transfer payments, has become an increasingly important source of income in rural areas. The share of rural workers falling below the poverty line for a family of four in 1987 was 42 percent as compared to 23 percent for urban workers (Galston, 1992). In the rural poverty population, around 46 percent of the heads of households and unrelated individuals worked at least part-time during the year, indicating a sizable working poor population (Deavers and Hoppe, 1991). Rural unemployment was one percentage point higher than that for urban areas for most of the 1980s (Galston, 1992).

The rate of rural poverty reached 18 percent in the early in 1980s but declined to 16 percent in 1990; it remained about 50 percent greater than that found in metropolitan areas throughout the decade (Galston, 1992; Rural Sociological Society Task Force on Persistent Poverty, 1993). In 1990, among the rural poor, about 30 percent lived in single-parent family households; 44 percent were in married-couple households; and the remainder were unrelated individuals (Rural Sociological Society Task Force on Persistent Poverty, 1993). In recent years the most significant increase in poverty has occurred in female-headed households.

The severity of these discouraging trends is not uniformly distributed across rural America. The distance a rural county is from a metropolitan area is inversely related to the economic conditions of the area. Nonmetropolitan counties that are adjacent to metro areas perform better economically than those more distant.

Diversity in Rural Economies

Natural resource endowments and historical patterns of settlement have generated substantial diversity among the rural areas of the country. The resources of an area, including soil, climate, mineral, and other extractive resources, lead to diverse products, with each requiring variation in types of production system. For example, mineral extraction generally requires a more spatially concentrated type of production system than that required by agriculture production.

Additionally, there is a substantial range of production systems among agriculture products—the labor and capital requirements for wheat production are vastly different than those for producing vegetables or fruit. Spatially extensive cultivation, say of wheat, will lead to very low population densities and relatively low levels of urbanization, while other types of production systems can lead to higher population densities and higher levels of urbanization.

The success of a rural economy will be partially related to the success of its product (or products) in export markets. The effect of these export products on the broader economy of a region will depend on the degree of linkages between the agriculture or mineral extraction sector, local processing of these resources, and the local economy. In some instances the rural economy will be strictly dependent upon the success of exporting the area's product. But if production requires relatively little labor, processing occurs elsewhere, or production occurs with nonlocal ownership and a leakage of profits occurs, the impact on the local economy will be less.

Diversity has historically been a characteristic of rural America. Local economies, or broader regional economies, were specialized on specific agricultural products—wheat, corn, cotton, cattle, chickens, sheep, etc.—or on natural resources—lumber, oil, coal, fisheries—for export. Many factors contributing to change in rural America can be traced to changes occurring broadly in American society, but that have had accentuated effects in rural America.

The Economic Research Service of the United States Department of Agriculture has developed a classification of nonmetropolitan counties by their economic specialization; this clearly reflects a trend toward greater economic diversity among counties (Hady and Ross, 1990). In 1979, of the 2,300 nonmetropolitan counties in the country, 716 counties specialized in farming, 630 in manufacturing, and 160 in mining. In 1986, all three types of nonmetropolitan counties had declined in number; farming to 516, manufacturing to 580, and mining to 130. The number of government-specialized counties had increased by over 100 and the number of unclassified counties, indicating no specialization in the local economy, increased by 150 to 550. This means that many counties were no longer relying on their traditional economic bases, but rather were diversifying internally. Thus, looking across all nonmetropolitan counties, more diversity in economic structure of counties is observed.

Even within a single state the degree of diversity may be marked and meaningful. In California, for example, rural areas tend to be one of two types: those experiencing heavy developmental pressures and those suffering from unemployment and weakened economies. The first group includes areas located along the coast or in the fertile central valley. The second group includes the timber-dependent areas in the remote northern mountains of the state (Sears et al., 1992). The two types of rural communities face vastly different problems and require fundamentally different solutions.

Rural areas that have special scenic beauty and climatic conditions can benefit from tourism. Ski resorts, parks, and dude ranches attract a substantial number of tourists and this tourism can serve as the economic base. Nonmetropolitan counties specialized in retirement and recreational activities number more than 500 and these accounted for most of the nonmetropolitan population growth after 1982 (Deavers, 1992b).

Rural Development Policy

As discussed in Chapter 1, the federal government has a long history of involvement in rural development. But, as noted, at the turn of the century, almost 40 percent of the population lived on farms; thus rural development was virtually synonymous with agricultural development (Rasmussen, 1985).

States are much newer to the rural development arena. A review of state strategic plans indicates that rural development has not been central to state strategies (Wilson, 1993). The explanation for the inattention to rural issues is political. Reapportionment has meant that state legislatures are increasingly dominated by urban and suburban members. In addition, as Bonnen (1992, p. 198) argues, "there are few if any effective and influential interest groups working in the interest of rural communities . . ." Consequently, with the exception of agribusiness, rural constituencies have not played key roles in state development policy (Wilson, 1993). In a variation on the "rising tide lifts all boats" theme, state policymakers have tended to assume that rural areas would benefit automatically from an improvement in the economic health of the state as a whole, as have federal policymakers (Gillis, 1991). Given that, the question asked in a recent article is especially provocative: "Why should the state devote special attention to the rural portion of its economy?" (Sears et al., 1993). The authors of the article offer several reasons: to improve the efficiency of the state's economy, make full use of fixed investments, improve rural-urban equity, and preservation of a rural "way of life." Whatever the rationale, states are increasingly expected to play a more active role in rural development policy.

Contemporary strategies for increasing rural competitiveness contain a number of recommendations for state governments (Bonnett, 1993). Foremost among them is investment in human capital, that is, in education and training. The argument is quite simple: by upgrading the skill levels of their residents, rural areas will be able to attract and spawn jobs. Despite the simplicity of the argument, the task is formidable. A second recommendation involves the development of telecommunications systems and advanced technologies as a rural revitalization strategy. In other words, have the information highway take farm-to-market roads. Rural communities would benefit, not only from being linked to global and national economies but also from the improved business networks within the area.

A third recommendation, one that is common in contemporary development circles, be they rural or urban, is the promotion of entrepreneurship. Creating an environment supportive of entrepreneurial behavior requires several elements, including leadership, talent, opportunities, innovation, capital, and spirit (Gregerman, 1991). It is no wonder then, that most communities fall short. Most state programs aimed at entrepreneurship have focused upon small business development. Increasing access to capital is the fourth recommendation (Bonnett, 1993). Rural communities, along with inner-city neighborhoods, have traditionally lacked access to capital. Recognizing that, several states have instituted programs such as state bond banks, community reinvestment regulations, linked deposit programs, and venture capital pools to ameliorate the problem.

The wealth of many rural communities lies in their natural resources. The fifth recommendation for improving rural competitiveness is natural resource development. This broad-based strategy typically involves enhancing the productivity of resource assets, expanding natural resource-based primary industries, and creating new natural resource enterprises (Nothdurft, 1984). Interestingly, one popular new enterprise for rural areas is tourism. Another recommendation is the use of collaborative efforts to promote rural development (Bonnett, 1993). Collaboration can be across government levels, agencies, and communities. The establishment of networks facilitates not only the accomplishment of development projects but also the exchange of information. State rural development councils are a primary example of collaboration in action.

Community leadership and capacity building is the seventh recommendation for improving rural competitiveness. As discussed in the next section, this is a necessary condition for the survival of rural communities. Leadership training, along with community assessment programs, are well under way in many states. Wisconsin has an extensive program in which community resource development specialists are placed in county extension offices to nurture local leadership (Sears et al., 1992). The final recommendation is a familiar one: improve the public infrastructure in rural areas. Here, however, the emphasis is upon a broader conception of infrastructure to include quality of life concerns.

In a similar vein, the director of Pennsylvania's Rural Center calls for innovative programs specifically tailored for rural communities (Gillis, 1991). These policy options can be grouped into three categories, depending on their focus. Policies focusing on rural people should aim at improving their productivity and employability; these include education and skill training, health care, and child care. Community-focused policies should have as their goal the attraction of new residents and businesses; these include infrastructure improvements, community facilities and services, main street revitalization, and planning assistance. Policies oriented toward rural businesses should target start-up firms as well as the retention and expansion of existing enterprises; these policies include providing financial capital, supporting competitive technologies, and international market development.

The Local Community

When the local public school is consolidated with one in a nearby community, a small town in rural America knows that it is in trouble. The demise of the school—a traditional source of identity and unity for a town—is emblematic of the tough times that a lot of rural communities face. In fact, some analysts argue that the major distinctions in regional economics are no longer between sunbelt and frostbelt or east coast and west coast but between metropolitan America and the countryside (John, 1988).

Much of the research on rural development has focused on communities in decline, that is, those places that are losing both population and economic base. As a rule, *declining communities* have had economies based on farming, mining, or manufacturing. It is important to note, however, that disinvestment and decay do not characterize all rural areas. One recent analysis identified three other types of rural communities (Seroka, 1988). A *dynamic growth community*, as the label implies, is one in which both population and economic growth are occurring. *Strain communities* are those places that are experiencing population growth without proportionate gains in personal income. On the other hand, *preservation communities* have stable or declining populations but enjoy growth in personal income. Although the challenges facing the declining communities are the most severe, even the more prosperous places have difficulties, such as the likelihood that growth will disturb their rural flavor and identity.

Demographic and economic trends aside, declining communities face an additional challenge. Local leadership and organizational capacity have been shown to be critical components in successful economic development efforts (Blair and Reed, 1995). Compared to the other types, local leaders in declining communities are the least supportive of administrative modernization and change (Seroka, 1988). Local governments in these communities are less capable of responding creatively to the problems they face. Consequently, the gap between places where dynamic growth is occurring and the declining communities is likely to increase. The fear is that this will become a self-perpetuating phenomenon, until some communities simply disappear. Research on rural communities in the Midwest lent some credibility to this contention: the communities that have withstood economic downturns are those that have had the administrative capacity to identify and pursue opportunities. Macon County, Missouri, is an example. With "hard work, luck, and heads-up opportunism," Macon County transformed itself from a declining community into a dynamic growth community. But administrative capacity is often in short supply in declining communities.

An additional concern in these communities, regardless of type, is sustainable development. As noted earlier, sustainable development is a loose term. In most usages, it refers to economic progress "that protects and restores the quality of the natural environment, improves the quality of life for individuals, and broadens the prospects for future generations" (*Choosing a Sustainable Future*, 1992, p. v). In its practical application, it means that communities are increasingly wary of trading long-term environmental quality for short-term economic gain. Even in some declining communities in which economic revival is the dominant goal, greater attention is being accorded to sustainability. Natural resource depletion and ecosystem destruction are no longer alien concepts in rural communities. However, these concerns complicate policy-making.

What can state governments do to reverse the decline in rural areas? Short of pumping enormous amounts of money into the local economy, they can encourage the expansion of local intergovernmental cooperation, so that small rural governments join together to increase their administrative capacity to deliver services and achieve economies of scale. The constraints on rural development—isolation, low population density, mobility disadvantages, scarcity of fiscal resources, personal familiarity (which affects objectivity and confidentiality), resistance to innovation, and lack of support services—can be minimized by increased intergovernmental cooperation. Two state actions facilitate such cooperation. One is reform of state tax codes, so that jurisdictions can share locally generated tax revenues. Rather than competing with each other for a new manufacturing plant or a shopping mall, local governments can cooperate to bring the new facility to the area; regardless of where it is located, all jurisdictions can receive a portion of the tax revenue. A second useful state action is the promotion of countywide and especially, statewide, land-use planning. As one observer has noted, "Currently too many rural local governments engage in wasteful inter-community competition, mutually antagonistic zoning, and contradic-tory development plans" (Seroka, 1988, p. 45). In other words, the state's role in promoting the development of rural communities is one of enabling them, freeing them up to do it themselves.

Once free from these constraints, then what? One promising option for communities in trouble is multijurisdictional collaborative efforts, or, in less grand language, rural partnerships (Cigler et al., 1994). The promise of collaboration lies in its ability to overcome two classic rural conditions: limited local capacity and weak linkages to economic and political centers. Multicommunity collaboration may not reverse these conditions, but it certainly improves upon them. And by doing so, it helps make rural communities economically viable alternatives to cities. One successful collaborative venture has taken place in eastern Kentucky. The twenty-seven rural counties making up the state's fifth congressional dis-trict joined together to improve the quality of public education in the region. Called "Forward in the Fifth," the nonprofit organization spun off local affiliate groups that developed and shared a series of programs that have had a measurable effect in improving schools (Eager, 1995).

Conclusions

The challenges facing rural communities are substantial. Economic transition and political change have taken their toll on rural America. "The environment for local economic development in rural communi-ties has undergone a fundamental change over the past few decades. International competition, economic restructuring, deregulation, and New Federalism make it increasingly difficult for rural communities to compete for capital" (Green et al., 1993, p. 1). New strategies are needed. Wade and Pulver (1991, p. 115) identify four implications:

> First, community leadership is much more important and requires a far greater level of knowledge and understanding of the community econ-omy and the changes occurring. Second, the role of the professional shifts from delivering predetermined programs to rural communities to being a resource available to rural communities to carry out locally defined policy. Third, policy education shifts from informing communi-

ties about policy to empowering communities to develop policy. Fourth, the policy emphasis of state and federal government shifts from policy that results in specific programs to policy designed to create an environment supportive of communities implementing their own policies.

In keeping with Wade and Pulver's argument, interest is growing in "self-development" strategies. These are strategies in which local organizations (typically, governments) invest substantial local resources in the creation of an enterprise or activity that remains locally controlled (Green et al., 1994). If the evolution of state development policy is characterized in terms of waves, as presented earlier in this chapter, then these self-development efforts may represent an incipient fourth wave.

Some communities, those positioned to take advantage of a changing global economy, will likely flourish; for others, the future could be one of stagnation and decline. State governments occupy a curious place in the rural development network. Over time, states have fashioned an eclectic development policy, cobbling together approaches and tactics from all three of the so-called waves. Increasingly, states are rethinking their development strategies in a more coherent and comprehensive manner. The key question is the emphasis that states will accord rural development in the reinvented policy domain.

References

Ambrosius, Margery Marzahn, and Steven Maynard-Moody. 1991. "Normative Models of Federalism in Economic Development." Paper presented at the Annual Meeting of the American Political Science Association, Washington, D.C.

Bacas, Harry. 1990. "Allies for Growth." *Nation's Business* 78 (November), 40–43.

Barabcik, S. 1990. "The Rural Disadvantage: Growing Income Disparities Between Rural and Urban Areas." Washington, D.C.: Center on Budget and Policy Priorities, 9.

Barringer, Felicity. 1993. "Population Grows in Rural America, Studies Say." *New York Times* (May 25), A6.

Beale, Calvin L., and G. V. Fuguitt. 1990. "Decade of Pessimistic Nonmetro Population Trends End on Optimistic Note." *Rural Development Perspective* 6 (3), 14–18.

Beaumont, Enid F., and Harold A. Hovey. 1985. "State, Local, and Federal Economic Development Policies: New Federal Patterns, Chaos or What?" *Public Administration Review* 45 (March / April), 327–32.

Blair, Robert, and B. J. Reed. 1995. "Applying Strategic Planning to Rural Economic Development." In David W. Sears and J. Norman Reid, eds., *Rural Development Strategies*. Chicago: Nelson-Hall, 29–58.

Bonnen, James T. 1992. "Why Is There No Coherent U.S. Rural Policy?" *Policy Studies Journal* 20(2), 190–201.

Bonnett, Thomas W. 1993. *Strategies for Rural Competitiveness: Policy Options for State Governments*. Washington, D.C.: Council of Governors' Policy Advisors.

Bowman, Ann O'M. 1988. "Competition for Economic Development among Southeastern Cities." *Urban Affairs Quarterly* 24 (June), 511–27.

Bowman, Ann O'M., and Richard C. Kearney. 1993. *State and Local Government*. 2nd ed. Boston: Houghton Mifflin.

Brace, Paul. 1989. "Isolating the Economies of States." *American Politics Quarterly* 17 (July), 256–76.

Brace, Paul. 1993. *State Government and Economic Performance*. Baltimore: Johns Hopkins University Press.

Carlson, Eugene. 1983. "Great Lakes Governors Split over Truce on Industry Raids." *Wall Street Journal* (July 12), 41.

Cigler, Beverly A., Anicca C. Jansen, Vernon D. Ryan, and Jack C. Stabler. 1994. *Toward an Understanding of Multicommunity Collaboration*. Staff Report AGES 9403, USDA Economic Research Service (February).

Clarke, Marianne K. 1986. *Revitalizing State Economies*. Washington, D.C.: National Governors' Association.

Committee for Economic Development. 1986. *Leadership for Dynamic State Economies*. New York: Committee for Economic Development.

Deavers, Ken. 1992a. "What Is Rural?" *Policy Studies Journal* 20(2), 184–89.

Deavers, Ken. 1992b. As reported in General Accounting Office, "Rural Development: Rural American Faces Many Challenges." Washington, D.C.: General Accounting Office, 31.

Deavers, Ken, and Robert A. Hoppe. 1991. "The Rural Poor: The Past as Prologue." In Cornelia B. Flora and James A. Christenson, eds., *Rural Policies for the 1990s*. Boulder, Colo.: Westview Press.

Eager, Ginny. 1995. "Community Involvement in Education as a Rural Development Strategy." In David W. Sears and J. Norman Reid, eds., *Rural Development Strategies*. Chicago: Nelson Hall, 102–15.

"Economic Development Potpourri." 1993. *State Policy Reports* 11 (July), 6–10.

Economic Research Service. 1995. *Understanding Rural America*. Washington, D.C.: U.S. Department of Agriculture (February).

Eisinger, Peter K. 1988. *The Rise of the Entrepreneurial State*. Madison: University of Wisconsin Press.

Flora, Cornelia B., and James A. Christenson. 1991. "Critical Times in Rural America." In Cornelia B. Flora and James A. Christenson, eds., *Rural Policies for the 1990s*. Boulder, Colo.: Westview Press.

Fosler, R. Scott. 1988. *The New Economic Role of American States*. New York: Oxford University Press.

Fosler, R. Scott. 1991. As quoted in Dan Pilcher, "The Third Wave of Economic Development." *State Legislatures* 17 (November), 34.

Galston, William A. 1992. "Rural America in the 1990s: Trends and Choices." *Policy Studies Journal* 20 (2), 202–11.

Gillis, William R. 1991. "Encouraging Economic Development in Rural America." In Kenneth E. Pigg, ed., *The Future of Rural America*. Boulder, Colo.: Westview Press, 119–36.

Goodman, Robert. 1979., *The Last Entrepreneurs: America's Regional Wars for Jobs and Dollars*. Boston: South End Press.

Green, Gary P. et al. 1993. *From the Grassroots: Case Studies of Eight Rural Self-Development Projects*. Staff Report AGES9325, USDA Economic Research Service (November).

Gregerman, Alan S. 1991. "Rekindling the Future." *Commentary*, Winter, 91.

Hady, Thomas F., and Peggy Ross. 1990. *An Update: The Diverse Social and Economic Structure of Nonmetropolitan America*. Staff Report AGES 9036, USDA Economic Research Service (May), 2.

Hanson, Russell L. 1993. "The Development of Development Policy in the American States." In Fred A. Meyer, Jr., and Ralph Baker, eds., *State Policy Problems*. Chicago: Nelson-Hall.

Herbers, John. 1990. "A Third Wave of Economic Development." *Governing* 3 (June), 43–50.

Holmes, Mac R. 1993. As quoted in Peter Applebome, "States Raise Stakes in Fight for Jobs." *New York Times* (October 4), A10.

"The Invaders Are Welcome." 1994. *The Economist* 330 (January 8), 32.

John, DeWitt. 1994a. As quoted in William K. Stevens, "Struggle for Recovery Altering Rural America." *New York Times*, (February 5), 8.

John, DeWitt. 1994b. *Civic Environmentalism*. Washington, D.C.: Congressional Quarterly Press.

Jones, Bryan D. 1990. "Public Policies and Economic Growth in the American States." *Journal of Politics* 52 (February), 219–33.

Kane, Matt, and Peggy Sand. 1988. *Economic Development: What Works at the Local Level*. Washington, D.C.: National League of Cities.

Ledebur, Larry C., and William W. Hamilton. 1986. *Tax Concessions in State and Local Economic Development*. Washington, D.C.: Aslan Press.

Mahtesian, Charles. 1994. "Romancing the Smokestack." *Governing* 8 (November), 36–40.

National Association of Counties. "Economic Development Survey: Urban Counties." Unpublished report, no date.

National Association of State Development Agencies. 1987. *The NASDAA Newsletter* (January 21), 1–7.

National Commission on Agriculture and Rural Development Policy. 1990. "Future Directions in Rural Development Policy" (December), 1.

National Commission on the Environment. 1992. *Choosing a Sustainable Future: The Report of the National Commission on the Environment.* Washington, D.C.: World Wildlife Fund.

Nothdurft, William E. 1984. *Renewing America: Natural Resource Assets and State Economic Development.* Washington, D.C.: Council of State Planning Agencies.

Osborne, David. 1988. *Laboratories of Democracy.* Cambridge, Mass.: Harvard Business School Press.

Osborne, David, and Ted Gaebler. 1992. *Reinventing Government.* Reading, Mass.: Addison-Wesley.

Pilcher, Dan. 1991. "The Third Wave of Economic Development." *State Legislatures* 17(November), 34.

Porter, Gareth, and Janet Welsh Brown. 1992. *Global Environmental Politics.* Boulder, Colo.: Westview Press, 30–32.

Rasmussen, Wayne D. 1985. "90 Years of Rural Development Programs." *Rural Development Perspectives* 1 (October), 2–9.

Reid, J. Norman, and David W. Sears. 1992. "Symposium on Rural Development Strategies: Introduction." *Policy Studies Journal* 20 (2), 214–17.

Ross, Doug, and Robert E. Friedman. 1991. "The Emerging New Wave: New Economic Development Strategies." In R. Scott Fosler, ed., *Local Economic Development.* Washington, D.C.: International City Management Association, 125–37.

Rural Sociological Society Task Force on Persistent Poverty. 1993. *Persistent Poverty in Rural America.* Boulder, Colo.: Westview Press.

Schmandt, Jurgen, Frederick Williams, Robert H. Wilson, and Sharon Strover, eds. 1991. *Telecommunications and Rural Development: A Study of Private and Public Sector Innovation.* New York: Praeger.

Sears, David W., et al. 1992. *Gearing Up for Success: Organizing a State for Rural Development.* Washington, D.C.: The Aspen Institute.

Sears, David W., et al. 1993. "State Leadership in Rural Development: The Rationale." *Rural Development Perspectives* 9 (October), 32.

Seroka, Jim. 1988. "Community Growth and Administrative Capacity." *National Civic Review* 77 (January/February), 42–46.

Wade, Jerry L., and Glen C. Pulver. 1991. "The Role of Community in Rural Economic Development." In Kenneth E. Pigg, ed., *The Future of Rural America.* Boulder, Colo: Westview Press, 105–17.

Wilson, Robert H. 1993. *States and the Economy: Policymaking and Decentralization.* Westport, Conn.: Praeger.

3 | The Case Study States
A Study in Diversity

THE GOVERNMENTAL RESPONSE to the problems and challenges of rural America has undergone a significant change during the last decade. The nature of rural America itself has changed, as described in the previous chapter, as has the role of the public sector. But very significant variation in the governmental response can be seen across states. For this reason, this analysis has undertaken substantial field research in sixteen states. The experience of the State Rural Development Councils (SRDCs) in these states provides the empirical base.

This chapter provides basic background on economic and political structures in the sixteen states. The first two sections describe the diversity of the rural sectors and variance in the systems of governance that operate. The relative size of the rural sector in a state and its prospects for development provide an important element for the context of the SRDCs. The governmental structure, particularly the relative power of the various branches of government and the political culture of states, sets the context for factors that may condition the sixteen councils.

The second purpose of the chapter is to characterize rural policymaking and to identify past rural development efforts that provide the specific context in which the councils emerge. Policymaking in states, for rural development or any other issue, involves a complex interplay of many factors, including the nature of the problem being addressed, availability of resources, institutional capabilities, political leadership, political culture, and interest group participation, among others.

Policymaking in states has become more problematic in recent decades as these factors have changed. In addition, rural development policy involves federal activities; thus intergovernmental relations becomes a central issue. The section includes a discussion of federal activities, particularly in terms of federal collaboration and coordination with other units of government. The final section provides short profiles of the sixteen rural development councils.

The Rural Sector

The sixteen states studied in this project represent a cross section of the regions of the country, providing good variation in the types of rural economies. The empirical analysis of rural areas confronts a problem of geographic definition, especially when changes over time are to be studied. Most demographic and economic data are available by county, but a geographic definition masks rural-urban distinctions within a single county. In addition, a rural county may grow over time and eventually become urban. Data from such a community would be classified as rural in one time period and urban the next, complicating the analysis of changes in the rural area. One solution to this problem is to use the same geographic definition, based on counties, for two points in time. Using the metropolitan/nonmetropolitan definition developed by the Office of Management and Budget in 1983, comparisons are consistent in terms of the geographic definition. However, this method results in the loss of information about rural areas in metropolitan counties and does not provide a means to recognize that a nonmetropolitan county in 1980 may have grown and been reclassified to metropolitan category by 1990.

Demographic Characteristics

The rural population was observed in Chapter 2 to have declined nationally during the 1980s. The nonmetropolitan population actually increased in the sixteen states studied by just over 700,000 individuals, although six states registered a decline. A regional variation to the pattern can be observed. The Midwestern states—Iowa, Kansas, North Dakota, and South Dakota—lost population while the New England, southern, and western states recorded increases in nonmetropolitan population. Even so, all states but one had a somewhat smaller share of state population in nonmetropolitan counties in 1990 than in 1980, indicating an increasingly urban population in the states (see Appendix A).

With respect to the distribution of the nonmetropolitan population within a state, great variation is found. In most states, the share of the nonmetropolitan population residing in counties with less than 2,500 population declined slightly and the Midwestern states had the highest shares of nonmetropolitan population in such counties. With the exception of Iowa, the Midwestern states show substantially lower shares of the nonmetropolitan population residing in counties not adjacent to metropolitan counties than the other states, indicating a sparsely populated rural environment, remote from metropolitan areas.

New Mexico, Oregon, Washington, New York, and Maine have a majority of their nonmetropolitan population living in counties with between 250,000 and 20,000 population while the remaining states have majorities living in smaller counties. In seven states, the share living in the larger nonmetropolitan counties increased, reflecting a national trend of the relative rapid growth of larger nonmetropolitan counties. In twelve states, the share of nonmetropolitan counties adjacent to metropolitan counties increased their share of the nonmetropolitan population, again reflecting the trend observed nationally.

The age distribution of the nonmetropolitan population in our states followed the national trend. The share of the population over sixty-five years of age increased in all states and the share less than eighteen years of age decreased in all states. The highest levels of the over-sixty-five population were found in the Midwestern states (15 to 18 percent) and in Texas, Oregon, and Washington (around 15.5 percent) (see Appendix B).

The education levels of the nonmetropolitan population improved in all states, although significant differences in levels remain. Starting from quite low shares of individuals with at least a high school degree, the southern states improved dramatically in the 1980s. Overall, the high school dropout rates have dropped in virtually all states; however, the Southern states, Texas, New Mexico, Washington, Oregon, and New York have significantly higher rates than the others.

The racial/ethnic composition of the nonmetropolitan population, although overwhelmingly white, does show some regional variation. The three southern states have around a one-third African-American population (Texas has around 9 percent) in nonmetropolitan areas and the share changed little during the 1980s. Texas and, especially, New Mexico have large shares of Hispanic population in nonmetropolitan areas. A sizable Native American population is found in New Mexico (13 percent of nonmetropolitan population in 1990) and smaller, but notable, shares are found in Utah, Washington, Oregon, North Carolina, South Dakota, and North Dakota (see Appendix C).

The Rural Economy

The general pattern of relative decline in the rural sector, described in Chapter 2 for the country as whole, is visible in the sixteen states. In all regions, the share of the state's income originating in nonmetropolitan counties declined between 1979 and 1989, and the declines ranged from three to four percentage points in most states. This result actually overestimates the importance of the economic base of these counties; the relative share of income in nonmetropolitan counties resulting from transfer payments (one type of passive income) increased from two to four percentage points in most states; transfer payments are not the result from local economic activity (see Appendix D).

The sources of nonmetropolitan county income demonstrate the diversity of the economic base in rural America. Although the farm contribution to nonmetropolitan county income declined in most states, substantially higher levels were found in Midwestern states. Similarly, income derived from manufacturing declined in most states; southern states continued to show the highest levels, with New England states and northwestern states somewhat lower. Income attributed to the service sectors increased in all states, by two to three percentage points.

Employment trends in the nonmetropolitan counties also reflect patterns of national economic change. The nonmetropolitan share of total state employment declined between 1979 and 1989 in most states (with the exception of New York and Wyoming). The relative employment in agricultural and natural resource extraction industries declined in all states but Oregon, where forestry was the natural resource form. Most states experienced a substantial decline in this share, in the range of three to five percentage points. The share of employment in the manufacturing sector declined in nine of the sixteen states; the other states showed very modest increases in manufacturing employment. Employment in government represents a sizable share of nonmetropolitan government —ranging from about 16 percent to 23 percent of total nonmetropolitan employment —and its shares in the states changed little during the decade. The largest employment generator in all states was the services sector. Its share of relative employment increased by three and a half to five percentage points in most states (see Appendix E).

State/Regional Patterns

Demographic and economic characteristics of the rural sector in the sixteen state study demonstrate a pattern largely regional in nature. States in the same region have similar characteristics. These regional patterns are quite distinct in two regions, the Midwest and South, but noticeable in all.

The rural economy of the Midwestern states (Iowa, Kansas, North Dakota, and South Dakota) is highly dependent upon agriculture for income generation and employment, but both demonstrated a relative decline between 1979 and 1989. A loss in nonmetropolitan population resulted. The region is sparsely populated, has aged significantly during the decade, is virtually all white, but is relatively well-educated.

The southern states (Mississippi, North Carolina, and South Carolina) are quite distinct in both their demographic characteristics and rural economies. All are heavily rural and the nonmetropolitan population has grown substantially in North Carolina and South Carolina, although not in Mississippi. These states have a large share of African-American population (around 30 percent) and the rural populations are relatively poorly educated although substantial improvements in educational attainment occurred during the 1980s. The rural economies have much higher shares of income and employment generated by the manufacturing sector than in any other region, even though the role of the manufacturing sector declined somewhat during the decade. Although substantial growth occurred in nonmetropolitan counties, the relative share these counties represented in total state activities declined in all three states.

The two New England states (Maine and Vermont) are unlike New York with respect to the relative importance of nonmetropolitan counties in the state as a whole. Only 9 percent of New York's population resides in rural areas, compared with 76 percent in Maine and 60 percent in Vermont. The demographic characteristics are somewhat different as well. The New England states have higher educational attainment and although few minorities are found in the rural areas of all three states, their share is somewhat higher in New York. In terms of the rural economy of the three states, substantial similarities are seen. In all three states, very little employment and income are generated by the agriculture and natural resource sectors. Relatively high levels of income and employment are found in rural manufacturing, and quite high levels are found in the services sector. Nonmetropolitan counties adjacent to metropolitan populations have tended to increase their share of the non-metropolitan population.

The patterns among the remaining, western states are complex. In all states but Utah, the nonmetropolitan population grew in absolute terms, but declined in terms of relative share of the total state population. There was a tendency for the nonmetropolitan counties adjacent to metropolitan counties to grow somewhat more quickly than nonadjacent counties. Educational levels were quite high in the far western states but lower in New Mexico and Texas.

All western states had somewhat large shares of income and employment linked to agriculture and natural resource extraction, although farming itself was of average size, and manufacturing sector was significant in three (Washington, Oregon, and Utah). The relative importance of all three sectors in the rural economies of these states experienced a decline between 1979 and 1989. New Mexico and, to a lesser extent, Utah and Wyoming had significant specialization in the government sector. Compared with the three other regional groupings, these western states had somewhat more diversified and stronger rural economies.

Political Structure and Culture

Structure of State Governments

During the last two decades, performance of state government has improved for a variety of institutional and political reasons. Institutional reform has tended to strengthen the executive branch of government (Wilson, 1993). Reform of administrative structures and budgeting has enhanced the authority and responsibility of governors. Strengthened gubernatorial powers, however, cannot explain the emergence of a large number of strong and active governors during the last two decades. The relative decline in federal activism has also contributed to the growing prominence of governors. The importance of gubernatorial leadership is also reflected in the increased prominence of the National Governors' Association in policymaking. Although the general trend toward enhanced gubernatorial leadership is clear, there is a substantial degree of variation among states in terms of formal powers. In the sixteen states studied, there is considerable evidence of the formal powers of governors (see Table 3.1).

TABLE 3.1. *Powers of Governors*

Weak	Moderate	Moderate to Strong	Strong
North Carolina	Maine	Iowa	New York
Texas	Mississippi	Kansas	South Dakota
Vermont	South Carolina	New Mexico	
	Washington	North Dakota	
		Oregon	
		Utah	
		Wyoming	

Note: Values for Power of Governor are calculated by averaging Beyle scores for the following categories: tenure potential, appointment power, removal power, governor controls budget, legislature can change budget, and veto power.

Source: Beyle, 1990, pp. 121–129.

A governor gains formal strength through the power of appointment (especially in a cabinet-style state government), control of the budget process, and veto power. In some states, such as New Mexico, relatively strong formal powers are diluted by the inability of a governor to be reelected and succeed himself or herself. The policy agenda of a state may fluctuate as the governorship changes hands.

In addition to the relative strength of the governor, which may be the primary structuring element of a state's government, the formal powers of the branches of government and of local government are important in policymaking. Again, substantial variation among the states exists. In the absence of a strong governor, states are likely to have a strong legislature, such as in the southern states (North Carolina, South Carolina, Mississippi, and Texas), which exert great influence over state government. Some legislatures, such as those in Washington, have developed very sophisticated policy analysis capabilities and influence outcomes in this fashion. A number of states have legislatures that meet infrequently, thus reducing their roles in policymaking. The Vermont legislature prides itself on being citizen-driven, rather than professional politician–driven.

In a number of states, executive branch agencies are relatively independent and powerful. This most frequently results from the so-called long ballot where directors of some agencies are elected in statewide elections, especially in the southern states, giving them an independent political base. State legislatures may also create special links to agencies, again giving them a somewhat independent base, as in North Carolina. Such states can give the appearance of a quite fragmented, decentralized state government. Further variation is found in those states with large Native American populations and reservations, such as New Mexico.

The relative sovereignty of reservations continues to be a major point of contention, but one that must be confronted in a rural policy initiative.

States are affected by partisan politics in quite different ways. With the decline in the internal coherence and discipline of the two national political parties, governors in recent decades have tended to become less tied to national parties and more pragmatic in their efforts within states. Nevertheless, in some states partisan competition greatly influences policymaking. In the southern states, the move from the domination by the Democratic party to a bipartisan political system, with the strengthening of the Republican party, has made state policymaking quite contentious. In this region, the growth of the political power of African Americans (and Mexican Americans in Texas) has further complicated policymaking in that more and diverse interests are represented in the process. In other regions, bipartisan competition in states may lead to policy gridlock, as in Maine, but in other states, such as Kansas, cooperation between the two parties, at least in state policymaking, may exist. In a number of western states, Republican domination of state politics reduces contentiousness.

The State Rural Development Council initiative is intended to enhance cooperation among all three levels of government and with the private sector, including the nonprofit sector. The formal and informal relations between state government and local government varies quite widely in the sixteen states, as a result of both formal powers and the political process. In all states, the powers of local government are specified by state government; that specification, however, varies widely among states. In some states, local governments are fairly independent with respect to financial capabilities and/or ordinance-making authority. Two states (South Dakota and Texas) provide strong powers to municipal government, but counties are weak.

Beyond the formal powers and relations between state and local governments, the practice of governance varies greatly. In some states, councils of governments (COGs) provide the principal link between state governments and local governments. In other states, such as Oregon, the connection between state and local governments varies among subregions and depends on the actions of local officials. In a number of states, significant antagonism exits between state and local officials (New Mexico and Kansas). Local officials may feel that state government is distant and unconcerned. Diversity in the rural sector of the state (as in New Mexico and Texas) may make it difficult for state government to respond to individual community needs (that is, targeting of state policy is difficult because of diversity in the rural sector of a state) and local governments feel neglected.

Political Culture

Political culture refers to the attitudes, values, and beliefs that people hold toward government. As developed by political scientist Daniel Elazar (1984, 1994) in the 1960s, the term refers to the way in which people think about their government and the manner in which the political system operates. According to Elazar, the United States is a synthesis of three major political subcultures, each of which has distinctive characteristics. These political subcultures developed out of the sociocultural differences among the peoples who settled this country. As Elazar (1984, p. 122) puts it, "Sectional concentrations of distinctive cultural groups have helped create the social interests that tie contiguous states to one another even in the face of marked differences in the standard measures of similarity." Within a region, states that may vary widely on socioeconomic dimensions share a common character that unites them. The three political subcultures are individualistic, moralistic, and traditionalistic. In an individualistic setting, politics is an open marketplace in which people participate because of essentially private motivations. A very different orientation exists in a moralistic community, where politics is an effort to establish a good and just society. Citizens are expected to be active in public affairs. In a traditionalistic political culture, politics functions to maintain the existing order, and political participation may be confined to social elites. These differing conceptions about the purpose of government and the role of politics lead to different behaviors. For example, with regard to the initiation of a new program, officials in the three subcultures will react differently. In an individualistic community, officials will resist initiating a program unless public opinion demands it. However, leaders in moralistic areas would adopt the new program, even without pressure, if they believed it to be in the public interest. Rulers of traditionalistic communities would initiate the program only if they thought it would serve the interests of the governing elite.

Few states are characterized by a single subculture. Instead, cultural change and synthesis have produced a mixture within most states. In Elazar's framework, although sixteen states tend toward traditionalism,

TABLE 3.2. *The Political Subcultures of the Sixteen States*

Traditionalistic	Traditionalistic/ Moralistic	Traditionalistic/ Individualistic	Individualistic/ Moralistic	Moralistic/ Individualistic	Moralistic
Mississippi	North Carolina	New Mexico	New York	Iowa	Maine
South Dakota		Texas	Wyoming	Kansas	Oregon
				S. Dakota	Utah
				Washington	Vermont
					N. Dakota

Source: Adapted from Elazar. 1984.

only eight are purely traditionalistic. Six others have pockets of individualism; two are influenced by moralistic subcultures. To account for the shifts, Elazar added five hybrid subcultures to the original three. Nine states are dominated by a moralistic subculture; in eight states, moralism is modified by strains of individualism. Of the seventeen states tending toward individualism, in nine states the individualistic subculture predominates. In two states, traditionalism is an important secondary influence and in six states, moralism plays a strong role. Generally, traditionalistic cultures have characterized the South, individualistic cultures have developed in the middle and southwestern sections of the country, and moralistic cultures have predominated in the far North, the Northwest, and the Pacific Coast. Table 2.3 lists the political subcultures for the sixteen states.

One of the most difficult aspects of political culture is its measurement. How can a concept so intangible be operationalized for use in statistical analysis? Substantial work has been undertaken to operationalize the concept. The first effort to quantify the concept was by Ira Sharkansky (1969), who developed an additive scale ranging from one (purely moralistic) to nine (more traditionalistic). Although the Sharkansky scale has been employed by subsequent researchers, it has not been free of debate. For example, Charles Johnson (1976) has argued that by making political culture a unidimensional concept, Sharkansky has blurred the distinctiveness inherent in Elazar's notion of three separate cultures. Johnson adopts an alternative formulation to capture political culture: data on religious affiliation by state early in the twentieth century. Denominations are classified as moralistic, individualistic, or traditionalistic. Morgan and Watson (1991) borrowed Johnson's approach and updated it using 1980 data.

The most recent work on political culture shifts the unit of analysis from the state level to the county level. Lieske (1993) has identified ten regional subcultures using racial origin, ethnic ancestry, religious affiliation, and social structure. As Lieske (1993, p. 991) contends, regional subcultures result from "the cultural preferences of different ethno-religious settler groups and the nationally centripetal and regionally centrifugal demands of their environments." Using cultural indicators for the nation's counties, he is able to generate ten distinctive regional subcultures that are fairly homogeneous and contiguous. He gives them labels such as "rurban," "ethnic," "border," and "agrarian," among others.

The fascination with quantifying Elazar's concept lies in its compelling nature. Socioeconomic and political variables are limited in the degree to which they explain why states do what they do, why certain states adopt a particular public policy and others do not. Political culture, difficult as it is to get a handle on, remains a viable explanation for state behavior. Applying the work of various researchers to specific states yields some interesting outcomes. For example, Vermont is considered by Elazar to be moralistic. Johnson finds the state to be individualistic, as do Morgan and Watson. Florida is traditionalistic, according to Elazar and Johnson, but individualistic in the Morgan and Watson categorization. In fact, one of the trends in the data is the increase in individualistic states; the recent work by Morgan and Watson counts twenty-seven individualistic states.

The findings are tantalizing enough to keep the interest in political culture high. In general, political culture has been found to affect the level of political participation in a state, the operation of a state's political institutions, and the types of public policies that a state enacts (Morgan and Watson, 1991). One study, for example, found that political culture influenced the accessibility of state government structures and political processes to the public (Herzik, 1985). Other research has linked political culture to policy outcomes; for instance, moralistic states demonstrate the greatest tendency toward innovativeness, whereas traditionalistic states exhibit the least (Fitzpatrick and Hero, 1988).

Political culture has been shown to influence development policy in the states. Traditionalistic states pursue a strategy marked by business retention and attraction policies while moralistic states favor business creation tools (Boeckelman, 1991). Individualistic states tend toward more of a mixture of approaches and tools. Of course, political culture interacts with other factors in influencing state development policy. Boeckelman found a state's economic condition to be another important explanatory variable. However, other state characteristics (such as the level of partisan competition and the ideological bent of the public) are of little value in understanding development policy.

Hanson's (1991) research confirmed the importance of economic circumstances in determining state development policy. In his analysis, the importance of political culture is in its effect on the strategic choices made by states. For example, moralistic states adopt what Hanson calls "solidarity," or an inclusive orientation toward development. Policymakers in moralistic states not only offer capital subsidies to employers and tax concessions to investors, they also strongly protect workers' interests. In traditionalistic states, improvement of the business climate is accomplished through extensive subsidies and tax concessions to investors. Although the antilabor bent in traditionalistic states has declined over time, it remains higher than in states dominated by other political cultures. Individualistic states tend to act in a more particularistic manner by conferring benefits on specific firms or enterprises. These states rely more heavily on the provision of capital subsidies.

Rural Policymaking and Past Rural Development Activities

State Efforts

Most states substantially increased their economic development activities in the 1980s, as discussed in Chapter 2. The national pattern is reflected in many of the sixteen states studied here. Iowa, New York, North Carolina, South Carolina, and Vermont adopted major development initiatives. The extent of initiatives targeted on rural initiatives were less common and generally less significant. The level of rural development initiatives in the 1980s can be partially explained by several political factors, including the importance of the rural sector in a state's legislature and nature of the rural sector in a state.

A number of the sixteen states, including Iowa, Maine, South Dakota, and Wyoming, are predominately rural and rural interests dominate the state legislature. This pattern is unlike the broader national trend of increasing urban and suburban orientation in state government. Although such states do not necessarily expect the public sector to promote development—Wyoming, in particular, has historically adopted a fairly minimalist vision for public sector—to the extent that economic development is promoted, it has a decidedly rural, if not agricultural, orientation.

A substantial number of the sixteen states, including Kansas, New Mexico, North Carolina, Texas, and Washington, have witnessed a relative decline in rural population and subsequently a decline in the representation of rural interests in state legislatures. The extent of the decline of rural influence varies, but the overall tendency in these states during the 1980s was less attention and resources devoted to rural issues as compared to the urban interests in the state.

In some states, the heterogeneity in the rural sector complicates the formation of rural policy. States such as New Mexico, Mississippi, Texas, North Carolina, and Washington have diverse rural sectors, resulting from agricultural specialization and/or the racial/ethnic composition in various subregions, and thus consensus building at the state level is difficult. In at least two states, New Mexico and Texas, the lack of targeted rural policy in the past is in part explained by the difficulty in forming consensus, given the diversity of interests in their rural sectors.

Many states have given priority to human resource development in their rural sectors in order that communities can be self-sustaining. States such as Kansas, Oregon, South Carolina, and Texas have adopted efforts to improve the capacity of local communities, which will empower them to develop their own initiatives. In a variation of this concept, some states, including Iowa, Maine, and South Carolina, focus efforts on leadership development in rural communities and these efforts are frequently funded from nongovernmental sources.

Six of the sixteen states (Iowa, Maine, Mississippi, New Mexico, North Dakota, and Wyoming) participated in the Rural Academy of the Council of Governors' Policy Advisors (CGPA). The academy was designed to bring diverse interests from rural communities in a state, including governmental officials and private sector representatives, to assess and develop strategies for rural development. This experience was found to have a very important impact on the rural development councils. In several states, the overall direction established in the academy was adopted by state council. A number of states have a tradition of open and inclusive policymaking process (such as Iowa, Oregon, Vermont, and Washington) which can similarly have a positive impact on the Rural Development Councils.

Federal Efforts

The federal government became heavily involved in rural America during the last century. As discussed in Chapter 1, the range of activities is quite extensive; some are organized sectorally, such as the U.S. Department of Agriculture, and others result from the delivery of services to rural populations in programs that are not area-specific, such as programs of the Department of Health and Human Services (DHHS). Although the extent and nature of cooperation and collaboration may vary among states, in most of the states considered in this project the overall pattern is similar.

With respect to federal-state relations, three different types of interaction can be identified. Some federal delivery systems require little programmatic contact with state systems, such as Farmers Home Administration (FmHA) and other USDA programs, and this limits the need for interaction with state government. In instances of shared funding and program administration, where federal and state funds are utilized in a single activity, there is more cooperation. The County Extension Service is such a program and although the federal partner frequently dominates policy direction, with limited influence or oversight by state officials, its activities produce very extensive contact and cooperation among federal, state, and local levels of government and with the private sector. In the third type of relation, federal funds are transferred to state agencies for administration. State agencies that implement the Small Cities Community Development Block Grant (CDBG) program, for example, have substantial discretion in program administration, but there is little formal cooperation between federal and state agencies. In fact, decentralization of the administration of federal programs, such as in health and human services, EPA, and CDBG, has diminished the opportunities for cooperation between federal and state agencies because state agencies now have more discretion and autonomy in the administration of programs.

Cooperation among federal and state agencies on rural projects often occurs. For example, a rural project might include funding from EDA, FmHA, and the state agency that administers the CDBG program, when no one agency has sufficient funds to undertake the project on its own. Another federal agency, Small Business Administration (SBA), has an extensive field organization throughout the country and is generally viewed as an agency that cooperates with a broad range of institutions and organizations. While its specific mandate is to provide loans to private sector businesses, it fulfills this mandate in a fairly entrepreneurial fashion and works with many local groups (governments, chambers of commerce, utility companies, and banks), state agencies, and other federal agencies.

There are a number of federal efforts intended to promote cooperation between state administrators of federal programs and local governments. An early example of this type of federal initiative, from the 1960s,
was the section 304 planning grants from the EDA to states. These
grants had to be matched by state funds and frequently involved the participation of FmHA. A contemporary version of this type of initiative is
HUD's requirement for the development of a Comprehensive Housing
Assessment Study (CHAS) by the state agency responsible for administering HUD's programs. The development of the CHAS produces extensive contact between state officials and local officials even though the
level of funding available to communities has been relatively modest,
given the level of need.

In social services, there has been a good deal of cooperation and
coordination between state and federal agencies. The rural health programs of the Public Health Service, for example, have an extensive history of very significant relations with state and local agencies. Many
federal centers and institutes provide important technical information,
largely through professional relationships with state officials. While federal dominance has dissipated with decentralization, federal agencies
nevertheless still play a facilitative role.

The Resource Conservation and Development Program (RC&D) of
the Soil Conservation Service (SCS) has created service areas throughout
the country. The purpose of this program is to accelerate the conservation,
development, and utilization of natural resources in order to improve the
level of economic activity, enhance the environment, and raise the standard of living of the areas in which it operates. The membership of the
RC&D councils consists of local community, county, and area leaders and
has a full-time administrator from the SCS. The councils utilize the
resources of federal, state, county, and local agencies in their efforts.

The degree of cooperation among federal programs and officials in
rural areas in an individual state, a goal of the State Rural Development
Councils, is conditioned by a number of institutional factors. Agencies
have distinct missions and constituencies which may restrict the opportunity for coordination and cooperation. Federal agencies and officials tend
to be program-oriented and, consequently, cooperation is problematic.
Also the training received in some federal agencies may be not conducive
to approaching rural issues in the holistic framework suggested by the federal initiative. One factor that contributes to this problem is the congressional committee structure, which tends to create overlapping jurisdictions

in program design. For example, construction of rural health facilities can be funded by DHHS, Farmers Home Administration, or HUD.

In the land and resource management agencies of the Department of Interior and USDA—including the Forest Service (FS), Bureau of Land Management (BLM), and Soil Conservation Service (SCS)—significant coordination has occurred in the past. For example, the FS, BLM, and the Bureau of Indian Affairs (BIA) have exchanged information and undertaken joint projects. The public land agencies, especially BLM and the FS, have had fairly extensive interaction resulting from the common and complementary functions. The permitting process for individuals or local governments frequently brings federal agencies into contact. Tourism strategies that involve public lands bring not only federal agencies together but also state and local governments. Coordination of these federal agencies may also involve the extension service and state departments of agriculture.

Council Profiles

The sixteen states that have been studied intensively represent three different generations of Rural Development Council activity. Eight of the states—Kansas, Maine, Mississippi, Oregon, South Carolina, South Dakota, Texas, and Washington—were a part of the original pilot states; they have been classified as the first generation of activity. Four states—Iowa, New Mexico, North Carolina and Vermont—are viewed as the second generation of states since they responded to the initial request for expansion. Four states—New York, North Dakota, Utah, and Wyoming—were more recent entrants into council activity. The profiles that follow represent a glimpse of these councils as of summer 1994.

First-Generation Councils

Kansas Rural Development Council. The Kansas Rural Development Council (KRDC) Steering Committee was convened on November 8, 1990, by the state director of the Farmers Home Administration (FmHA). The council held its first meeting in the spring of 1991. The steering committee drafted the KRDC bylaws which were adopted by the full KRDC in spring 1991 and have since been amended. The initial KRDC structure included a cochair arrangement (one federal and one state member) but experience proved this to be unwieldy. Current KRDC bylaws provide for the election of a chair, vice chair, treasurer, and an eleven-member executive committee. For the executive committee, federal members elect three of their members as representatives; the governor appoints three state representatives; private/local government members elect three representatives; and the entire council elects two at-large members (these can be federal, state, local, or private-sector members).

From the beginning, the membership of the council has been broad and inclusive. Within a few months of its organization, state groups included the governor's office, the legislature, and a range of state agencies, including the community action agency. While local government representatives are members, they do not play active roles. Tribal governments are not involved at all. The council had forty-nine members in 1991; it had sixty-four in 1993, including the executive director. Of these, nineteen are federal members, twenty-seven are state actors, two are local government members, and fifteen are from the private sector.

The KRDC has defined its mission as that of an interorganizational network that will tackle problems of rural development that are beyond the scope of any one agency. One of its early demonstration projects was the consolidation of a common loan application form for Farmers Home, Small Business Administration (SBA), and the Kansas Department of Commerce and Housing's (KDCH) Community Development Block Grant program. The executive committee and standing committees play pivotal roles in the development of activities for the Kansas council. The executive committee develops agendas prior to the quarterly meetings and action plans for implementing decisions of the full council.

Both the initial executive director for the KRDC (who served from 1991 through 1992) and the current executive director (who joined the council in May 1993) have had extensive backgrounds as federal employees within the state of Kansas. The office of the council is located within the KDCH, a state agency located near the capitol and with easy access to other state agencies.

As of mid-1994, there were four committees active within the council: natural resources, infrastructure, community services, and economic development. All council activities are funneled through these committees. The council is currently involved in the High Plains Trade Project, which seeks collaboration among states in the High Plains region to advance regional trade opportunities in global markets.

Maine Rural Development Council. The Maine Rural Development Council (MRDC) was one of the eight pilot councils. It evolved from the 1979 Governor's Committee on Rural Development which had membership representing state and federal agency heads, elected officials, and representatives from rural areas. The Governor's Committee was disbanded by a 1992 executive order and folded into MRDC.

MRDC's first organizing meetings were held in November and December 1990, and the first full council meeting in May 1991. Acting cochairs were appointed in December 1990. Permanent officers and an executive committee were elected at an August 1991 summer institute. Six action plan themes were adopted and assigned to standing committees in 1991: coordination and cooperation, human resources, physical infrastructure, business, development, leadership, and natural resource development.

From the outset, participation and membership in MRDC have been open and inclusive. Meetings of the full council are held quarterly and usually have attracted between twenty-five and sixty participants from federal, state, and local government units as well as nonprofit organizations and private businesses.

MRDC business is conducted by its (now) eighteen-member executive committee that meets monthly. The executive committee includes representatives of federal, state, and local government and "other." Formal leadership positions include a federal cochair, state cochair, and secretary-treasurer. The current federal cochair represents EDA; the state cochair is the commissioner of the State Department of Agriculture; the secretary-treasurer is the state economist and director of the State Office of Planning and Budgeting.

MRDC's first and only executive director was hired in April 1991 through the Cooperative Extension Service on the campus of the University of Maine, where MRDC's primary office remains. Previously, the executive director had extensive community and economic development experience in Maine (including with tribal governments), and grant writing and grant management experience with a wide variety of federal programs.

In 1992, MRDC adopted strategic planning principles to guide its selection of project activities. Annual work plans are prepared at retreats and are implemented by project-specific work groups that have replaced the original standing committees. In summer 1992, one project of note was operational, cranberry industry permitting. In summer 1993, four major project working groups were active: value-added wood products, leadership, the rural health care initiative, and impediments removal. Additional project areas became operational during the second half of 1993: visioning/futuring for the potato industry, strategic planning for a community that is being heavily impacted by a military base closure, interagency business mentoring, resources to assist communities in distress, a "one-stop" job creation and job training linkage model, and a single credit application project.

Mississippi Council on Rural Development. The Mississippi Council on Rural Development (MCRD) was organized as one of the eight original pilot states in the fall of 1990. The first executive director for the council was selected in Washington before the council itself was actually formed. The State Farmers Home Administration representative had the official responsibility for convening the first meeting but the executive director effectively played the lead role in the first phase of the organization. The council has actually gone through three different phases that reflect both federal and state political changes. The second phase of the council occurred when there was a change in governor in the state; the third occurred when there was a change in the White House.

When the council first began meeting, membership on the council was expected to total no more than thirty individuals, of whom half would be federal officials. By the end of May 1991, however, approximately fifty individuals were involved in some way in the council; the core group, however, was defined as twenty-six state or federal agency members. Although there has been an expansion in the membership of the council, there continues to be some disagreement within the group about the extent to which it would be broad and inclusive, particularly involving representatives from the substate regions, the private sector, and community-based organizations. By the end of 1993, however, the council membership was larger and more diverse than it had been earlier. More than fifty-five individuals attended at least one of the meetings.

The original bylaws of the council defined a broad approach to rural development: "to improve the quality of life in rural Mississippi through addressing the economic, infrastructure, medical, educational, and environmental needs of Mississippi's rural people." Objectives included providing leadership in making strategic use of available resources, serving as a focal point for identifying interdepartmental/intergovernmental barriers to rural development, and elevating national issues to the federal working group. The bylaws established a sixteen-member executive committee that included officers and the executive director, four task force chairs, chairs of the finance, membership, and bylaws committees, and four individuals at-large.

The first executive director for the Mississippi council was a native of the state and an individual who, as a political appointee in the Bush administration, had been a participant in the Washington-based activities. He saw himself as an expert in rural development and wanted to play the overt leadership role in the council. He resigned to become the regional director of Rural Development Administration. For most of 1992, there was no executive director and little activity of the council. In May 1993, a new executive director was chosen who was also a native of the state and had extensive Washington experience. However, she was selected by the council. During the early days of the council its office was located in the Farm Bureau. When the current executive director began, it was moved to the Institutions of Higher Learning, the state higher education coordinating body.

In mid-1994, four task forces were active: social/community development, physical infrastructure development, business development, and work force development. These groups meet on their own and report back to the board.

Oregon Rural Development Council. Oregon was one of the pilot states under the rural development initiative. Twenty-six people attended the first meeting of the Oregon Rural Development Council (ORDC) in December 1990. At the outset, most members represented the federal government, but there was also representation from the private sector and state and local governments.

It was always intended that the ORDC be an inclusive group that would include representation of five key constituencies: federal, state, and local governments, the private (including not-for-profit) sector, and Oregon tribal governments. Significant state involvement was slow in coming; however, the Oregon Economic Development Department has provided some level of support from the beginning. The governor gave her full backing to the council in mid-1993. As of this writing, all five constituencies are represented and fully engaged. Membership on the council now numbers eighty-six. This includes twenty-nine federal, nineteen state, fourteen local, five tribal, and nineteen private-sector representatives.

The full council meets monthly as does its executive committee. Most full council meetings are held in rural communities where community members make presentations on their development needs and concerns. Relevant council members and the executive director are assigned follow-up responsibilities as the council attempts to address the concerns raised. The council's agenda is set by the executive committee with input from the full council, and is driven by the information gleaned from the community meetings.

The ORDC has expressed its vision for rural Oregon as "a strong dynamic community that provides a safe, quality living environment for work and family and is responsive to changing conditions." This leads to its mission, which is "to promote rural development by focusing governmental, private, and non-profit resources to assist rural Oregon in building long-term viability."

The executive director, hired as a federal employee, came from the state of Washington, where she had been employed in local economic development for eight years. She is the council's second director. The ORDC office is located in space provided by U.S. Bank in Portland.

Council standing committees include the executive committee and a nominating committee. Ad hoc working groups are formed to deal with specific issues identified in community meetings. The council has dedicated its time and resources to work on five major issues: the development of a rural information network; assistance to timber dependent communities and businesses wishing to bid on government contracts; the need for local communities to hire rural development staff; excessive paperwork requirements in federal grant applications; and federal and state mandates without money (primarily environmental regulations).

South Carolina Rural Development Council. One of the eight pilot states, South Carolina organized its council during the fall of 1990. The state director of the Farmers Home Administration and the economic development director in the governor's office brought together existing networks of rurally-focused actors and agencies from the federal and state levels, respectively. In its formative stages, the council used a cochair (one federal and one state) structure to convey the partnership nature of the rural initiative. That structure has remained in place.

In terms of membership, the SCRDC initially tended toward exclusivity. Members were selected because of a central, not tangential, interest in rural development. In 1991, the Council had forty-one members (fourteen federal, seventeen state, and ten "other"); the number had grown to fifty-three by early 1994. The increase in membership has come from two categories: state government and "other." An invitation to membership for nonfederal, nonstate "others" has been on the basis of their ability to bring resources to the council. SCRDC meets quarterly, usually in the state capitol.

Officially, the mission of the council is "to improve the opportunities, income and well-being of South Carolina's rural people by strengthening the capacity of rural America to compete in the global economy." That rather expansive sentiment is narrowed in a goals statement: "The goal of the Council is to provide an institutional framework with which federal government resources can be used, in combination with those of state and local government, private businesses, and non-profit organizations, to promote rural development." SCRDC is committed to an activist posture but aimed at policy issues, not programs.

Leadership in the council is provided by the federal and state cochairs (who serve one-year [renewable once] terms) and the executive director. At the July 1993 quarterly meeting, one of the cochairs announced that he, the other cochair, and the executive director had met to reflect on "where the Council's been and where it's going." That reflection resulted in the design of the ensuing year's action plan (presented as a draft) and the realignment (and reduction) of committees. He then asked the question: any objection? After some clarification, the threesome had council agreement on their proposal. The executive committee and the working committee chairs (a few council members do double duty on the executive committee and chairing a working committee) occupy a "second-tier" leadership role. Working committee chairs can carve out a more or less activist role for themselves.

The executive director for SCRDC served as rural transportation policy coordinator for the U.S. Department of Transportation in the office of the assistant secretary for policy and international affairs for nine years prior to assuming the South Carolina job. In addition to his federal-level employment, the executive director worked as a health planner in the office of the governor of West Virginia. He is the first (and only) executive director that the council has had. After three years on the job, his description of his role is that of "collaborator," blending both leadership and administrative functions.

SCRDC is a three-and-a-half-year-old organization that spent the first year and a half getting organized. Its activities over the past two years have emanated from the strategic planning process. One of the benefits of this process was a relatively comprehensive airing of fundamental issues and concerns regarding rural development. Council members were forced to weigh the relative importance of competing activities. As such, this was a catalytic event, that is, it caused rurally involved agencies to take stock of their approaches and activities. And it showcased SCRDC as more than another player; in this case, it was the hub of the wheel. Some of SCRDC's subsequent accomplishments include the identification (and forwarding to Washington) of several rural development impediments, publication of the *South Carolina Rural Resources Directory*, and a demonstration project that resulted in a multijurisdictional sewage treatment system. As of spring 1994, the council was considering the feasibility of a new demonstration project, "Earn Your Enterprise," a plan to improve the self-sufficiency of rural welfare recipients.

South Dakota Rural Council. The South Dakota Rural Council (SDRC) held its initial meeting in October of 1990. Participants at that meeting included the federal, state, and private sectors. The executive committee, comprised of officers from all three of these sectors, was elected to set meeting agendas and to hire a director.

Membership has followed this three-sector pattern from the founding period. Membership is by position, including state cabinet secretaries (including environment and natural resources), and the governor's office, particularly its Economic Development Office. Statewide associations representing local government, commerce, banking, retail, and rural cooperatives were originally involved. Later other associations, planning and development districts, and tribal organization representatives were added. The group expanded from a core of fifteen members to forty-five and later to sixty-two. The current council includes twenty-one federal officials, fifteen state officials, six tribal members, and twenty private members. Meetings of the full council are held on a quarterly basis.

The South Dakota Council has defined its mission as "to strengthen rural South Dakota." It defines rural as all areas outside of the Sioux Falls Metropolitan Statistical Area (MSA), the only one in the state.

The executive committee of the council originally played the key role in developing their agenda. The initial focus of the group was on building a database of development resources for communities and in removing federal impediments. As of mid-1993, a series of work groups were established that now share a role with the executive committee in shaping the activities.

The executive director for the council is the former deputy director of the Governor's Office of Economic Development. He is now a federal employee. The council offices occupy space in the state capitol.

As of late 1993, the council restructured its subcommittee effort to reflect a shift in focus away from federal impediments removal toward problem-focused research. The committees reflect the current substantive focus: rural capacity building, infrastructure, partnering in government, and value-added agricultural activity. These working groups are exploring strategic issues and developing agendas for federal-state collaboration.

Texas Rural Development Council. The Texas Federal Rural Development Council was formed (formally instituted) in February of 1991 (a name change, dropping "Federal," was approved in December 1992). The leadership responsible for establishing the council was largely federal (two key individuals were from Farmers Home Administration). Nonfederal members received an associate status and could not serve on the executive committee, although nonfederal members did have important assignments as committee chairs.

The federal leadership became quite concerned with the lack of participation and degree of commitment of state and local officials and the membership definition was perceived to be an important impediment to broader participation. A change in the bylaws in December of 1992 removed the associate status designation. The election of new officers resulted in a chair from a federal agency (EDA) and a cochair from the governor's office. The appointment of chairs to standing committees insures that leadership is shared by representatives from different groups. Several of the founders were federal political appointees. In spite of the change in presidential administration and Democratic appointments to federal positions, the leadership transition in the council was made with very little loss in momentum.

Membership in TRDC is open and has grown very dramatically, reporting 2,800 in its membership database in the fall of 1993. The number of active members, in terms of frequent participation in council and committee meetings, is substantially less. Substantial care has been given to developing materials for prospective and new members. The quarterly meetings draw from sixty to ninety participants.

The council operated for more than a year without an executive director. The woman appointed to the position came with an extensive background in rural Texas, where she served in many different types of capacities. Her role has been largely determined by the council's decision to expand membership, which has required the management of a very large flow of information in the council and largely defines the day-to-day activities of the staff.

The administrative and budgetary functions of the TRDC are the responsibility of the five-person executive committee [the chair (federal) and cochair (state), secretary (federal), treasurer (nonprofit organization), and counsel (federal)]. This committee establishes meeting dates and agenda. The substantive activities are conducted largely through standing committees (membership, leadership, Partnership and entrepreneurial development, strategic planning, think tank). Each standing committee has three cochairs, one federal official, one state member, and one private or local member. The activities of the standing committees are coordinated through a strategic planning committee whose membership consists of officers and chairs of the standing committees and other ad hoc members.

The early years of the TRDC were devoted to process and membership issues. The strategic planning process adopted in the spring of 1993 produced a more action- and activity-oriented agenda for the council.

Washington State Rural Development Council. The Washington State Rural Development Council (WSRDC) began its activities through an informal meeting of participants representing federal, state, and local governments in November 1990. By May 1991, six constituency groups from nonprofit organizations, the private sector, tribal governments, local governments, state agencies, and federal agencies formed the core of the council. Washington was the first state to include representatives from tribal governments in the organizing efforts of its council—a move that other states have emulated.

The council's mission: "According to locally conceived and driven strategies, coordinate and apply private, local, state, tribal, nonprofit, and federal resources to support the development of viable, self-reliant rural communities."

From its inception, Washington's council was broad and inclusive. An executive committee of thirty, made up of five members from each of the six constituency groups, provides continuity of both membership and issue management. The executive committee meets three times a year, in February, May, and October. Meetings are open to anyone who wishes to attend. The May and October meetings are held in rural communities to consider issues from a local perspective. Active membership numbers about fifty, representing all of the constituency groups and most rural regions of the state.

State agencies, especially the Washington Departments of Community Development, Health, and Employment Security, provided much of the council's early impetus. Continuity has also been maintained through the presence of key career officials from federal agencies located in the state, notably the Forest Service, Farmers Home Administration, Soil Conservation Service, Economic Development Administration, Small Business Administration, and, more recently, the Rural Development Administration and the Environmental Protection Agency.

Washington's council interacts with other organizations having a stake in the development interests of rural communities, including the Governor's Timber Team, which plays a key role in the implementation of the presidential timber initiative, Affiliated Tribes of Northwest Indians, representing tribal governments across the Pacific Northwest, and Washington's resource, conservation, and development councils.

The executive director, lead staff person to the council's executive officers and executive committee, was an employee of Washington's Department of Community Development, where the council's office is located.

As of March 1994, three standing committees consolidate issues and carry out some of the work of the council. These committee are: communications linkages, responsible for building and developing an effective electronic mail link among council members; policy, building and developing linkages with other organizations and agencies, including the state legislature; and resources, organizing efforts among all the council's partners to design and implement streamlined planning requirements for local jurisdictions to apply for state and federal resources. These committees meet regularly — in person or electronically.

Second Generation Councils

Iowa Rural Development Council. The Iowa Rural Development Council (IRDC) held its organization meeting in October of 1992. The meeting was planned by a steering committee of persons who had been active on state-level rural projects, with staff support from the Iowa Department of Economic Development (DED). Participants at this meeting elected permanent members of the steering committee and work groups were selected.

Membership on the Iowa council and its steering committee is balanced evenly between federal government, state government, and private sector individuals. Selection to the council is by position in some cases, but most members are active individuals who have worked on previous rural development projects. Nongovernmental organizations, such as local government, farm, and business associations, are represented, but not necessarily by their chief executive officers. The forty-six member council is equally divided by the three sectors. There has been difficulty in achieving tribal representation.

The Iowa council's mission is to examine and develop solutions for rural problems of a federal-state nature. The council envisions its role as more of a research and demonstration body, working on problems that are not the exclusive province of any single agency, as opposed to a policymaking group.

The steering committee was not only essential in establishment of the committee, but performed administrative functions during its first year, when the council had no director. The seven-member committee includes two federal, two state, and three private-sector members. The chair is a private member, a female farm operator. The committee meets monthly, between quarterly council meetings.

The executive director is a former planning staff member in DED. He was involved in developing the early strategic planning for the council. He is officially a contract employee of DED, but spends full time on the council. The office is located within the DED.

Three working groups are developing issues for the council: leadership and development; water, sewer, and infrastructure; and housing. New groups in quality of life, value-added agriculture, and restructuring local government/networking are in various development stages. The existing groups have explored different models of problem solving and services delivery and plan to develop pilot or demonstration projects in the future.

New Mexico Rural Development Response Council. In early 1992, Governor Bruce King proposed that New Mexico be included in the second round of the federal initiative for rural development. The proposal was accepted and the first partnership meeting was held in July of 1992. An executive committee was established and started meeting monthly. The first full council meeting was held at the end of November 1992.

The council was founded with a formal structure. The governor appoints the chair and all state members of the council (which totaled 105 in July of 1993). Most decision-making authority rests with the executive committee, which has expanded its membership to ensure participation of various groups, such as the federal agencies. Each of the various groups in the council—federal and state agencies, local and private sector—elect members to serve on the executive committee. The executive director, a man with substantial previous experience in state government and in New Mexico, reports to the executive committee and is housed in the state's Department of Economic Development (DED).

The organizational structure and founding of the council, dominated by gubernatorial leadership, created initial difficulties with respect to the participation of federal officials. Compounding the problem was that the lead federal official was from the Small Business Administration, outside the chain of command of the USDA and with little leverage for inducing federal participation of rural-oriented federal agencies. To remedy this situation, in July of 1993 the federal officials organized a "caucus" within the council and two new seats for federal officials were created on the executive committee. The council has also attempted to attract the participation of tribal governments. Seats on the executive committee and in the council are reserved for tribal representation but active participation, on the level desired, has not yet been achieved.

The work of the council is organized in seven issue areas and response teams are organized within each area to address specific issues: infrastructure, health, agriculture/land use, economic development, regulation and legislation, environmental/natural resources, and education/job training. The chair of each response team is a member of the executive committee and members are drawn from the council and outside experts are brought in as needed. The response teams are fairly autonomous in establishing their action plans and in conducting their own activities.

The quarterly council meetings (with roughly fifty members attending) are held in small communities throughout the state. The council makes a point of holding one session with the members of the local community, where their problems and activities are presented. The council has been action-oriented and has already accomplished a great deal. Many important council activities were undertaken in response to problems raised in the community meetings.

North Carolina Rural Development Council. The first meeting of the North Carolina Rural Development Council (NCRDC) was held in September 1992 and was planned by an interim steering committee selected by the representative of the Federal Highway Administration and the governor's office. While seventy individuals participated in the first meeting, the group just began its organizational activity and had not formed an executive committee before the November election. At that time, a Democrat was elected as governor and the White House changed hands. The first meeting of the newly reconfigured council was held in July 1993, planned by the new state and federal administrations, particularly by the director of the North Carolina Rural Economic Development Center.

Although the group invited to participate in the original council was relatively inclusive, a number of individuals did not choose to participate until after the election, believing that the council was dominated by a state agency agenda. By July 1993, however, the new council included individuals from the legislature, the state community development agency, the state highway and transportation agency, and the state education agency, who had not been involved earlier. There was somewhat less involvement from USDA agencies but new participation from the RDA staff, EDA, and congressional staff. Community development corporations and foundation staff were involved for the first time.

The North Carolina council describes its mission "as a collaborative, cooperative initiative by groups representing private, non-profit, tribal, federal, state, and local governmental units. The mission of the NCRDC is to serve as a forum through which public and private groups can promote rural development by strengthening communities."

The general membership of the council elected its first executive committee during the July 1993 meeting. It was composed of three federal, three state, and one tribal government representatives, one representative from the North Carolina State Commission of Indian Affairs, one person representing COGs, four representing nonprofit organizations, three representing education, three representing the private sector, one representing agriculture, and three individuals appointed by the chair (two of whom were from the state legislature). A chair (at this writing, the executive director of the Rural Center), the secretary (from

Farmers Home), and a treasurer (from the governor's office) were elected for one-year terms.

The North Carolina council decided not to hire a full-time director as it began its activities but, rather, to operate out of the Rural Center with consultant assistance.

The council decided to work closely with the governor's office and play a role as a partner in the state's Rural Initiative, particularly focusing on housing, infrastructure, and business development. It focused on efforts to increase local economic development through ongoing information and training programs offered to a network of locally designated partners.

Vermont Council on Rural Development. The Vermont Council on Rural Development (VCRD) held its organizational meeting in October 1992. Participants at that meeting, planned by an interim steering committee, elected a board of directors with representatives from six constituent groups: federal, state, and local government, the education sector, the private sector, and the nonprofit community.

From the beginning, the membership of the council was broad and inclusive. Within a few months of its organization, state groups included the governor's office, the legislature, and a range of state agencies (including the community action agency). Cities and towns, substate areas, and associations of specific localities represented the local government sector. The active membership included fifteen state agencies, thirteen nonprofit, nine federal, seven local, five private-sector, and three education groups. Approximately 170 individuals have been involved in the activity. Meetings of the full council are expected to occur once or twice yearly; the first meeting was attended by more than 100 persons.

The Vermont council has defined its mission to "enable and empower all Vermonters and Vermont communities to create a prosperous future through coordination, collaboration, and the effective use of local, state, federal, educational, and private resources. The council holds, as a central value, the integration of the working landscape with the social, economic, cultural, and environmental fabric of Vermont."

The board of directors of the council played the pivotal role in the development of activities for the group. Composed of twenty-four individuals (for persons representing each of the six partnership groups), the board as a whole assumed collective responsibility for leadership. Two officers were established: a chair (as of this writing, an individual from a nonprofit development group) and a vice-chair (an individual from the governor's office). The board meets at least quarterly.

The executive director for the Vermont council, hired as a state employee, was a native Vermonter whose background included a variety of state agency, education, and nonprofit organization jobs. The office for the council is located within the Vermont Agency of Development and Community Assistance, a state agency located in the shadow of the capitol and with easy access to other state agencies.

As of mid-1994, there are thirteen working groups active within the council. Some involve organizational issues: strategic action planning, marketing/PR, organizational guidelines, membership, rural development special assistants, local leadership/citizen involvement, personnel, and finance committees. Others relate to substantive programs: rural arts, rural fire protection, small business finance response team, agricultural services network, and forestry and wood products. These groups meet regularly and pull in a variety of interested members.

Third Generation

The New York Rural Development Council. In December of 1991, former governor Mario Cuomo responded to the invitation to participate in the Rural Development Partnership. Although state and federal contacts were named soon after, little was done to move the New York council to an active role. The council itself did not develop into a serious organization until October 1993.

The interim steering committee met in December 1993, with approximately twenty-five individuals in attendance. Office of Rural Affairs director June O'Neill served as the chair for the meeting. Attendees at the December planning meeting included some federal officials (Farmers Home, St. Lawrence Seaway, and RDA), two tribal representatives, several private-sector groups, and a sprinkling of representatives from the education sector and local government. State agency representatives were the predominant group at this meeting.

During this session, committees were appointed, including a search committee for an executive director. Although initial plans called for a meeting in mid-1994, delays in recruiting the executive director postponed the first meeting until after the November 1994 gubernatorial election. However, representatives from the state were active participants in the national meetings.

Participants in the planning meeting decided that the council could benefit the state in a number of ways: provide greater access to Washington; foster an environment for working together; develop relationships; bring necessary players together to solve complex problems; provide a connection to "customers"; plug rural economic development efforts into the overall state effort; link rural and urban efforts; create job development; enhance communities; generate and share ideas; serve people in more ways; help set priorities; provide access to state policymakers; promote small business development; and develop infrastructure.

The recommended structure for the council included an open, inclusive membership. Specific plans were made to reach out to organizations and individuals in each of the six partnership groups. Criteria were developed to choose who was to be invited, including geography, adequate representation, and balance among partners; "real" people and "customer" groups would be included.

As of spring 1994, it is too early to determine the agenda and activities of the New York council. The relationship between the council and the ongoing activities of the Office of Rural Affairs has yet to be devised. Similarly it is not clear how the council will mesh with the ongoing activities of the very active state Legislative Commission on Rural Resources and other groups (particularly those associated with the Cooperative Extension Service).

North Dakota Rural Development Council. In the summer of 1991, former governor Sinner responded to the invitation from President Bush to participate in what was then called the President's Initiative on Rural Development. A Memorandum of Understanding was signed in April 1992 and the NDRDC was established.

Representatives of the unofficial NDRDC attended national meetings and networked with established RDCs during the fall of 1992. In late 1992, an executive director position description was circulated and advertised. An interim committee formed by primary state contact Charles Fleming, chief of staff to the governor and leader of the CGPA policy academy effort, screened applicants and reduced candidates to three prospective interviewees in January 1993. However, the committee could not hire an executive director until the new administration moved into the statehouse. The NDRDC was put on hold for several months while the new administration became established.

In mid-1993, new plans were put into place to form an interim steering committee, comprised of the six federally expected constituent groups. The membership included five federal agencies (FmHA, Farm Credit, SCS, SBA, EDA), state officials (governor's office, EDF, Intergovernmental Assistance), regional councils, local government representatives, the nonprofit sector, private business, and tribal representation. Task forces were formed in four areas: empowerment, educational material, mailing list, and bylaws. An interim executive committee was selected with two state, federal, private, tribal and at-large representatives each and one representative each of local government and the governor's office. It was decided at the first full committee meeting to build the council through an inclusive approach, and new groups would be invited to participate in the expansion.

Initially, the twenty-seven-member steering committee was cochaired by the Executive Director of the State Association of Counties and a representative of the Association of Regional Councils. This interim committee has met only once, in November of 1993. Twenty-five members were present and the group discussed the mission of the NDRDC. The executive committee met for a half day in January 1994 and discussed work plans and reviewed a draft for a council brochure. The difficulties in hiring an executive director were also discussed, and it was decided that the NDRDC annual meeting would be postponed until several months after an executive director was hired. At this writing no meeting has been scheduled. Meanwhile, NDRDC members have attended the national leadership conferences.

The participants at the interim NDRDC Steering Committee planning meeting decided that the council could benefit the state by working on projects in one or more of several areas discussed during a brainstorming session. These issue areas included: Native American issues, such as in-state job formation for Native Americans and the creation of a special Native American–owned and operated bank; the development of an in-state, on-line database system; an investigation of venture capital possibilities in rural regions; and a review of regulatory issues at HUD which may impact rural areas.

Currently, a brochure on the council has been prepared in draft form, and mailing lists are being compiled. The NDRDC has been working with the National Partnership office since 1992 on administrative matters and the selection of a director. As of spring 1994, it is too early to determine the activities or the work agenda of the NDRDC. An executive director has not been selected, and the future relationship of the council with the governor's office or to EDF may depend on who is hired.

Utah Rural Development Council. The governor-elect of Utah signed a memorandum of understanding (MOU) to participate in the national initiative in December 1992. This formal effort to establish a Utah Rural Development Council (URDC) had been preceded by several public-private partnership ventures, including the designation and activation of a rural development steering committee in summer 1992. URDC development activities, however, were hardly noticeable until the original URDC organizing meeting in October 1993. Approximately 500 invitations to the original organizing meeting attracted 175 participants.

At the October 1993 organizing meeting, participants were divided into six constituency groups to select members of a new forty-four-member steering committee: six federal, seven state, ten local, and three tribal governments; thirteen private for-profit and nonprofit organizations; and four education (combined elementary/secondary and higher education). Elected cochairs included the president of a state junior college and the director of the Utah Department of Agriculture (a former rural state legislator). Working groups were established to develop structure, budget, and selection guides and processes to hire an executive director.

The formal URDC organizing meeting was held in January 1994. Participants adopted a mission, goals and objectives; approved organization and structure; decided to proceed with hiring an executive director; and selected members of a fifteen-person executive committee. A procedure was established for accepting proposals to house the executive director. Composition of the executive committee is: two federal, two state, four local, two tribal government; two private for-profit; two private nonprofit; one education. Administratively, the executive director will be an exempt employee of the Utah Department of Community and Economic Development.

URDC's six major goal areas are: encourage and sustain capable rural community leaders and provide improvement opportunities for current and future rural leaders; assist rural communities to communicate and collaborate effectively among themselves and with state, local, and federal agencies; assist rural communities to improve community infrastructure resources, including water, waste treatment, transportation, roads, telecommunications, culture and education, health care, and traditional community services; assist rural communities and businesses to develop fair access to a complete range of financial services; assist rural communities with tax policy and tax base challenges; and assist rural communities to meet their training and education needs.

Membership in URDC is open. Participation is accessed through seven caucuses representing URDC's identified partnership groups.

The Wyoming Rural Development Council. Wyoming has a long history of economic development planning, as well as a programmatic history that goes back several years. None of the past efforts have focused specifically on rural development. However, economic and rural development are almost synonymous in this second most rural state in the country. Wyoming's connection to rural development comes not from agriculture, service, forestry, or fisheries (these account for roughly 1 percent of their total gross industrial product) but rather from energy resources and mineral development, which account for more than 60 percent of the state's gross product.

Perhaps most important is Wyoming's inclusion in the Council of Governors' Policy Advisors (CGPA) 1990 Rural Policy Academy. Governor Sullivan was appointed as the national chair of the CGPA Rural Development Policy Academy in 1989, and Wyoming's participation is an example of a state's ability to seize opportunities to use outside assistance in planning and developing strategies. There are also numerous examples of bilateral relationships between Wyoming's key actors in economic and community development, as well as extensive networking.

As of late spring 1994, the Wyoming Rural Development Council was not yet formally organized and had not held its first meeting. A job description for the executive director's position has been written, but negotiations as to salary level, reporting relationships, and other structural and personal considerations are continuing. A six-member steering committee was formed and met in January 1994. It is recruiting council members, and the plan is for the WRDC to have an inclusive membership.

Conclusions

As this chapter has indicated, the SRDC activity took form in states with very different demographic, structural, programmatic, and cultural histories. The challenge for the effort was to create a design that would take account of this diversity, yet at the same time provide a framework to move state activity in a way that acknowledged some of the shared problems across rural areas in the United States.

References

Beyle, Thad (ed.). 1990. The powers of the governors. In *State Government, CQ's Guide to Current Issues and Activities, 1990–1991*. Washington, D.C.: Congressional Quarterly Press.

Elazar, Daniel J. 1984. *American Federalism: A View from the States*. 3rd ed. New York: Harper and Row.

Fitzpatrick, Jody L., and Rodney E. Hero. 1988. "Political Culture and Political Characteristics of the American States: A Consideration of Some Old and New Questions." *Western Political Quarterly* 41 (March), 145–53.

Hanson, Russell L. 1991. "Political Culture Variations in State Economic Development Explanation." *Publius* 21 (spring), 63–81.

Herzik, Eric B. 1985. "The Legal-Formal Structuring of State Politics: A Cultural Explanation." *Western Political Quarterly* 38 (September), 413–23.

Johnson, Charles A. 1976. "Political Cultures in American States: Elazar's Formulation Examined." *American Journal of Political Science* 20 (August), 491–509.

Lieske, Joel. 1993. "Regional Subcultures of the United States." *Journal of Politics* 55 (November), 888–913.

Morgan, David R., and Sheilah S. Watson. 1991. "Political Culture, Political System Characteristics and Public Policies among the American States." *Publius* 21 (spring), 31–48.

Sharkansky, Ira. 1969. "The Utility of Elazar's Political Culture." *Polity* 2 (fall), 66–83.

Wilson, Robert H. 1993. *States and the Economy: Policymaking and Decentralization.* Westport, Conn.: Praeger.

Additional Readings

Boesckelman, Keith. 1991. "Political Culture and State Development Policy." *Publius* 21 (spring), 49–62.

Elazar, Daniel J. 1994. *The American Mosaic: The Impact of Space, Time and Culture on American Politics.* Boulder, Colo.: Westview Press.

4 | The National Rural Development Partnership

A New Approach to Intergovernmental Relations

THIS CHAPTER EXAMINES the design and assumptions behind the National Rural Development Partnership, focusing on policy context for the experimental effort and elements and assumptions contained within the design. The discussion emphasizes the concept of collaboration and the development of this idea within a changing political context.

The Challenge of Rural Development as Stimulus for Change

Rural America enjoyed a renaissance in the 1970s as many people sought less congested and less complicated surroundings than urban areas afforded (Cornman and Kincaid, 1984). Unfortunately the economic growth that the American economy enjoyed during the 1980s was not shared in rural communities; rural economies in most states plummeted in the 1980s (Flora and Christenson, 1991; Galston, 1992; Reid and Frederick, 1990). Small rural communities have experienced declines in employment, population, and revenues for more than a decade (Reid and Sears, 1992).

As discussed in Chapter 2, fundamental shifts in the national and international economies and influences of these macroforces on markets made rural communities increasingly vulnerable to changes beyond their horizons. Declining rural populations and economies left severe personal, social, and economic burdens for residents who remained. Rural outmigration has been particularly characteristic of younger people and disproportionately so among younger people with more years of formal education (Shribman, 1991). Tax bases erode, an aging population is left without younger family supports, and services shrink as the customer-clientele base diminishes. People who remain have less purchasing power. The community becomes less desirable for new industrial and commercial ventures. Such downward cycles are difficult to reverse. As Reid and Sears (1992, p. 215) note, there must be "an expansion in the ability of an area to sustain, largely through its own efforts and with its own resources, improved performance along one or more key economic and social dimensions."

This was the context within which rural development became part of America's national agenda. Indications of early interest in energizing rural America were visible in the poverty programs and the Rural Development Act of 1972. The Carter administration's approach emphasized a continued federal role in rural development, including program coordination and improved service delivery (Osbourn, 1988a,b). There was some recognition of the limits of this perspective in the Reagan administration.

The Bush administration took a different approach. Early efforts to reverse the downward cycles in rural communities were modest and tied to presidential politics, for example, President Bush's reelection effort. The Bush administration launched its initiative in 1990 to address the needs of rural economies in a way that was philosophically consistent with its agenda of reducing the role of the federal government in rural economies, increasing the role of the private sector in rural economies, and building political support in rural America for the Bush reelection campaign. Such a rural initiative appeared to be a program that could be implemented without much controversy and at low cost.

In many ways, President Bush's rural initiative was a modest but politically and substantively an agenda that was ideal in support of his reelection bid. It spoke to important rural constituents but did not require major resources. New thinking, however, was required. First, it was necessary to break the mind-set that equated rural economies with agricultural economies. Second, new strategies were needed that were consistent with the Bush administration agenda that precluded solutions requiring transfer payments or economic development subsidies.

Recognizing the problem but having no solution, the Bush administration hit upon a process approach that utilized State Rural Development Councils (SRDCs). These councils would broaden economic development participation within the states, let rural communities define their own problems, and accept responsibility for their own solutions. Hopefully these councils would yield uniquely tailored strategies for rural development based on local initiatives, intergovernmental collaboration, and public/private cooperation.

The modest nature of the financial support and the programmatic priority of reducing the role of the federal government combined to set the stage for some new ways of approaching rural development. The lack of new program dollars meant that state and local participants did not have recourse to the old "reactive" posture vis-à-vis the federal government. Self-reliance, local autonomy, and public/private collaboration were the only strategies that had any likelihood of success.

Something considerably more complicated and innovative evolved from these early Bush administration ambitions than is typical of initiatives launched in Washington. The Rural Initiative, renamed the National Rural Development Partnership in 1993, continues as a work in progress both in the nation's capital and in the states. The rural development enterprise has been one of change and redefinition. Indeed, keeping track of the number of name changes presents a challenge, let alone keeping abreast of the subtle changes in emphasis and orientation that the name changes reflect.

The Nature of the Experiment

There are a number of elements within the Partnership that are basic to its development: the concept of collaboration, commitment to broad-based participation, and constant change (or a "work in progress").

Collaboration

The earlier Bush administration President's Initiative on Rural Development and the Clinton administration's Rural Development Partnership have relied on restructured intergovernmental relations. The Partnership represents a new way of public policymaking that has involved shifts away from the traditional command and control approach of intergovernmental relationships noted in Chapter 1. That model of federalism emphasizes formal lines of authority that separate one level of government from another and programs that emphasize one definition of a problem and a specified range of solutions. In contrast, the Partnership emphasizes intergovernmental collaboration in problem definition and problem solving rather than a top-down, federal-to-state or federal-to-local flow of directives. The emphasis is on a combination of a bottom-up and top-down approach to problem definition. In this, federal, state, local, private, and not-for-profit sector actors with rural policy interests collaborate and collectively assume the initiative for rural development.

The complexities of collaborating within the federal government, between levels of government, and between government and non-governmental organizations have raised myriad opportunities and constraints. The scope of the Partnership's activities has expanded as its key actors have become more open to expressions of diverse purposes, expectations, and perceptions in Washington, state capitals, and rural communities.

The Partnership's changes reflect something more than the normal problems that should be expected during the early stages of creating and implementing any new program. They also reflect the need to wrestle with a classical dilemma of intergovernmental relations: pursuit of national goals through induced compliance with federal government directives (usually issued by a single lead agency), while preserving local, state, and other federal agencies' autonomy to pursue (or ignore) national goals, using self-selected strategies. Although the trial-and-error learning processes have caused inconsistencies, the initiative has emphasized collaboration among independent and—at least in theory—coequal agencies rather than the federal government's familiar top-down way of doing business through imposed program requirements backed with grant dollars.

The federal role in this endeavor has two different dynamics: one that is top-down and another that is responsive to initiatives from the states. Federal actors in Washington, D.C., especially the National Partnership Office (the staff office established to support the activities) and the National Rural Development Council (the organization of federal agencies and national organizations interested in this effort) have adopted a top-down approach to facilitating the various bottom-up initiatives. Inside the beltway and within federal agencies, a top-down approach was used to announce the program direction and communicate the expectation that federal agencies would participate. Federal actors within the states participate in state rural development councils' collaborative activities as one among equals.

The bottom-up aspect of the Partnership derives from the belief that collaboration among rural development actors within the states is the primary source of ideas and initiatives. D.C.-based federal actors play a facilitative role in response to these SRDC-originated ideas. An example of this facilitative role is seen in the support role played by the National Rural Development Council in the removal of federal impediments.

Broad-Based Participation

The Partnership has benefited from growing recognition that rural development is not a simple endeavor. Wide-ranging participation has contributed to the realization that rural development cannot be imposed unilaterally, and it involves more than support for agribusiness or economic development programs to recruit new industries into withering communities. Trials, errors, corrections, and after-the-fact justifications for activities have provided valuable learning experiences—and high levels of frustration.

The cornerstone of the experiment is the State Rural Development Council. While each council has its own idiosyncrasies and dynamics, the overall pattern is one of networking and reliance on inclusive, collaborative methods of participation and problem solving. In most instances, any governmental or private-sector actor with an interest in rural development and the willingness to participate in state rural development councils has been welcome to do so. The broad-based nature of the rural development partnerships has necessarily incorporated diverse expectations and perspectives. This has resulted in definitions of rural development that are broader than job creation. And the diversity has created pressure to occasionally sidestep controversial issues where no consensus position is possible.

Work in Progress

Since its origination, the Partnership has been in a state of constant change and many of the changes have been fundamental. It continues to experience change in its philosophy, structure, implementation approach, and key actors. One early structural approach, for example, would have created federal rural development councils in states that mirrored earlier councils made up of federal agricultural agencies. Thus, the original concept of the SRDC envisioned voting membership open only to representatives of federal government agencies. All other state, local, and private-sector actors were limited to secondary nonvoting roles.

The rural development enterprise is best characterized by continued change. The latest manifestation of this change is the Clinton administration's embrace of the Bush initiative in 1993, touting it as a shining example of its own "reinventing government" agenda at work. In fact, the Rural Initiative already was *doing* new governance before President Clinton charged Vice President Gore to undertake a National Performance Review (Gore, 1993). Since then, the enterprise has been renamed the National Rural Development Partnership and has expanded substantially.

Evolution of a Concept of Collaboration

Changing rural circumstances required new ways of stimulating rural development. The self-help provisions of the Bush administration's initiative, launched in 1990, with the goal of creating a leadership capacity for economic development in rural communities through State Rural Development Councils (SRDCs), had consequences for problem definition and solution generation. New ways of thinking about rural development and new strategies for promoting rural economic development were explored. SRDCs were intended to become collaborative structures where intergovernmental and public-private networks would develop. Collaboration within these networks would lead to the identification of problems and barriers, strategizing, problem solving, and leadership development in pursuit of self-sustaining rural development. In short, SRDCs were to create and implement their own agendas.

SRDCs are the centerpiece of the Rural Partnership. They are the vehicles for implementing rural development through new governance principles. Each SRDC includes federal, state, local, private for-profit, nonprofit, and (in most states where there are significant numbers) tribal members. The flexibility to respond to specific rural interests in each state guarantees that each SRDC is different. Each creates its own identity and implements its own agenda.

Realization of SRDC autonomy was slow to develop among the pilot SRDCs. Federal and state participants in SRDCs were accustomed to top-down imposition of priorities and requirements by the federal government in exchange for financial support. Several of the pilot councils were created as federal councils—not partnerships. For example, until 1992, only federal administrators were full voting members of the Texas council, officially known as the Texas Federal Rural Development Council. All other participants were "associate members." In December of 1992 the word "Federal" was dropped from the name and the associate membership category was eliminated. By mid-1993 only 7 percent of the TRDC membership was drawn from federal agencies, down from 48 percent of the membership in 1991.

Deliberations in SRDCs during the early years revealed a tendency to conceive of opportunities in conventional, categorical, federal control–state compliance terms. SRDCs looked to their federal members to be told what was expected and how to do it. It was not uncommon for an SRDC to ask its assigned federal government liaison person ("desk officer") to clarify expectations, rules, regulations, and requirements, only to find that such particulars did not exist. Early on there was a great deal of emphasis on State Rural Development Councils creating deliverables for federal government review.

Most of the SRDCs are in the process of evolving into more self-initiating, flexible, and collaborative bodies. It has not been an easy process, however. Four years into the Rural Partnership experiment, participants are beginning to realize that this initiative and the SRDCs have been constructed on the principle of local/rural problem definition and solution generation. Federal agencies and actors are viewed as potential resources, not sources of rules and regulations. The role of the federal government in rural development is evolving into that of facilitator, not controller.

The Rural Partnership's evolving principles in action have provided the Clinton administration with a "living laboratory" for its new governance. Those new governance principles include:

- Local customer satisfaction
- Government flexibility and responsiveness
- Empowerment of rural development policy actors and rural communities themselves
- Public-private partnerships
- Entrepreneurship in government
- Elimination of red tape in program administration
- Intergovernmental problem definition and strategy development

The State Rural Development Councils have been working under these principles since their earliest operations. A mission-driven rather than program-driven effort, the Partnership has defined itself as an activity focused on results rather than various inputs. It has emphasized flexible, responsive, and forward-looking approaches to problem identification and strategic planning. The emphasis is on an approach to problem definition where federal, state, local, tribal, private, and nonprofit sector actors with rural interests collaborate. The Department of Agriculture's Rural Development Partnership was mentioned favorably in Vice President Gore's National Performance Review (1993, p. 49) as an example of the flexible, decentralized approach to policy-making that will be needed for governance in the 1990s. In short, what started out as a Bush administration substantive agenda of economic development, diminished government involvement, and increased private sector roles evolved into a process agenda regarding how rural economic development should be approached.

With the Clinton administration, the Rural Partnership is moving back toward a substantive agenda—how government should be "reinvented." The challenge facing the Partnership is the lack of policy leadership from within the Clinton administration. The Clinton administration has embraced the concept of reinventing government and the Rural Partnership as an example of it. At this writing, it has begun to give the kind of supports perceived as necessary to meet the challenge of rural development in this complex environment. The NRDC/SRDC intergovernmental networks have presented themselves as ready to make a difference in the rural sector's capacity for focusing on mission and results using interagency collaboration, entrepreneurial management, and decentralization in policy-making.

Setting the Policy Stage for the NRDP

State Rural Development Councils, the cornerstones of the rural initiative, were not the first interagency coordinating body active in the rural sector. The states had prior experience working with interagency coordinating bodies through their exposure to USDA's Food and Agriculture Councils (FAC). FACs were created in 1982 to serve as interagency forums through which USDA agency heads would coordinate departmental objectives at the state level. USDA agencies participating in FACs included: Agricultural Stabilization and Conservation Service, Extension Service, Farmers Home Administration, Federal Crop Insurance Corporation, Food and Nutrition Service, Forest Service, Rural

Electrification Administration, Soil Conservation Service, and the National Agricultural Statistics Service.

FACs also were to serve as links between committees of the Policy and Coordinating Council and the states. In 1983, FACS were directed to emphasize support for the department's rural development functions, including regulations, policy development, and coordination among USDA agencies (Musgrave, 1989). The Rural Revitalization Task Force found that FACs had not been very active and recommended that they should be renamed "State Rural Development Councils" and reinvigorated by refocusing them on rural development issues.

The Carter administration's approach to rural development envisioned a continued federal role to improve the availability of basic human services. A few isolated developments also occurred during the Reagan administration. The Food Security Act of 1985, for example, established a National Commission on Agriculture and Rural Development Policy (NCARDP) with a two-year mission: "to provide a broad and long-range perspective on U.S. agriculture and rural development policy . . . [and be a] source of policy goals and initiatives and as a sounding board between state and national policy makers" (Knigge, 1990, p. iv). The fifteen-member NCARDP was appointed by President Reagan, but its contributions to rural development were minimal until 1989, the first year of the Bush administration.

On a second front, the National Governors' Association issued a 1988 clarion call for a "new alliance" between the federal government and other organizations, including state and local governments as full partners in the SRDCs (National Governors' Association, 1988). In 1990 the Council of Governors' Policy Advisors conducted a Rural Policy Academy which brought together top-level policy teams from ten states: Arkansas, California, Iowa, Maine, Michigan, Missouri, Mississippi, North Dakota, Pennsylvania, and Wyoming. These initiatives provided some energy and focus that helped the rural initiative get underway in the Bush administration.

The reports of the National Commission on Agriculture and Rural Development Policy (NCARDP), published during the first two years of the Bush administration, articulated the challenges facing agriculture and rural economies and thus set the stage for any national rural development initiatives. In 1989, NCARDP examined agricultural policy issues, including: international competitiveness, production flexibility and efficiency, resource conservation, environmental quality, farm financial well-being equity, and marketing and productivity (NCARDP, 1989). In 1990, NCARDP reports focused on rural development policy issues. Its primary observation was that the fate of rural America lay in the hands of rural citizens. Although the federal government could support rural development, it could not make rural development happen. NCARDP articulated the concern for rural America, recognized that rural economies were more diverse than agriculture, and noted that the long-term vitality of rural economies required attention to that diversity.

NCARDP called for a review of all federal policies to determine their effects on rural areas and improvement in the information available about rural conditions and development strategies. It also had advocated a more comprehensive approach to rural development, including education as a major component. NCARDP recommended processes that were more flexible, collaborative, and cooperative, with an eye toward more strategic, innovative, and experimental efforts in pursuit of rural economic development (Knigge, 1990). The recommendations of NCARDP were thus a seedbed for the Bush administration's rural initiative.

The early Bush administration's emphasis for the rural initiative was on helping rural America catch up with the rest of the nation's economic growth. Recognizing that rural America is home to 25 percent of American citizens and comprises 75 percent of the nation's land area, President Bush's initiative sought to "improve the employment opportunities, incomes and well-being of the Nation's rural people by strengthening the capacity of rural America to compete in the global economy" (Madigan, 1991, p. 3).

The initiative's substantive thrust was threefold: downscale or change the Department of Agriculture into the Department of Rural Affairs, diminish the federal role in domestic policy, and increase the role of the private sector in economic development. The Bush administration sought to provide a new framework for conceiving and carrying out public policy for rural economic development. Its intent was to reorient rural program delivery to meet challenges identified by NCARDP in its 1990 report (Osbourn, 1988a).

In its report, "Rural Economic Development in the '90s: A Presidential Initiative," the National Rural Initiative Office identified its guiding principles as the following: the private sector must participate actively; the benefits of rural development must be shared; new partnerships are needed; and a strategic approach is required (Madigan, 1991). The report explicitly recognized that "rural economic development implies a healthy private sector economy able to provide jobs and raising incomes for rural residents . . . enhancing the rural environment in which the private economy can flourish" (Madigan, 1991, p. 6). The rural initiative's ultimate goal was "to increase the level of economic and social well-being of rural people by overcoming the difficulties of rurality . . . by addressing the institutional constraints faced by rural areas" (Madigan and Vautour, 1991, p. 5). Specific principles included: active participation of the private sector; a better targeting of rural development resources; closer collaboration among federal departments, agencies, and state and local governments; and a strategic approach to development.

The official purposes for the rural initiative were:

> Improve the employment opportunities, incomes and well-being of the Nation's rural people by strengthening the capacity of rural America to compete in the national and international economy . . . to achieve short- and long-term rural economic development goals. State councils will identify the full scope of natural, human, and economic resources available within the State, and develop a long-term, comprehensive strategy for rural development. (Madigan, 1990, p. 5)

Three distinct agendas lie behind these official words: substantive, political, and process agendas (Radin, 1992). The substantive agenda had several components. First, the Bush administration was committed to reducing the role of the federal government in domestic policy arenas. Thus the initiative's emphasis on the primacy of state government leadership, the importance of private enterprise participation, and deregulation evolved naturally. Second, goals-oriented strategic planning processes were considered essential to rational economic development. Third, the rural initiative could "be viewed as a first step in a move either to scale down the [U.S.] Department [of Agriculture] or to refocus it as a Department of Rural Affairs" (Radin, 1992, p. 113).

The rural initiative was to demonstrate sensitivity to the issues of rural development with a minimal expenditure of federal monies in order to garner rural reelection support. This political agenda "demanded that the efforts be visible, developed quickly, and that the White House (rather than Congress) shape the agenda" (Radin, 1992, p. 113).

The 1990 Food, Agriculture, Conservation, and Trade Act (FACT) (PL 101-624) was the second major initiative used to signal how important rural America was to the president. FACT created the Rural Development Administration (RDA) within the U.S. Department of Agriculture. RDA was created from several existing agencies in USDA to provide overall leadership to USDA's rural development effort (Madigan and Vautour, 1991).

The process agenda was to change the role that federal agencies played in rural development from that of director and implementor to that of catalyst, enabler, and collaborative partner. This change, however, required a "new paradigm" of intergovernmental relations: a non-hierarchical model consisting of networks that reached across public-private boundaries as well as federal-state-local lines.

The Structure of the Initiative at Start-up

The Federal Government in Washington, D.C.

The president's rural initiative was announced in January 1990. Its six major components were action-oriented. They were designed for quick visibility or to support rapid implementation. They included (Madigan, 1991):

- Form a presidential council on rural America
- Establish state rural development councils
- Conduct rural development demonstrations
- Expand the Rural Information Center
- Target federal rural development programs
- Make the Working Group on Rural Development, chaired by Agriculture Secretary Madigan, a permanent standing committee of the President's Economic Policy Council

By the end of 1990, action had been taken on all six of these components. The governors of eight pilot states had been invited to participate in the State Rural Development Council experiment that would include federal, state, local, and private actors as full partners. The eight pilot SRDCs were asked to identify rural development demonstration projects. The Rural Information Center was expanded to include a Rural Development Technical Assistance Center and Hot Line.

In Washington, a relatively nonhierarchical structure was put into place to implement the rural initiative and support the SRDCs, including: the President's Council on Rural America, the Economic Policy Council's Working Group on Rural Development, the Monday Management Group, the National Rural Initiative Office, and the Rural Information Center.

The President's Council on Rural America (PCRA). PCRA, a "blue-ribbon" citizen's council, held its first meeting on January 23–24, 1991. PCRA membership included nineteen private-sector members with roots in rural communities. Its chair was Winthrop Rockefeller (Arkansas), and vice chair was Kay Orr (Nebraska) (Rockefeller, 1992). Although PCRA's mission was to improve the quality of life in rural America, its role as seen by the Bush administration was to bring the private sector into the rural initiative.

PCRA met twenty-five times in communities across rural America before issuing its final report, *Revitalizing Rural America through Collaboration: A Report to the President* (Rockefeller, 1992). Its primary conclusions were consistent with the Bush administration agendas for the rural initiative and did not provide any surprises. Those conclusions included: economic development improves the quality of life; economic development requires community development, the destiny of communities must be determined by residents; the federal government should be more collaborative and responsive in fostering rural economic development; the federal government should not establish new farm programs or new agencies, instead it should establish a permanent President's Advisory Council on Rural America to advise and monitor the achievement of rural development goals and objectives; and many existing federal rural programs were misdirected and too prescriptive (Rockefeller, 1992). PCRA also offered a vision for rural America's future (Rockefeller, 1992, p. 3):

- Empowered individuals
- Caring communities
- Skilled visionary leadership
- Resourceful collaboration
- A future sustained through local initiative

The President's Economic Policy Council (subsequently renamed the Policy Coordinating Group) established a standing committee devoted to rural economic development, known as the *Working Group on Rural Develop-*

ment (PCG-WGRD). These policy-level decision-makers represented virtually all federal departments, free-standing agencies, and commissions that had "rural" policies in their missions (Madigan and Vautour, 1991). Originally, the PCG-WGRD only had authority to recommend, but its powers were expanded when it became a permanent interdepartmental policy body with oversight responsibilities. The PCG-WGRD began to demonstrate its policy-making capability when it became involved in attempting to remove real and perceived impediments to effective governance that were identified, documented, and sent to Washington by SRDCs. The PCG-WGRD provided policy oversight of the rural initiative at the federal level, opportunities for joint rural development planning and policy implementation, and a mechanism for the elimination of unnecessary governmental barriers to economic development. This group terminated at the end of the Bush administration.

The National Partnership Office (NPO) (originally the National Initiative Office, NIO), operates as one hub in the web of Rural Partnership networks that exist in states and within the federal government in Washington, D.C. The NPO is small, minimally hierarchical, and interactions are peer-based. "The NIO [now NPO] demonstrates that a governmental entity can be trusted to operate in a system of accountability which is flexible, not rigid, and which is based on outcomes rather than procedures" (NIRA, 1993).

The National Council on Rural Development (NRDC), (earlier known as the Monday Management Group, MMG) has been a key element in the management support structure since the beginning of the initiative. The NRDC is a group of senior career and appointed officers who meet on alternate Mondays to resolve operational problems, monitor SRDC outcomes, and provide operational linkages among the PCG-WGRD, participating federal agencies, the National Partnership Office, and the SRDCs.

The basic elements of the group took form in early 1990 when Deputy Undersecretary of Agriculture for Rural Development and Small Communities Walter Hill experienced a sense of frustration over the number of committees and meetings that were being held as a part of an interagency policy development task through the Presidential Initiative on Rural Development (Radin, forthcoming). He observed that every time he called a meeting, different people showed up. His solution was to combine all of the committees into one group and schedule the meetings of the group every Monday morning. After about six weeks, between eighteen and twenty people showed up every time.

By September 1990, this group took on a more permanent status and was described as a staff-level management group with representation from all participating federal programs that convened regularly to provide detailed definition to the initiative and to design a strategy for implementation. By December 1990, the management group had four management teams centered on organizational, staffing, and training assistance to the state councils (known as the SRDCs).

The Monday Management Group, the precursor to the NRDC, initially established five management teams to focus on functions that were deemed most crucial to the rural initiative in 1990. They included: a state council coordinating team, a Rural Economic Development Institute team, a federal employee training team, a pilot project evaluation team, and a public affairs management team (PIRD, 1990). Progress toward a collaborative approach to rural policy-making within the executive branch had been made by sponsoring activities involving multiple departments and agencies. With support of the MMG, the PCG-WGRD began to serve a policy-making role to resolve impediments to effective governance that are identified by individual SRDCs (Rural Development, 1992; 1993).

Three issues have been paramount for the Rural Partnership's management support structure: How to maintain flexibility as the SRDCs and their tasks became more complex; division of leadership responsibility among the federal-level agencies and support structures and between Washington, D.C., and the SRDCs; and how the support structure could respond to external pressures (Outcome Monitoring Team, 1993). The National Rural Development Council's "impediment process" is illustrative of how the roles and functions of the management support structure have evolved (Radin, forthcoming).

The "impediments process" provides a highly visible example of how the Rural Partnership has tried to address paramount issues. It seeks to identify and redress barriers to effective rural development that are caused by federal law, regulations, or administrative practices (NIRA, 1992). The process is activated if an impediment is linked to rural development and is highly specific. Procedurally, efforts are made to resolve impediments at the state level first. When an SRDC identifies practices that it perceives as unjustifiable impediments to rural development that cannot be resolved at the state level, it brings them to the attention of the NRDC. Obvious state- or regional-level solutions must not be evident, and it must entail significant costs (Springer, 1992). When such efforts are unsuccessful, the Steering Committee of the NRDC tries to clarify the problem before referring it to the affected members of the PCG-WGRD for action. If necessary, an issue is referred to the PCG-WGRD as a whole, or it may choose to create a task force to work toward resolution (Springer, 1992). In one such case involving the creation of a single-loan application for businesses seeking to use multiple federal programs for rural development, the impediments group in Washington was able to facilitate requests by the Kansas Rural Development Council.

At an October 1992 conference on "New Approaches to Rural Development and Changing Perspectives on Governance," the then–deputy undersecretary of agriculture for small community and rural development differentiated between the roles of the PCG-WGRD, the NRDC, and the SRDCs. He identified the PCG-WGRD as the political level where policy decisions were made. The NRDC (then MMG) is the arena where structures are developed and Washington operations are coordinated. SRDCs are where the bottom-up approach to rural development takes place (NAPA, 1992, p. 17). Within the states a bottom-up approach was to be used to generate ideas and energy for rural development (NAPA, 1992). These relationships circa 1992 are summarized below.

Partner	*Area of Responsibility*
Policy Coordinating Group—Working Group on Rural Development in the White House	Policy role
National Rural Development Council (then called the Monday Management Group)	Development of structures, coordinate operations
State Rural Development Councils	Generate ideas, define rural development initiatives

The Rural Information Center. The rural initiative included a response to the call for improving rural policymakers' access to information by strengthening the Rural Information Center (RIC). The RIC is operated by the National Agricultural Library (NAL) in partnership with the

Extension Service. Since January 1992 it has expanded its staff and its range of duties greatly through cooperative arrangements between NAL and the Department of Health and Human Service, the Farmers Home Administration, the Forest Service, and the Small Business Administration (Madigan and Vautour, 1991). The Department of Health and Human Services established a Rural Information Clearinghouse for Health Services as part of the RIC. The Small Business Administration's Service Corps of Retired Executives (SCORE) and Farmers Home Administration provided resources to support the RIC.

Despite the efforts to structure the rural initiative in Washington, however, the Bush administration never clearly signaled its importance to the federal agencies. Walt Hill, the USDA deputy undersecretary for small community and rural development at the U.S. Department of Agriculture, guided the rural initiative largely without institutionalized support. Funding for the rural initiative and the SRDCs was obtained solely by voluntary contributions from agencies and programs. The budget situation was unstable. NRDC members are responsible for building federal support for the SRDCs in their home agencies. Confusion about the relationship between the MMG and the rural initiative office created some tensions between the two key Washington components (Outcome Monitoring Team, 1993).

The Rural Development Institute

Because SRDC members operate in an environment of interagency and intersectorial influence and decision making, new skills of collaboration, information sharing, and network building and maintenance were required. Thus, the Rural Development Institute (RDI) was established to provide leadership and strategic planning training and technical assistance for all actors in the rural initiative. The first two RDI training sessions were held in New Orleans and San Diego in March 1991. The purpose was to train SRDC members so that they could participate in the process of intergovernmental rural economic development (PIRD, 1990). Rural economic development and strategic planning were emphasized. The original RDI conferences, however, were deemed abject failures by many participants and were not repeated. Since then, the RDI appears to have found its niche working mostly by request with individual SRDCs on specific projects that require facilitation and by facilitating the initiative's annual national leadership conferences. These conferences serve as major conduits for the exchange of ideas among rural development councils.

Demonstration Projects

The rural initiative was expected to demonstrate effective programs and practices. To further this end, the 1990 Food, Agriculture, Conservation, and Trade Act (FACT) established two five-year pilot projects to test new models for improving rural development program delivery. Rural Economic Development Review Panels were available to help five states obtain state and local input in planning, prioritizing, and evaluating community business programs. Other sources of support for rural demonstration projects included the Rural Partnerships Investments Boards and a Rural Business Investment Fund, which were available to finance local rural business development projects in (up to) five states (Madigan and Vautour, 1991).

Organizing the SRDCs: the Pilot States

Although the early rural initiative spokespersons were proclaiming a "new paradigm" of responsive, intergovernmental, collaborative, and public-private partnerships to attack rural development, the early stages of implementation followed an all-too-familiar pattern. States were invited by the president to establish SRDCs. Once states accepted the invitations, the federal government convened the initial organizing meetings. Speakers and many of the participants at the organizing meetings were federal officials and state actors who were known by the meeting organizers. Three of the eight pilot state SRDC executive directors initially were "detailed" from federal agencies.

People who attended the original organizing meetings wanted answers to one overriding conventional question: What did the state need to do in order to secure future federal funds for rural development? The Rural Development Institute developed training programs for SRDC members without state input and paid (most of the) expenses for SRDC representatives to attend.

The pilot state SRDC organizing meetings were held in October 1990. The U.S. Department of Agriculture appointed organizers in each of the pilot states. In most instances, the organizer was the highest ranking in-state official in the Farmers Home Administration. Following directives from Washington, the organizers blanketed their states with invitations to participate in the organizing meetings. Representatives from the rural initiative in Washington, led by the USDA deputy undersecretary of agriculture for small community and rural development, flew to the pilot states to join with governors, locally based federal officials, and other in-state notables from the private and public sectors to announce the launching of the rural initiative and SRDCs.

As one might expect, skepticism abounded at the organizing meetings. Few if any participants truly believed that the federal government would ever let go of its top-down powers to join SRDCs as equal partners. The experienced, in-state federal government agency managers who had established careers under a more traditional model of federalism were among the most skeptical. It is unlikely that *anyone* who attended the first eight pilot SRDC organizing meetings truly believed that the words "new paradigms," "collaboration," and "equal partnerships" that were being pronounced from the front of the meeting rooms would become operating principles. Instead, state and local people were there for practical reasons. Some had been directed to participate by their superiors, particularly in-state federal government officials. Others were there to protect turf, to be sure that their own agencies and agendas were not adversely impacted by any SRDC initiatives. The primary motivation, however, was the belief that future federal money to states for rural economic development would require participation in a SRDC; this expectation never materialized. People attended because they wanted to know what had to be done in order to access money from Washington for rural economic development projects.

During 1991, the original SRDCs struggled to establish themselves. The historical patterns of federal-state domination were in evidence during the first year of SRDC operations. The pilot SRDCs were instructed to develop mission statements, assess the economic development needs of rural areas in their states, develop an inventory of available rural development resources, and create a strategic plan. The pilot states interpreted these suggestions as further evidence of federal control. These products constituted a "bill of deliverables." A few SRDCs took the mandates seriously, anticipating that compliance would improve their funding potential. Other states merely went through the motions, in some cases doing no more than photocopying documents produced by other SRDCs. Progress reports were submitted to the PCG-WGRD at the end of fiscal year 1991.

Overall, the early strategies employed by the rural initiative were reflective of a self-help approach to economic development. States and the private sector were encouraged to develop strategic plans for economic development that utilized new federal-state-local-private collaboration to overcome historical government agency rigidity and turf protection. The emphasis was on bottom-up identification of rural development problems and solutions (Reid and Lovan, 1993).

Beyond the Pilot Phase

In October 1991, President Bush once again tried to promote his political agenda for the rural initiative. Bush invited the governors of all other states and territories (forty-five total) to participate (Hill, 1991). There was a reluctance in some states where the word "rural" did not carry positive political currency. Nonetheless, by spring of 1994, thirty-seven SRDCs are under way and another six states are considering establishing one. Despite these efforts, the Bush administration never gave the rural initiative much attention or visibility. The substantive and process agendas never really took hold, and the political agenda did not pay off.

One of the developments characteristic of the SRDCs that followed the pilot states is that they have been able to build upon the experience of the pilot states. Executive director meetings and annual rural development leadership meetings have provided forums for exchanging ideas. For instance, second-generation SRDCs have avoided the problem of SRDC co-chairs, which on the surface appeared to be a perfect symbol of the new collaborative relationship that SRDCs aspire to develop between federal and state actors. Yet the experience of the pilot states shows it to be unworkable. There has been liberal borrowing of strategies and exchanging of ideas between first- and second-generation SRDCs.

Another aspect of this second phase of the Rural Partnership has been moving toward collaboration among different state councils. One example of this is the emergence of the High Plains Trade Region. Key actors involved include the SRDCs of each of the states on a north-south line from North Dakota to Texas as well as the eastern ranges of Colorado, Wyoming, and Montana. Partnership participants from the various states have been cooperating to increase the regional, national, and international trade prospects for enterprises in the High Plains Trade Region. In addition to a survey of present and potential programs to enhance export trade among the High Plains states, the SRDCs in those states have published a catalog of public and private export programs and an inventory of public assistance programs and innovative approaches to trade enhancement, including those that are available in urban areas but are not available in rural areas.

Principles for the Partnership: Change through Evolution

Although the rural initiative has been cloaked in the language, concepts, and symbols of new governance since the arrival of the Clinton administration, these were not its original principles or expectations. Some of its guiding principles have evolved, while others have been articulated after the fact in order to justify approaches taken and decisions made. Nor were the original principles articulated in Washington necessarily the same as the principles and expectations held in the states.

Evolving Principles in Washington, D.C.

The earliest hope for the rural initiative was that the federal government would become interested enough to address rural development—at all. It was not until 1990, for example, that NCARDP articulated what was all too evident: USDA devoted all of its time and resources to agricultural matters and was not doing enough (anything?) for the nonagricultural interests in rural communities. The rural initiative was conceived to change the way the federal government addressed rural development issues and make it more responsive to the needs of rural communities (NAPA, 1992, pp. 13–14).

Early on, the rural initiative was politically vulnerable because it was a George Bush, Republican initiative. Thus, its intergovernmental collaboration strategy served an important political purpose: it provided a way to skirt traditional political arenas and processes. Most of the action within the D.C. offices came through the support of undersecretary of agriculture Walt Hill and his staff by working without formal mechanisms to encourage interagency collaboration and encouraging rural actors within the states to get on with their deliberations.

Over time the rural initiative's management support structures and roles have largely shifted from bureaucratic principles that emphasized command and control, state dependence on the federal government, mass production efficiencies, and standardized responses to public issues regarding rural economic development (NIRA, 1992) to a broader, more encompassing concern with quality of life factors in rural communities. The Partnership has instigated new management approaches to collective enterprises through the structures, roles, and process of the SRDCs, NPO, and the NRDC. In general, the support structures reflect current realities: no single agency nor any level of government has full responsibility or authority for rural development. Structures, processes, and roles emerge with the evolution of the Rural Partnership's guiding principles. Using the language of 1994, rural development is being reinvented.

Rural Partnership evolved from an interagency working group under the jurisdiction of the Economic Policy Council into a restructured White House policy coordinating group. Ongoing management has been delegated to the National Rural Development Council. The NRDC—an interagency council, not a single federal agency — administers federal support for the SRDCs, including budgets, personnel practices, and evaluation (Springer, 1992). Many of the reinventing government notions that were popularized by Osborne and Gaebler (1992) "have been part of the Initiative from its very beginning" (NIRA, 1992, p. 3). The Partnership is mission-driven, not program-driven; results-oriented, not input-oriented; and it emphasizes a flexible, responsive, and forward-looking approach to problem identification and strategic planning. The Clinton administration has been trying actively to implement this type of management approach in other programs (Gore, 1993).

During the first eighteen months of the Clinton administration, there was some question among the National Rural Development Council whether it was prepared to back up its rhetoric with the political and managerial support needed to move the NRDC to another level of effectiveness. In spring 1994, a group of state and federal participants met with representatives from the Clinton administration and devised a compact of principles that would tie the NRDP to elements of the Clinton agenda and, at the same time, provide support for the effort. And individual NRDC members are acutely aware of the lack of recognition that their time spent on NRDC duties may legitimately substitute for their other agency-specific duties. At present, NRDC members perceive that agency-based supervisors view their duties to be a lower priority "add-on" to their regular agency-specific duties (NRDC, 1994b). NRDC members are also aware that they lack visibility within the federal government and the nation as a whole—a circumstance that also is true of many State Rural Development Councils in their respective states (NRDC, 1994a).

Evolution of Principles in the States

SRDC Structure and Process

The SRDCs were the initial laboratories for designing and implementing the rural initiative. While the PCG-WGRD and the MMG were struggling to balance interests in Washington, the SRDCs faced a plethora of philosophical and practical decisions. There were no categorical grant guidelines or funds that could be used to mandate or entice skeptical state government administrators, bankers, farmers, or county commissioners into participating. There were no road maps to guide them in their searches for new ways to *do* federal-state-local-private collaborative problem solving. Each had to find ways to overcome or circumvent histories of failed federal-state-local "partnership" ventures, skepticism (if not outright cynicism), agency turf protectionism, and distinctive emotionally charged contexts that included spotted owls, severe economic recessions, and racial discrimination.

SRDCs learned quickly that problems could not be solved by calling Washington. For the most part, solutions from Washington were rejected in the various SRDCs. It also did not take long for people to discover that ideas and strategies that appeared to work in other states often were dismal failures when imported. Yet learning occurred from experiences within SRDCs and states, and among SRDCs and the various rural initiative offices and groups in Washington. Thus, the evolution of each SRDC is a unique story about people in a few states who invested themselves in these early SRDC experiments—experiments in what would be labeled a few years later as new governance.

Even though early participants in the rural initiative had some previous experience with federal-state partnership ventures, each had to develop a new vision of rural development as well as the structures and processes for implementing the vision. Thus all SRDCs have had to struggle with complex philosophical-practical issues of: *participation rights* (membership), *entitlement rights and formal leadership* (allocation of power among participants), *operating structures* (committee of the whole, permanent committees, project-specific task groups), *decision processes, SRDC in-state role* (particularly in relationship to existing substate economic development groups, governors, and state agencies), *council-staff roles, autonomy with accountability, self-sustaining momentum, and distinctive identity* (strategic foci).

At this writing, the SRDC experiments are ongoing. Searches for new workable "partnership" solutions continue. With time, a few solutions have been institutionalized but many others have been discarded. Structural concerns have been resolved by process innovations and vice versa. The breadth and magnitude of these issues and the diversity of SRDC solutions are impressive.

Participation Rights (Membership). Although the Bush administration envisioned the rural initiative as a federal-state-local-private partnership, few SRDC participants could envision federal government administrators or agencies "coming to the table" as equal partners. There were too few exceptions to the history of money and control "flowing downhill from Washington."

Inclusive versus exclusive membership is an additional dimension of the participation rights issue that has been addressed in different ways by SRDCs. Texas and New Mexico's exclusiveness were mentioned earlier, and South Carolina followed the same pattern. Originally, the South Carolina SRDC was an "insider's club." Membership was restricted to cabinet-level federal agencies and appointees of the governor, who were connected to informal networks of rurally-focused actors and agencies.

Most of the other SRDCs, however, opted for inclusiveness from the beginning. Oregon's criteria for membership, for example, were an interest in rural development, holding a policy level or decision-making position, and having the time and willingness to serve. Anyone who expresses interest in or attends a meeting of the Maine SRDC is added to the mailing list and considered a member. Operationally, membership on the Maine SRDC is defined as an individual's or organization's decision to participate in some activities. Oregon and Maine would never have considered or tolerated the control over entry to membership that were adopted initially in New Mexico, South Carolina, or Texas.

Structures evolve as participants learn and conditions change. Texas and South Carolina are examples of SRDCs that decided their original designs were not adequate. Both have become more inclusive bodies.

Entitlement Rights and Formal Leadership. Membership does not necessarily guarantee rights of entitlement—to participate in decisions that affect the allocation of resources. The opportunity to exert leadership often was limited to SRDC members who represented certain constituencies with significant stakes in the issues, usually federal or state agencies. For example, in Texas, at first only federal agency representatives could be elected as chair or to the executive committee. In contrast, in New Mexico, the lieutenant governor chairs the council. Few executive committee positions were allocated to federal agency persons until the federal officials decided to organize a caucus, elect caucus officers, and began to meet monthly. Shortly thereafter, the New Mexico council decided to allocate two additional seats to federal agencies. Although federal agency members of the South Dakota council are eligible for executive committee positions, they have tended to be somewhat passive, often deferring to more influential state officials and private-sector representatives.

Access to formal leadership positions varies widely among SRDCs. Most SRDC executive councils have representatives from at least three sectors. Several states have opened formal leadership positions to federal and state agency representatives—but not to representatives of any other sector. The bylaws of the Kansas and Maine RDCs, for example, originally specified federal and state co-chairs in order to facilitate federal-state coordination of funds and programs. When the cochair arrangement proved unwieldy in Kansas, it was dropped. Maine continues with cochairs; access to leadership continues to reflect the realities of the political power of state government and the importance of federal funding for rural development in this state.

Washington State's history of leadership further illustrates the process of SRDC evolution through never-completed searches for workable strategies. During the first year of the council, federal agencies were dominant. During the second year, however, the notion of "constituency groups in equal partnership" evolved. Ever since, the chair position has rotated among representatives of the RDC's six major sectors. The 1992–1993 chair represented nonprofit organizations: The 1993–1994 chair was a member of the tribal government of the Squaxin Island Nation.

Operating Structures. Most SRDC committee structures have evolved through distinct stages. Structures that were instituted in an SRDC's first year often were found lacking in its second or third year. For example, the pilot SRDCs were urged to develop strategic plans during their first year (1991). They formed committees to produce draft mission statements, conducted needs assessments, identified demonstration projects, and drafted strategic plans that were submitted to Washington.

By mid-1991, most of the SRDCs had begun to develop a loose initial sense of strategic direction. A second stage of committee development thus reflected the results of these early attempts at strategic planning. For example, the Maine Council adopted six "action plan" themes in summer 1991: coordination/cooperation, human resources, physical infrastructure, business development, leadership, and natural resources development. Six permanent committees were formed to develop and implement each action plan theme. One year later (summer 1992), the permanent committee structure was declared a failure and was abandoned. It had never worked as planned. The permanent committees (except the executive committee) were abandoned and replaced with project-specific working groups. In this third stage of committee development, working groups disband when projects are completed.

In contrast to the broad-scope 1992 permanent committees, the 1994 working group titles reflect clear purposes, narrower scopes, and an action orientation. For example: secondary forest products value-added; technical assistance in leadership development for the Maine potato industry; and strategic planning for a military base closure community.

Commitment to balance among constituencies' interests also has been played out in many ways, as in Washington State. Oftentimes during the early years, assignments to committees were based upon individuals' expressed interest in a topic rather than expertise in the area. This particular form of participative egalitarianism proved to be unworkable. Although committees of people who recognized the importance of a particular issue as it related to development usually were highly motivated, too often members did not possess adequate expertise. Committee work lacked legitimacy. The Kansas Council committee assignment criteria thus evolved to assignments based on expertise and the centrality of agency involvement in program implementation. Individuals are invited to serve on committees where they can make strong contributions.

Decision Processes. Most SRDCs have operated with a consensus model of decision making, recognizing that SRDCs lack formal power or authority, and that the nature of their actions requires broad support from all major actors. The Oregon council uses a consensual decision model. Other SRDCs, including Kansas, follow a loosely structured parliamentary process that invokes motions and voting only after lengthy deliberations.

Council-Staff Roles. Each SRDC has had to face numerous thorny questions about council-staff roles, relationships, and accountabilities. The executive director position has been at the center of many difficult decisions. Is the paid director staff to the executive officers and to the executive committee? To what extent are SRDCs to be led by elected leaders who represent major constituencies or by paid executive directors? To what extent should executive directors be out-front visible leaders or behind-the-scenes support staff to elected SRDC leadership? Can executive directors be responsive and accountable to their council when their administrative base is in "a home agency"—federal or state—especially since the future of funding for SRDCs has been uncertain ever since their inception?

In several pilot states (including Kansas, Mississippi, and South Carolina), executive directors were detailed from—and paid by—their federal agencies. This practice allowed the SRDCs to avoid paying their executive directors from budgeted funds. The arrangement, though, raised complex questions about equity and accountability. For example, the U.S. Department of Agriculture has recommended that SRDC executive directors should be appointed at the level of GS-14 or GS-15 (if they are federal employees, or at an equivalent salary level if they are state employees). This level of grade and salary expectation has caused considerable difficulty and resentment in several states. The pay scale for federal officials is vastly out of line with local pay scales in most rural states. Complaints about a "GS 15 executive director being paid $70,000 a year to run the photocopy machine" were not uncommon. Also, executive directors who hold federal appointments must be evaluated according to federal guidelines using appropriate federal forms. Even the executive directors who hold state government appointments must have their performance evaluation "signed off" by federal officials in Washington. To whom are they most responsive and accountable? In New Mexico, where the lieutenant governor chairs the council and the governor appoints all state members, accountability and loyalty are unambiguous.

Vermont, Utah, and Maine SRDCs conducted open searches for executive directors to be hired as state employees, largely to prevent these types of problems. Once an executive director is assigned administratively to an agency (a practice that is required by the Rural Partnership Office), however, similar questions of accountability and loyalty almost always resurface.

Self-Sustaining Momentum. From the first, SRDCs have had to live with uncertain futures. They have needed to develop self-sustaining momentum. There is some question about whether and how SRDCs would survive if federal funding were to cease. SRDCs are still new enough to be vulnerable during leadership transitions within the SRDCs and, perhaps more important, among governors and national administrations. These issues remain as challenges for SRDCs.

Distinctive Identity/Strategic Foci. The focus of the Rural Partnership has been on knowledge-driven decision processes in pursuit of new ways to stimulate rural development through intergovernmental and public-private partnerships. The SRDCs have developed their own approaches, strategies, and "identities" in pursuit of this vision. In most SRDCs, deliberations have tended to yield much broader definitions of rural development than the original Bush administration emphasis on rural economic development. Once again, however, SRDC solutions have varied with changes in leadership and swings in state economic conditions, as well as among SRDCs. For example, Washington State has needed to face up to the presence of natural resource and rural issues on a grand scale, while its agricultural industries have fared well in the 1990s. Thus, its SRDC has had difficulty finding a role and identity for itself in areas that affect rural counties.

When the South Carolina council emerged from its initial strategic planning process in 1992, it adopted an ambitious action plan that included twelve "strategies" that collectively comprised a broad definition of rural development. The Maine council has followed a circular path toward establishing its niche or identity. Initially, it adopted a broad definition of rural development that included community climate, health care, transportation, and public education as integral components of long-term rural development. With the onset of a severe recession late in 1991, however, economically-driven political pressure forced the council to refocus on short-term, highly visible, economic development projects. It was not until the recession bottomed in 1993–1994 that the SRDC was able to once again begin to expand its operational definition of rural development.

This tension between a short-term project approach and a longer-term planning process approach has confronted most SRDCs. Some have tried to circumvent it, while others have faced up to it directly. Vermont, for example, employs a strategy that consciously includes a mix of short- and long-term projects—hard and soft projects. Short-term projects and long-term planning are iterative, allowing each to inform the other.

For several years, the South Dakota council devoted almost all of its energy to the elimination of federal barriers to rural development. There is a strong anti-federal regulation feeling on the part of many South Dakotans, and they have seen the council as a vehicle to help reduce such "impediments to their freedom." South Dakota's impediments removal process has involved serious deliberation and action on some fifteen barriers, mostly concentrated in environmental protection regulations and regulations affecting private business. Thus, the South Dakota SRDC's identity was inexorably linked with one strategic focus at least through 1993. "Impediments removal" was the overriding motivation for forming an SRDC in several states, including Washington and Utah. Unlike South Dakota, though, Washington State broadened its focus during its first year. The Utah council did not become operational until 1994, thus its directions are not yet clear.

Finally, several SRDCs have wrestled with the question of whether they are (or should be) entities with identities, missions, and operational structures—in essence superagencies. Proponents of SRDCs as entities argue, for example, for allocating energy and resources to newsletters and other activities that increase SRDC visibility and public recognition. An alternative view that predominates in Kansas and several other states holds that SRDCs are links between agencies (permanent systems) on issues that cross agency or jurisdictional boundaries. Thus, SRDCs are temporary systems or organizational networks that exist only to meet specific needs that are broader than any single agency mandate.

New Governance and Intergovernmental Relations

As noted earlier, the Bush administration rural initiative was experimenting with intergovernmental collaboration and a decentralized approach to problem definition and solution before the Clinton administration came into power. When the Clinton administration announced its focus on new governance as its strategy for invigorating the public policy process, it noted the rural development focused reforms within the U.S. Department of Agriculture as an example of new governance at work.

In many regards, the Rural Partnership's management support structure has reflected guiding principles that have evolved in Washington, D.C., and in the states. Early on, the pilot states tended to be highly dependent on their assigned desk officers in D.C. As the SRDCs matured, however, the principles of federal-state cooperation and state autonomy evolved into realities, and the role of the desk officers changed. Several management practices initiated by the National Partnership Office supported the transition from SRDC dependence to interdependent relationships. Loaned desk officers, for example, were rotated back to their home agencies. In short order, SRDCs began to realize that they knew as much—if not more—about the rural initiative than their desk officers. Dependence decreased.

The Partnership has provided an opportunity for national leadership in crafting strategies that are not limited to rural development. The significance of the Partnership is for intergovernmental relations: structures, roles, and processes for twenty-first-century challenges. The new governance principles that have evolved with the Rural Partnership include the notions of:

- Government as enabler in consensus-building process
- Government as proactive
- Government acting entrepreneurially to achieve a mission
- Citizens as customers
- Measure success by results achieved
- Focus on long-term planning
- Form alliances and collaborative partnerships
- Decentralize authority (NIRA, 1992, p. 4)

The Rural Partnership has resulted in significant decentralization of responsibility to state-level entities. Barriers to long-term rural economic enhancements have been targeted. Steps have been taken to introduce new governance principles into the management of rural development policies and programs (NIRA, 1992).

Major challenges remain, however. Too many federal agencies continue to operate from a program-driven mentality. Short-term projects rather than long-term strategies guide governmental actions. Most of government remains rigid and lacking in innovativeness (NIRA, 1992). The challenge of changing organizational cultures from program-focused, risk-averse cultures to those that encourage and reward entrepreneurial behavior is a substantial one (Light, 1995).

New governance has emerged from public impatience with government. Citizen expectations are changing, government responses are lagging, and there are mismatches and fragmentations in policy process (John and Lovan, 1992). New governance focuses on *participants, purposes, means,* and *politics.* As a mini-laboratory of new governance, the Rural Partnership focuses on:

- Participants. The participants are federal, state, local, tribal, private, and not-for-profit sector agency representatives.
- Purposes. Their purposes are to build a knowledge-based information system to strengthen rural development.
- Means. Their means is bottom-up collaboration and training for managers to adopt more entrepreneurial approaches to problem definition and problem solving.

In the language of new governance, the federal government can steer but it cannot row (Osborne and Gaebler, 1992). The politics are those of expanding political bases by engaging new participants (John and Lovan, 1992). The Clinton administration has been striving to build the capacity for new governance among departments and agencies of the federal government, within individual departments and agencies, among levels of government, and with the private sector. An August 1993 memo from Vice President Gore to cabinet-level secretaries regarding Community Empowerment Initiatives provides an example. This initiative would involve the U.S. Treasury, Small Business Administration, Commerce, Environmental Protection Agency, Housing and Urban Development, Agriculture, Office of Management and Budget, Transportation, Labor, Justice, Education, and Health and Human Services (Gore, 1993).

The rural development challenge is to revitalize local and regional areas by responding to changing economic conditions. The intergovernmental "challenge [is] to find indicators of success in accomplishing missions and goals so that state or federal authorities can hold implementors accountable for results, rather than just for trying" (John et al., 1994, p. 172). In order to do so, new approaches are needed to overcome barriers to rural development, including better access to information regarding business planning and development and national and international competition and developing a more educated workforce. Federal efforts need to recognize the utility of local solutions and avoid the futile federal mind set of "one size fits all" (Harman, 1992).

The change of administration pushed the National Rural Development Partnership to define its own needs as it sought support from a new administration. It argued that it needed high-level policy leadership to build upon the success achieved thus far in developing interagency collaborative networks. In particular, according to the group, the Partnership needs "explicit policy support to provide legitimacy and responsibility for the Partnership to work across agency lines," a policy statement on expectations from the office of the undersecretary, Department of Agriculture, interdepartmental subcabinet recognition and support; and access to and participation of departmental policy decision makers as well as support for departmental staff to spend time on National Council activities (NRDC, 1994b, pp. 4–5).

Conclusions

The rural development enterprise, which started during the Bush administration and has continued under the Clinton administration, began as a modest initiative to signal an interest in rural economic development without spending too much political or financial capital. The interagency collaborative initiative has evolved a dynamic of its own, one that takes seriously a decentralized, collaborative, entrepreneurial approach to rural development. Not only has there been a participant-generated expansion of the roles they can play in rural development, but there has been a substantial broadening of the focus of rural development councils from the original, relatively narrow focus on economic development. Now the focus is on the multifaceted components of the quality of rural life, including health, education, and environment, as well as economic stimuli—with an emphasis on leadership development and building capacity to solve problems and influence the future quality of life for rural communities.

References

Cornman, John N., and Barbara K. Kincaid. 1984. *Lessons from Rural America.* Washington, D.C.: Seven Locks Press.

Flora, Cornelia B., and James A. Christenson 1991. "Critical Times for Rural America." In Cornelia B. Flora and James A. Christenson, eds., *Rural Policies for the 1990s.* Boulder, Colo.: Westview Press.

Galston, William A. 1992. "Rural America in the 1990s: Trends and Choices." *Policy Studies Journal* 20 (2), 202–11.

Gore, Albert. 1993. *Creating a Government that Works Better and Costs Less: Report of the National Performance Review.* Washington, D.C.: U.S. Government Printing Office (September 7).

Harmon, John W. 1992. *Rural Development: Rural America Faces Many Challenges.* Washington, D.C.: U.S. General Accounting Office, GAO / RCED-93-35 (November).

Hill, Walter E. 1991. "Making Rural Policy for the 1990s and Beyond: A Federal Government View." Paper presented at the Annual Agricultural Outlook Conference, Washington, D.C.

John, DeWitt, and Robert Lovan. 1992. New governance for rural development. Unpublished manuscript.

John, DeWitt, Donald E. Kettl, Barbara Dyer, and Bob Lovan. 1994. "What Will New Governance Mean for the Federal Government?" *Public Administration Review* 54 (2) (March / April), 170–75.

Knigge, Charles. 1990. *Future Directions in Rural Development Policy: Findings and Recommendations of the National Commission on Agriculture and Rural Development Policy.* Washington, D.C. (December).

Light, Paul C. 1995. *Thickening Government: Federal Hierarchy and the Diffusion of Accountability.* Washington, D.C.: The Brookings Institution.

Madigan, Edward. 1990. "State Rural Development Council Mission." Materials from the U.S. Secretary of Agriculture in support of President Bush's invitation to governors to establish SRDCS.

Madigan, Edward. 1991. An invitation from the U.S. Secretary of Agriculture to governors to participate in the presidential initiative for state rural development councils. (Bush letter dated October 31).

Madigan, Edward, and Rolad R. Vautour. 1991. *Putting the Pieces Together: Annual Rural Development Strategy Report.* Washington, D.C.: U.S. Department of Agriculture.

Musgrave, John C. 1989. *A Hard Look at USDA's Rural Development Programs: The Report of the Rural Revitalization Task Force.* Washington, D.C.: U.S. Department of Agriculture (June 30).

National Academy of Public Administration. 1992. New approaches to rural development and changing perspectives on governance. Conference co-sponsored by the National Academy of Public Administration and the U.S. Department of Agriculture. Baltimore, Md. (October 1–2).

National Commission on Agriculture and Rural Development Policy. 1989. *"Future Directions in Agricultural Policy.* Report to the President and Congress." Washington, D.C.: National Commission on Agriculture and Rural Development Policy. (December).

National Governors' Association. 1988. *"New Alliances for Rural America: Report of the Task Force on Rural Development."* Washington, D.C.: National Governors' Association.

National Initiative on Rural America. 1992. "Rural development in 1992: Summary of the National Rural Initiative." Washington, D.C." National Initiative on Rural America (November).

National Initiative on Rural America. 1993. "A Vision Statement: National Initiative Office in the Year 2000." Washington, D.C.: National Initiative on Rural America (January).

National Rural Development Council. 1994a. "Memorandum on NRDP Outreach Strategies." National Rural Development Council, Outreach Task Force (January).

National Rural Development Council. 1994b. *National Rural Development Partnership: A Structure for Effective Rural Development Programs.* National Rural Development Council, Challenge Task Force Report (April).

Osborne, David, and Ted Gaebler. 1992. *Reinventing Government.* Reading, Mass.: Addison-Wesley.

Osbourn, Sandra S. 1988a. "Rural Development Initiatives of the Bush Administration: A Report for Congress. Washington, D.C.: Congressional Research Service, Library of Congress (July 13).

Osbourn, Sandra S. 1988b. "Rural Policy in the United States: A History." Washington, D.C.: Congressional Research Service, Library of Congress (July 13).

Outcome Monitoring Team. 1993. "Preliminary Assessment of the Support Structure for the State Rural Development Councils: Abbreviated Version." Washington, D.C.: Monday Management Group, Outcome Monitoring Team (July 16).

Presidential Initiative on Rural Development. 1990. "Summary of Progress." Washington, D.C.: Presidential Initiative on Rural Development (September 18).

Radin, Beryl A. 1992. "Rural Development Councils: An Intergovernmental Coordination Experiment." *Publius* 22 (3) (summer), 111–28.

Radin, Beryl A. Forthcoming. "Managing Across Boundaries: The National Rural Development Council of the National Rural Development Partnership." In Donald F. Kettl and H. Brinton Milward, eds., *The State of Public Management*. Baltimore: John Hopkins University Press.

Reid, J. Norman, and M. Frederick. 1990. *Rural America: Economic Performance, 1989* (AIB-609). Washington, D.C.: U.S. Department of Agriculture, Economic Research Service.

Reid, J. Norman, and W. Robert Lovan. 1993. "Reinventing Rural America: 'The new governance.'" Presented at the Annual Conference of the American Planning Association, Chicago, Ill. (May 4).

Reid, J. Norman, and David W. Sears. 1992. "Symposium on Rural Development Strategies: Introduction." *Policy Studies Journal* 20 (2), 214–17.

Rockefeller, Winthrop P. 1992. *Revitalizing Rural America through Collaboration: A Report to the President*. Washington, D.C.: President's Council on Rural America. (August).

Shribman, D. 1991. Iowa towns shrivel as the young people head for the cities. *Wall Street Journal* (April 24), A1.

Springer, Michael. 1992. "Removing Federal Impediments to Local Rural Development Efforts: A Bottom-up Approach." Washington, D.C.: U.S. Department of Treasury, Office of Economic Policy (October).

Additional Readings

Green, Gary P., and K. T. McNamara. 1988. "Traditional and Nontraditional Opportunities and Alternatives for Local Economic Development." In L. J. Beaulieu, ed., *The Rural South in Crisis: Challenges for the Future*. Boulder, Colo: Westview, 288–303.

Sears, David W., John M. Redman, Richard L. Gardner, and Stephen Adams. 1992. *Gearing up for Success: Organizing a State for Rural Development*. Washington, D.C.: The Aspen Institute.

5 | New Governance in Action
Rural Development Councils as Networks

THIS CHAPTER FOCUSES on an important aspect of the rural development initiative: the creation of networks both within the State Rural Development Councils (SRDCs) and in the National Rural Development Council (NRDC) operating out of Washington, D.C. It discusses networking and networks within new governance concepts, relates the various definitions of the network concept to intergovernmental problem solving, and reviews the experience of the SRDCs and the NRDC within that literature.

From Hierarchies to Networks, Emergent Forms of Policy-Making

The New Governance

A critical aspect of the new governance is the role of bringing the various sectors together to work on problems that cross the domains of many organizations. Governments must not only focus on providing public services, "but on *catalizing* all sectors—public, private, and voluntary—into action to solve their community's problems" (Osborne and Gaebler 1992, p. 20). In a widely read book, the *New Economic Role of American States*, R. Scott Fosler (1988) argues that state governments must correctly read prevailing forces and reorient development strategies in three essential domains of activity:

1. Development should be viewed as a process that occurs inside and *outside* of government. States involve a wide range of actions: creation, expansion, relocation, contraction, regeneration.
2. Active strategies need to be engaged to improve competitiveness, activism of communities, natural advantages, strengths, etc.
3. Fundamentally different sets of institutional arrangements are required, involving numerous public and private organizations at different levels of government—*institutions that are more versatile and flexi-*

ble in permitting the state to anticipate, specialize, experiment, integrate, evaluate and adjust in dealing with emergent forces.

While these prescriptions focus on the new role of states, there is food for thought for all public entities in regard to stretching their boundaries, doing things differently, and engaging in actions that involve working with other entities. In rural community and economic development, many issues suggest the need for cooperative efforts because problems not only exceed the domain of any one organization but involve various levels of government and nongovernment sectors. In many ways, the SRDCs are an attempt to catalyze the various levels and sectors in order to address rural issues.

Among the underlying premises of the state SRDCs is that organizations and agencies cannot "afford to act independently," and thus must "break down the barriers which impede the public and private sectors from acting collectively," and to "provide forums to establish collaborative outcomes" (National Rural Development Partnership, 1994). This charge obviously refers to the networking activities of the SRDCs. The most obvious example of networking is the councils themselves, as bodies built from federal, state, and local governments, nonprofit organizations, and the private sector. Some SRDCs are launching extensive programs of networking, such as Vermont Collaborative Communities, which includes sharing of resources and using collaborative approaches, developing access on the information superhighway, and promoting rural self-help and community development. Other SRDCs have engaged in networking as a byproduct of their work in promoting strategic development activities, building inter- and intragovernmental relationships, expanding resource bases, solving problems facing communities and regions, and in addressing regulatory and administrative impediments. Thus, the SRDCs networking actions are adding to the new model of governance.

Networks and Networking

The concept of interorganizational relations emphasizes that organizations operate as subsets of larger institutional systems, and that there is a fairly high degree of interdependence within these systems. Alter and Hage (1993) argue that this interdependence and the complexity of modern economic and policy domains has led to the formation of "a wide variety of institutional arrangements which are being used to coordinate organizational activities across organizational boundaries" (p. 1). Accordingly, networks themselves are viewed as nonhierarchical clusters of organizations that permit interorganizational interactions of exchange, concerted action, and joint production.

In many ways, networks are interorganizational adaptations of intraorganizational "adhocracy" approaches, particularly matrix organizations. In such organizations, project teams come together to perform specific tasks which have been formalized into a matrix where functional departmental staff are organized in teams to encourage flexible, innovative, and adaptive behavior. Networks bring organizations together in a similar fashion. Like matrices within organizations, networks use multiple organizational contributions to break down the barriers of specialization, allowing organizations to focus on a common problem. Moreover, like matrices, networks of organizations increase adaptability to environmental influences, enhance coordination between functional units, and maximize the use of human resources (Davis and Lawrence, 1977; Morgan, 1986).

Networks span organizations to do what matrices do within organizations. They are unbounded or bounded clusters of organizations that are nonhierarchical collectives of separate units (Alter and Hage, 1993, p. 46). Alter and Hage (1993) point out that these systemic networks are emergent forms of social organization that are more effective and more efficient than traditional hierarchical structures. They "adjust more rapidly to changing technologies and market conditions, develop new products and services in a shorter time period, and provide more creative solutions in the process" (p. 46).

The key to understanding networks and networking involving public sector and nongovernment organizations is the notion of collaborative problem solving. These are not simply coordinating mechanisms that are in place because of some vague notion that it would be nice for agencies operating in the same policy arena to work together. Rather, collaboration is a method for solving interorganizational problems that cannot be successfully solved by single organizations, and a network is the organizational arrangement for doing so. "Collaboration is a process in which those parties with a stake in the problem actively seek a mutually determined solution. They join forces, pool information, knock heads, construct alternative solutions, and forge agreement" (Gray, 1989, p. xviii). In short, collaborations are dynamic processes intended to reframe issues or problems so that they can be solved jointly.

Networks as formally defined "constitute the basic social form that permits interorganizational interactions of exchange, concerted action and joint production. Networks are bounded or unbounded clusters of organizations that, by definition, are non-hierarchial collectives of legally separate units" (Alter and Hage, 1993, p. 46). Networking "is the act of creating and/or maintaining a cluster of organizations for the purpose of exchanging, acting, or producing among the member organizations" (Alter and Hage, 1993, p. 46).

Interagency collaboration, or networking, has been a regular activity in the public sector for some time. In the human services field, the services integration efforts of the 1960s and 1970s, comprehensive health planning in the 1970s, and even some of the war on poverty endeavors such as community action programs are early examples of collaborative problem solving and interagency coordination (Agranoff 1986; 1991). A more recent illustration involves the promotion of state interagency efforts to reduce the impact of prenatal alcohol and other drug use on families.

As Agranoff and McGuire (1993) point out,

> The one inalienable truth that has emerged from policy studies is that policy making in modern societies is characterized by mutual dependency among many different governments and organizations involved in the process. The basic problem and challenge of policy making in such settings is for multiple governmental and nongovernmental organizations to jointly steer courses of action and to deliver policy outputs that are consistent with the multiplicity of societal interests. (p. 8)

It is this mutual dependency and the need to satisfy multiple and often conflicting interests which give rise to the need for networking. As an example, consider the argument made for networking in the prenatal alcohol and drug use arena. Collaborative networks are needed in this field because no

> single agency or system of services can respond effectively to the complex needs presented by those involved in or at risk for alcohol and other drug dependency. The categorical nature of service programs demands parallel interagency cooperation at the Federal, State, and local levels if coherent approaches to alcohol and other drug use prevention and intervention are to be planned, implemented and evaluated. (Jones and Hutchins, 1993, p. 1)

Policy Networks, Policy Sectors, Intergovernmental Problem Solving: How the Rural Sector Encourages Networking

Properties of SRDCs as Networks

There have been numerous paradigms for the analysis of networks. An analytical scheme proposed by Agranoff and McGuire (1993) synthesizes the literature on policy implementation and networks, defined in terms of their properties. This six-part scheme is an attempt to blend conceptually the management of intergovernmental relations and policy implementation into network analysis. The framework argues that network analyses should be explained within their policy or program contexts; who are the partners and what are their foci?

Six distinct properties of managing interorganizational networks in policy settings are offered as a way to differentiate networks such as SRDCs and, ultimately, the associated network management strategies:

- Instrument. What are the policy (or program) instruments utilized by the network?
- Membership. What administrative arrangements are involved in the network?
- Focus of control. What organizations are central to the network?
- Analytical focus. Where in the network is the focal organization located?
- Distribution of resources. What do parties bring to the network?
- Focus of power. What are the interests served by the network?

This framework is consistent with some dominant theoretical concerns in interorganizational relations. For example, Benson (1982) suggests that one of the objectives of policy analysis is to "explain the emergence, the maintenance, and the transformation of interorganizational patterns" (p. 147). His model of policy sectors is based around the idea that a policy sector is an interorganizational political economy or, in more operational terms, a multilevel social structure.

It has been suggested that SRDCs as interorganizational networks lead to new structures while operating in their rural development policy sector. These implementation structures or program structures operate to adapt interdependent national programs at intermediate (state government) and local levels. They operate with representatives of different agencies, exercise considerable discretion in actual application, and are *distinct institutional arrangements* in which specific tasks are accomplished (Hanf, Hjern, and Porter 1978; Hjern and Porter, 1981; Mandell, 1991). Program structures are not merely aggregates of individual organizations. Networks like SRDCs themselves can become critical, and an analytical focus on the individual organizations is relevant in such cases only for understanding how and why each organization contributes to the overall effort (Provan and Milward, 1991). Program structures that emerge from systemic networks are characterized by:

- Multiple power centers with reciprocal relationships
- Many suppliers of resources
- Overlapping and dynamic divisions of labor
- Diffused responsibility for actions
- A high potential for imbalanced and/or poorly coordinated capacities among components
- Massive information exchanges among actors
- The need for information input from all actors. (Hanf, Hjern, and Porter, 1978)

In a number of important respects the SRDCs are another form of program structure. As networks SRDCs bring the various sectors together to look for new program approaches or to smooth the way for management of these interdependent programs.

Network Instruments. The content of the policy or program practices endemic to a particular sector is the substantive focus of the policy instrument component (see Chapter 1 for the discussion of intergovernmental policy instruments). In the case of the SRDCs this involves the means they choose to bring about changes. The changes sought are designed to achieve some ends such as the creation of employment opportunities, more accessible and affordable health care, physical infrastructure improvements, or education for employability in a high-technology world.

What Benson (1982) calls a "policy paradigm" refers to a commitment within the sector to a particular set of policy options. Policy paradigms are comprised of the sector's choice of policy instruments (Elmore, 1987) or tools of government action, for example, grants, demonstrations, and regulatory changes (Salamon, 1981). The policy instruments chosen by the SRDCs will be described more completely in Chapter 6. They are identified here as key network activities such as:

- Changing rural development policy
- Statutory relief
- Regulatory relief
- Management improvement systems
- Demonstrations and development projects
- Database development
- Community information improvements
- New funding sources
- Cooperative ventures
- Outreach activities
- Leadership development

As this list of instruments suggests, rarely did SRDCs set out to change basic rural policy or seek major new program initiatives. Rather, their primary instruments appeared to be seeking existing program relief, improving the operation of programs, developing databases, providing information, and mounting experiments to assist in rural development. Clearly, the predominant number of intergovernmental adjustments (relief) and information and demonstration projects appear to meet Salamon's criteria. Other sections of this chapter clearly describe not only the emphasis placed on these choices by the councils, but their individual characteristics and predictability in regard to intergovernmental management.

Membership, Focus of Control, and Analytical Focus. The administrative arrangements of the framework are "the patterns of differentiation and control over various activities in a policy sector" (Benson, 1982, p. 149). Until the emergent focus on interorganizational networks, the policy literature has typically reflected an overreliance on the simple distinction between markets and hierarchies. However, even though politics and markets yield many different arrangements for designing and administering public policies (Lindblom, 1977; McGregor, 1981), administrative arrangements in modern public sectors are rarely defined solely by law or by the traditional separation of public and private realms (Franz, 1991). The SRDCs constitute a typical example, where the administrative arrangements appear to be closer to those of voluntary mutual-aid organizations than either a market or hierarchy. Where a focal organization is located in a policy sector determines how the arrangements are analyzed; one's point of reference could be a community or locality, a region, or a state. The SRDCs are clearly state-focused; state government agencies are focal actors in every council, either by their action and degree of participation or nonaction or nonparticipation. Rural policy in a federal system is centered on states. The analytical focus of the SRDCs has been somewhat determined by the states' interest in the council effort. They can make them central parts of an important policy network, as is being done to some extent in South Carolina and New Mexico, they can make them support networks for broader strategies, as in the case of Iowa, Vermont, and North Carolina, or they can marginalize them from major state development activities, such as in South Dakota and Mississippi.

Distribution of Resources. The structure of organizational interdependencies in a policy sector is often dependent on the distribution of resources within the network. The resource dependency model asserts that organizations depend on other organizations to secure scarce resources (Benson, 1975). In the case of the SRDCs they were to some extent formed because of this recognition of resource interdependency. This model is based on the assumption that each organization in a sector acts solely as an independent entity (Mandell, 1988), but has the *potential* to contribute. Networking activity, such as SRDC efforts, enhance resource exchanges. Moreover, systemic production networks are necessary in policy sectors like rural development because the individual members cannot achieve their goals operating alone. Formally autonomous but functionally interdependent organizations require mechanisms for implementing tasks (Metcalfe, 1978), as is the case with virtually every effort undertaken by rural development networks. An argument can thus be made that SRDCs have smoothed the process of program implementation.

Focus of Power. The focus of power in systemic networks is best reflected in the interest structures and the formation of rules that provide the underlying institutional boundaries for the sector. Rogers and Mulford (1982) recognize four different interest groups identifiable in policy sectors: support groups, coordinating groups, administrative groups, and demand groups. In the SRDCs, all four of these have emerged. Federal officials, who in many cases have been quite passive or reactive to specific requests, have largely played a supportive role. Key state and interest group members, and in a few cases active citizens, have played important coordinating and administrative roles. Demand components have been rural communities or their representative organizations, and some state agency heads. The underlying interest-power structure of any policy sector acts to preserve a particular hegemonic model of policy; states have been reluctant to share policy development with SRDCs. Similarly, the structure of a policy sector also includes certain rules setting boundaries upon its operation (Benson, 1982), such as not stepping on agency turf. These rules restrict the range of policy choices within a sector. The concern with rules and structure in the policy sector framework is also essentially the underlying thesis of subgovernment theories. Resource dependencies among agency representatives, congressional members, and beneficiaries of legislation act to constrain attempts at reorganization or policy shifts, resulting in a strong and enduring preference for enacting distributive policies in certain sectors (Lowi, 1969; Meier, 1987). This may help explain the difficulties that SRDCs have had in getting involved in major efforts in rural policy redesign.

Interrelationships

The six properties that differentiate network structures are interrelated in a way such that a change in one often produces changes in the others. Different administrative and institutional arrangements may affect differently the position and power of various actors by altering the importance of the resources they possess (Majone, 1989). For example, the change in national administration altered the role of political appointees on the councils. The prior role of the Farmers Home Administration (FmHA) as convener agency shifted to the Rural Development Administration (RDA) as the National Rural Development Partnership (NRDP) effort was placed in this U.S. Department of Agriculture agency. Similarly, government reorganizations invite a new set of interdependencies among agencies traditionally distinct in strategic operations (Barzelay, 1992). In some states, the role of community and/or economic development departments shifted within the state government, changing the network configuration somewhat within SRDCs. However, the constraints may flow in the other direction as well. Existing organizational interdependencies may determine administrative arrangements and policy paradigms when such interdependencies constitute power structures or institutionalized interactive conduct. The councils have had a difficult time bringing certain recalcitrant independent agencies such as EPA to be regularly participating members. There is not a great deal that can be done about this. The six properties can be viewed as determinants of actions within the SRDC intergovernmental networks.

Types of Networks

The formation of networks results in the establishment of symbiotic relationships; integrations in which the whole is greater than the sum of the parts. Such networks are the result of a linking among a diverse number of organizations into a purposive whole (Mandell, 1988). Alter and Hage (1993, p. 73) have conceptualized a typology of networks that identifies three types distinguished by their increasing level of integration and interaction. Their framework includes:

> obligational networks (informal, loosely linked groups of organizations having relationships of preferred exchanges), promotional networks (quasi-formal clusters of organizations sharing and pooling resources to accomplish concerted action, and systemic networks (formal interorganizational units jointly producing a product or service in pursuit of a superorganizational goal).

The Alter and Hage typology is depicted in Table 5.1.

TABLE 5.1. Symbiotic Network Development

	Embryonic ⟶		Developed
Networks:	Obligational	Promotional	Systemic
Interorganizational activities:	Almost none; ad hoc	Peripheral; segmented	Essential; enduring
Emergent properties:	Boundary spanners	Pooling of resources	Division of labor
Goals:	Individual member needs	Supraordinate member problems	Supraordinate societal problems
Examples:	Patterned resource exchanges	Federations, coalitions	Service delivery systems
	Groups, supplier associations, interlocking directorates	Sematech Chip; United Way; AFL-CIO	Japanese systems; Keiretus

Source: Alter and Hage, 1992, p. 74.

Rural Councils as Networks in Operation: Federal-State Intergovernmental Networking

The SRDCs represent a form of promotional network as identified by Alter and Hage. They are an emergent type of networking representing governmental (and nonprofit) organizations that work on rural development. As will be described in Chapter 6, they are "intergovernmental bodies," comprised of sector elements involved in the chain of programming (grants, loans, regulatory) that cross governmental sectors. In regard to the scheme presented by Alter and Hage in Table 5.1, these networks appear to be promotional networks, in the intermediate categories identified above.

First, their interorganizational activities almost never involve the core activities of the agencies, but involve problem solving, demonstrations, or cooperative ventures that are at the periphery of the work of the participating agencies. Rather than being part of some comprehensive strategy or policy effort, the type of issues and problems undertaken by the networks are highly segmented. Indeed, the work of the SRDCs is an integral part of some comprehensive rural policy strategy in only a few cases. The issues they deal with come up one at a time or at least not in a systematic fashion.

Second, for the most part the resources of the SRDCs are pooled when a problem is being solved or a project is being tackled. The properties of these networks include more than the coordinative actions involved in boundary spanning but considerably less than a complete and integrated division of labor. Participating organizations, particularly federal agencies, actually commit funds for grants, waive rules and requirements, approve new managerial procedures, and so on. Moreover, the SRDCs have created some new efforts through demonstration and developmental projects, databases, and resource guides. In a few cases new cooperative ventures involving two or more agencies have been undertaken, but rarely with the type of sequential, interdependent processing operations that Alter and Hage (1993) refer to in terms of developed networks.

Finally, the operating goals of these networks are also of an intermediate nature. Generally speaking, the SRDCs as networks have worked on those systemic problems brought to them by member organizations or by individual communities. Generally the latter have also been of a systemic nature. Intersector problems, such as the need for a change of a grant requirement, a new way to deal with a regulation, or a demonstration of a new approach in the rural economy involve the network in problems that the individual member agencies cannot solve or deal with themselves. Individual organizations involve other organizations in the network. Although perhaps the SRDCs as networks may have been originally designed to deal with broader rural problems, in fact they have not really attacked rural development in such a fashion, but have limited their actions to selected problems generated by member organizations or from communities within the states.

As networks, SRDCs appear to stand between less formal and embryonic patterned resource exchange groups, and they develop service delivery or processing systems. They appear to be more like federations and coalitions that engage in interdependent activities that are selective, ad hoc, and member-driven.

Network-Building Activities

It is fair to say that the initial months and years of the SRDCs' existence have been spent in establishing themselves as networks. They were "contrived networks" in that they did not spontaneously rise out of mutually perceived needs; rather, the federal government stimulated them. On the other hand, they were not mandated in law, and states were not required to form SRDCs. No doubt because they came about through federal stimulation, they took some time in building. Nevertheless, the rapidity with which most SRDCs found a niche and began to work on rural problems suggests that these networks fulfilled a need.

One stage of network building involved creating the councils themselves. In some states a small nucleus of core, rural-serving agencies and organizations formed interim councils and new members were gradually added. The FmHA served as the nominally designated starter agency but councils emerged beyond this shadow quickly. Some states emerged out of the principal state agency having to do with rural development, often the department of economic development or its equivalent. Other states began with large representational bodies. One state, Texas, began only with federal agency staff as full members, with state government representatives being associate members. This designation was later changed to full membership. Most agencies built their networks by designating agencies and positions within organizations (e.g., commissioner, executive director). One state, Iowa, built on previous network activities, primarily choosing "activists" and working members. In many cases this meant organization members and agency program heads rather than directors of organizations. In every state the process of network definition—who to include—was gradual, as SRDCs expanded. Network building by membership expansion appears to be an ongoing process, even in the eight pilot councils.

Another network-building activity is through selection of council scope of work. What the group chooses to do obviously defines the parameters of the network as defined above. In this regard, the Washington SRDC appears to be in a constant state of network building, having undertaken not much more than a gradual strategic planning process including some elements of a needs assessment. Other states, such as New Mexico, South Dakota, and Oregon, appear to have encouraged communities within the state to largely determine their work and define the network. North Carolina, Iowa, and Vermont seem to have selected their targets of effort as a council, which is another means of strategy selection. Whichever route may have been chosen, it is clear that network-building activities and emerging council strategies are linked. What an SRDC chooses to do and who is active in defining council activity cannot easily be separated.

Project activities proved to be yet another significant set of network-building activities. As SRDCs actually began to work on databases, demonstration projects, and federal program changes, they were going through a process of learning how to work with one another, which agencies might contribute resources, and how to make changes. They were also learning who were the "workers," "talkers," and "passive partners." This trial by fire on actual project activities, so to speak, both tests and builds the network. If it is to move beyond the informal, and resources are to be contributed or pooled, then this network property must be put to the test early in the process. In turn, these testing actions have complemented the networking activities of the SRDCs.

Rural Council Network Maintaining Activities

The process of network building and maintaining appear to be simultaneous activities, and both are needed for the viability of network operation. Three maintaining activities appear to be key to the viability of SRDCs as networks:

1. Establishment of the housekeeping provisions of the councils as organizations emerging out of other organizations. This would include selection and rotation of officers, establishment of charters and bylaws, agenda-building activities, and the holding of regular meetings of the councils and their executive committees.
2. Strategies or work approaches pursued by the SRDCs. Each council was more or less expected to develop a strategic plan, in part to set them off on a course of work. In fact, not all councils engaged in fully formal strategic planning; many adopted work plans or another document that defined the scope of their activities. A few relied on previously developed strategic plans. Regardless of the course of action taken, the process of working on and formally adopting something that identified the type of work helped to solidify the network.
3. The projects themselves maintaining the councils as networks. Projects are important in that they allow participating organization representatives to feel that their time and effort is worthwhile. If a network is successful, from the time work plans come out, something is accomplished. For example, SRDC efforts in maintaining a rural hospital, establishing a wastewater treatment facility, developing a joint federal application, obtaining new cranberry permits, or creating a resource database sustain the network. (Chapter 6 provides a detailed explanation of each of these network products.) These outcomes nourish the catalytic efforts of participants.

Accomplishments are proof that a network can work, and then bring people back. Project results signify that something beyond merely talking about the need to coordinate is happening. This is a key factor in network maintenance.

Network Properties

Key Parties and Players. Each of the State Rural Development Councils has been organized to involve a membership of five "partner" constituencies with interests in rural issues: representatives from federal agencies, state governments, local governments, tribal councils, and private sector organizations, defined by the NPO as both nonprofit and businesses. A number of states have rejected this private-sector combination and have broadened it by dividing it into for-profit and nonprofit sectors. The belief here is that there are substantial differences between the two and both need representation. Generally, each of the five sectors is represented in the state SRDC's executive committee. Also, in most states representatives from each constituency are in the "inner circle" of decision makers, although the intensity of their involvement varies considerably from state to state.

An analysis of SRDC membership, focusing on participation by organizations in each of the partnership sectors, indicates shifting leadership roles over time. For example, while the Kansas governor's office was represented on the Kansas SRDC throughout its existence, it did not play a leadership role all of that time. Changes such as these reflect the dynamic nature of the SRDCs and of networks. Leadership and membership in these policy networks shift with changes in the salience of particular issues and particular problems which arise. The fact that very few organizations give up their seats on the councils may also be a reflection of the fact that they are indeed "doing something." Coordination is not an empty exercise for these entities, and the fruits of collaboration encourage continued involvement.

A number of states chose to broaden their membership beyond the five constituencies outlined by the NPO. Most of this occurred as a result of the division of the private sector representation into profit and nonprofit categories. Even then, there were often significant differences among associations of nonprofits, large nonprofits, and smaller community-based groups. There were attempts to secure direct representation of important private interests, particularly credit institutions, health, agriculture, food processing, commerce, and manufacturing organizations, as well as utilities.

Iowa's SRDC formalized this relationship by creating distinct categories of "nonprofit and local government" and "private sector" for purposes of council and steering committee membership. A number of states also made attempts to reach out to critical categories of membership for that state, such as timber in Washington, Oregon, and Maine. Because of the critical or potential role of education in rural development, most of the states added a variety of educational leaders to their councils. These often included state education agency officials, vocational and technical education representatives, and in a few states local school board or school district representation. Tribal representation was maintained as a special category in states with large Native American populations, such as Washington and South Dakota, whereas other states have much lower numbers of council members from tribes, in some states only one representative or no representation.

The only other pattern which emerges from the case studies is that members of council executive committees are key decision makers. In some states, Oregon, for example, the entire executive committee plays a central role in setting agendas and directing the business of the council. In other states there is an inner circle that includes some persons who are members of the executive committee and some who are not. In such states the "key person" test seems to be dependent upon one's organizational affiliation and position.

Those State Rural Development Councils that hold their meetings out in rural communities (such as Oregon and New Mexico) also bring to the table different sets of actors depending upon the location and the agenda of the meeting. In some sense, then, the answer to the question of who sits at the table and who decides is situational.

Map of Influence Patterns. In order to discern intensity and patterns of involvement SRDC executive directors from the states studied were asked to identify the most active members of their council and those whom they would like to see more actively involved. The data show that, in the aggregate, the Economic Development Administration and FmHA are the most active of the federal agencies. State economic development departments and governor's offices are the most active at the state level. COGs and local government departments are the most active of the locals, and they were judged most active in only one third of the SRDCs. Utilities are the most active from the business sector, and community-based organizations in the not-for-profit sector; albeit they were named by only one sixth of the executive directors. Tribal governments are among the most active in only a few SRDCs. Executive directors would most often like to see more involvement from local governments, business in general, tribal governments, and governor's offices. No other organizations on the list were named by more than two SRDCs.

While there are clearly people inside each council who consistently exhibit leadership, several different maps of influence patterns would have to be drawn in each state to accurately represent who is the most influential. Position (both in and outside the council), technical expertise, and personal characteristics are the most important determinants of leadership. The weight of these factors varies by state. For example, in Iowa influence is not dependent on council position, but in South Carolina the cochairs are the most influential members. For the Texas council, position is important, as is institutional affiliation. Technical expertise is significant in Kansas, while personal characteristics and technical expertise are major determinants of influence in Iowa and Oregon. Personal characteristics also play a central role in South Dakota. In Maine members who represent substate economic development and planning organizations gained influence when it appeared they were going to withdraw their participation. In most states it comes down to values and commitment, personal leadership skills, and one's ability to create an elegant solution for a given problem. The latter is a combination of technical expertise and personal characteristics, such as creativity and vision. The truth is, leadership and influence emerge in these states and they resides in different individuals depending upon the issue under consideration.

An example is found in Oregon's Rural INFO project. Eastern Oregon State College (which had representation on the council) had been operating an electronic information system for ten rural counties prior to the formation of the council. When it became apparent that the lack of information about rural development was an issue across the state, the then-council chair, the state director of the federal EDA, suggested that Eastern apply for additional funding to expand the network and the database. The entire council supported the idea and the project was subsequently funded—in part with funds from organizations with representation on the council.

Subjects of Discussion in the Council. The discussion that takes place in council meetings occurs both inside the formal meeting as well as through informal contacts. The South Carolina SRDC has been described as a meeting place with all sorts of crosscutting information systems. In terms of mental image, overlapping circles is an apt description of the intersecting networks on the South Carolina council. Council members in this and all other states truly do network when they come to meetings. Their informal discussions on matters related to rural development often take them well beyond the formal agenda, and these discussions go on before, during, and after meetings. The Oregon council has gone so far as to set aside time at its community meetings for such discussions.

New People, Linkages, Relationships. In most cases network actors are not people who are coming together for the first time. They do not need to establish their agency or interest turf, and already know how to work together. This is not to say that new linkages are not established or relationships are not improved, however. The New Mexico SRDC is illustrative. Reportedly, networks of individuals found within the council are not new, although the structured forum provided by the council allows for greater and more productive interaction among individuals.

Even so, federal officials in particular in several of the states report meeting new individuals and establishing working relationships with them. In Texas, for example, while a core of public officials concerned with rural development had well-established networks prior to the formation of the council, the networks have substantially expanded as a result of the council. Many individuals in that state mentioned that the council has provided the opportunity for either creating new relations or further developing old ones, and that being on a first name basis with others was very valuable to them in noncouncil business. The formation of the federal caucus of council members in New Mexico provided the opportunity for very substantial expansion of interaction among federal officials·there.

Issue networks are found in the Oregon council, and these networks expand as members discuss other rural issues and as they meet new people in the field. Several council members commented on how participation on the council exposed them to economic development people they did not know existed or who they had not had contact with previously. One local government representative said she has been able to educate federal officials—such as from FmHA, the Army Corps of Engineers, and the Forest Service—about local problems of which they were not aware. She and others commented on the fact that their involvement with Oregon SRDC has given them a lot of new, useful contacts. Another telling comment came from a member who said that participation has elevated relationships to the point where council members will bend over backward to get things done.

Another example from the South Carolina council illustrates the formation of new linkages around the issue of rural poverty. As of this writing, the SCRDC is considering a plan to improve the self-sufficiency of rural welfare recipients. If adopted, this plan would unite four groups: welfare recipients interested in owning a business, several retired business people, the SCRDC to coordinate the participation of appropriate federal and state agencies and to provide technical assistance, and the State Department of Social Services to recruit participants and provide appropriate counseling.

Effect on Own Organization. To date, networking activity has not had substantial impact on council member's own agencies in most of the states. However, in Oregon participation has had a definite positive effect. One federal council member representing the EPA said the decision to have council meetings in rural communities cemented his involvement because it put him face-to-face with community problems. He has learned that he can no longer simply sit in Portland and make decisions about what is best for rural Oregon. This in turn gave him a better understanding of development issues related to his agency, made him more accessible, and made it easier for him to solve problems.

On the other side of this coin, the current chair said that while the council has had a positive impact on members and their agencies the longer-term impact has yet to be realized. The council creates dialogue and improves communication, he said, but "singular events don't change how organizations function. The lack of communication among federal agencies is a long-term problem."

With respect to the Texas SRDC, many organizations are now devoting significant resources to council activity. All the chairs of committees devote a good deal of time and many organizations have taken on special projects for the council. In addition, a fair number of organizations have found that the council represents a viable forum or vehicle for the promotion of their activities.

Past Relationships. As noted, the networks formed by the councils are in the main made up of people who have worked together previously. Well-developed networks existed in the states prior to the existence of the SRDCs. Iowa is illustrative of this fact. Most members are either formalizing old contacts or extending their previous networking to a new venue. The entire IRDC (with very few exceptions), particularly the steering committee, is built largely on past relationships. Those who have proven themselves by contributing time, expertise, and energy in related rural or state program networks have been tapped for the council. Membership criteria are simply knowledge, political (but not partisan) connections, trust, and time commitment.

In New Mexico some federal agencies, especially those associated with land management, had well-developed networks prior to the formation of the council as a result of their common interests in public land. Others had similar programs, but had little common activity or coordination. Thus, there were some narrowly-defined networks and the absence of networks where some would have been expected.

There is little evidence that past relationships were an impediment to network formation. In a few isolated cases, mutual involvement in the same service delivery system or competition for state or federal funding roughed some edges before people came together. In no case were these sources of friction reported as an impasse to cooperation. It was reported that in Kansas past relationships may have contributed to some reluctance to work together among KRDC actors, although these problems were overcome. In South Carolina past relationships were characterized not so much by conflict as by "ships passing in the night."

South Dakota is one state where the council created a federal-state network where none existed before. While there was some dyadic contact before, the SDRDC represents the first time such networking efforts have been taken in such a comprehensive way.

View of Council Activity from Outside. It appears that many SRDCs studied must deal with a fair amount of skepticism about their activities. This is often found among federal officials where, as is the case in Iowa, they perceive the council to be of minor influence, given the limited scope of its work, the state's own sense of having a rural strategy, and their clear understanding of the state's concern about protecting its policy domain. In South Carolina federal officials are skeptical about the potential influence of the council. In response to a hypothetical question about whether people would notice if the SCRDC went away, they think the council's demise would be noticed, but not for long. In South Dakota the council has not created a great deal of visibility, except in communities where it has worked on specific problems. Also, legislators have very little knowledge of the council's presence or work, and virtually no problem-oriented networking has involved legislators. In Kansas there is also a report of general skepticism among nonmembers of the council. Maine participants experience little recognition for the activities because general economic development—not rural development—is the focus within the state and the council is viewed as outside the long-standing economic development network.

Skepticism in Oregon has come from state officials from the governor to several of her department heads. While the situation changed late in 1993, from the beginning the governor and other top state officials were taking a wait-and-see attitude. The governor was waiting for a signal from the Clinton administration that it supports the councils and the Rural Initiative. When it became clear that the administration was in support the governor quickly signed on. A similar dynamic was found in several other of the second- and third-generation states.

Network Strategies

SRDC work is bound up with various types of networking functions. Council activity itself involves a constant process of what is commonly called network-building; that is, creating constant patterns of interaction. A number of the SRDCs are, in fact, creating new networks to advance rural development. For example, the arts, wood products, and dry hydrant projects in Vermont all involve the creation of new networks. Likewise, Iowa's regulatory compliance and housing demonstration effort involves the network approach to rural development. The Texas on-line information system would appear to be the beginning of a new network. In other cases the network strategy is to utilize existing or ongoing networks. The New Mexico effort to preserve a rural hospital really tapped into an existing network, although to some extent the SRDC was able to effectuate a change in the operation of network elements. The Oregon Rural INFO project is an example of expanding a regional network to operate on a statewide basis. Yet other situations involve SRDC involvement in existing relationships. The North Carolina SRDC's participation in the state's Rural Initiative is a prime example of this type of activity.

The networking that has been conducted by the councils to date can be characterized as primarily interorganizational problem solving and brokering. Most project efforts in statutory and regulatory relief, demonstrations and developmental projects involve bridging the gaps and acquiring resources from the different organizations. There have been some technical assistance aspects to the database and resource directory efforts and, no doubt, a great deal of behind-the-scenes informal advice has been given on intergovernmental matters both involving SRDC matters and matters related to the partners' own agencies. Information such as how to contact agencies, how to secure grants, or how to make regulatory adjustments has been provided. A great deal of brokering activity has obviously followed these activities. The SRDCs have not generally been called upon to mediate interagency or intergovernmental disputes, or to otherwise resolve conflicts. It is possible that some have been approached informally but have chosen to avoid such a course of action.

Council network strategies are perceived as important but not generally influential. The importance of their scope of work is that there are few rural development project efforts that do not engender a high degree of interdependence and need a boost. But much of the work of the councils has been to support larger activities or to take on projects that, as mentioned, are not at the core of state rural development policy. The SRDCs have not been involved in many of the central activities that involve major rural community and/or economic development efforts. These initiatives are usually state government–centered, and no state seems to have delegated a piece of these activities to the SRDCs, or to have allowed the councils to capture or preempt such portions. On the other hand, there has been some willingness by state governments to share power. So long as the SRDC work remains within the limited parameters of interagency work, allowing the councils an intergovernmental management role appears comfortable to states. That would no doubt not be the case if the councils played a more significant role in policy change and/or funding.

Federal network participants, on the other hand, are less concerned about matters of power or power sharing. They appear to have a more circumscribed understanding of their agency's limited and legally defined role. They will always act within these limits. More importantly, since they view themselves more passively as reacting to state or private sector requests for action, and do not see the councils as policy actors, sharing of power is not an issue. Their influence on most councils is minimal by choice, except where the force of personality or where technical knowledge prevails. Power does not appear to loom as large of a concern.

Networking at the Federal Level

A number of mechanisms have been put into place at the Washington, D.C., level to support state-level activities. This national networking operates simultaneously within the Washington scene and between Washington and the state SRDCs. In addition to the staff office (the National Partnership Office) of the National Rural Development Partnership, a National Rural Development Council (NRDC) provides a venue for the Washington-based perspective for the Partnership and works on behalf of state councils. It is composed of senior program managers representing over forty federal agencies (from eighteen departments or independent agencies) as well as national representatives of public interest, community-based, and private sector organizations. The NDRC promotes interagency collaboration and cooperation with nonfederal programs, and advocates for the engagement of agency and interest group involvement in development. Its primary networking role is to work among the parties to promote change, reduce barriers, and to share information.

The federal interagency group had some of the same characteristics found within the SRDC networks (Radin, 1992; forthcoming). Membership in the group was never viewed in an exclusive way; indeed, the group was willing to include anyone who was interested in participating or whom they could cajole into attendance. Leadership was viewed as a shared experience. The traditional tension between career and political appointees never surfaced as a real issue. As one participant in the process observed, "The political people were different than usual; they didn't push a political agenda." As a result, the two sets of actors operated as a team and the career people were the individuals who assumed leadership roles in the process (Radin, forthcoming). Although the group could cloak itself in the rhetoric and symbolism of the White House, as one participant commented: "Both the White House and the Working Group [subcabinet political appointees] had a limited role. Their level of involvement and role was in promoting the Initiative, giving enough recognition and credibility to move forward."

The staff of the National Partnership Office was committed to openness, consultation, and cooperation. The design of the initiative—a combination of a bottom-up approach (where the SRDCs have control over their own agenda) and a top-down strategy utilizing the NRDC—provided an ongoing "market" for NRDC activities. State skepticism about the level of commitment by the federal actors, especially during the early stages of the process, pushed the interagency group to be attentive to participants in the state councils. However, both NRDC members and SRDC participants are concerned about inadequate communication between the two nodes of activity. At various times SRDC representatives were included in NRDC activities (for example, SRDC executive directors were invited to NRDC meetings), but as one NRDC participant put it, "Councils are still perplexed about the [group] and our expectations of each other are not realistic." Creation of task forces provided a vehicle for individual NRDC members to exert leadership and, as well, to assume responsibility for some part of the group's activities.

As the NRDC developed, its definition of tasks moved gradually away from organizational development activities (that is, providing support first to the pilot states and then to the second-generation states) to more substantive policy efforts. The NRDC has organized itself into four focus groups: natural resources and the environment, human resources, infrastructure and housing, and business support. These groups are addressing impediments within their respective areas, identifying arenas of potential action, strengthening policy linkages, looking for existing avenues of collaboration, and strengthening linkages with state SRDCs. Several national outreach strategies have also been identified by the National Partnership, including a rural development electronic communications network, regular reporting and interactions of the state SRDCs, extensive media contacts, educating policymakers, encouraging leveraging private-sector funds, and telecommunications and satellite projections. NRDC positioning allows it to have an important role in networking between federal agencies, and with states and political decision-makers. Consultant David Sanderson (1993, pp. 2–3) identified important networking aims as:

- SRDCs and NRDC. NRDC will become more proactive and solicit more guidance, advice, and input from SRDCs, especially on priority administration issues (e.g., health, telecommunications, business development, retraining, housing). Ongoing examples are the supporting work of the National Rural Economic Development Institute and the research assistance of the Economic Research Service (ERS).
- NPO and NRDC. We will ask ERS to broaden its efforts across NRDC agencies, involving more NRDC members in interagency research and creating a more formal network. We will include brief presentations of rural research reports in NRDC meetings, prepare fact sheets, provide a research-building agenda, and convene a gathering of researchers from various agencies and organizations.
- Federal agencies and NRDC. Convene a workshop/discussion meeting on marketing NRDC within agencies, focusing on a collaborative effort (e.g., a single reporting format that would require field-D.C. participation on reducing regulations, creating empowerment zones, and other projects from the National Performance Review).

- Policy levels in the Administration, Congress, and NRDC.

   a. NRDC members will brief their agency policy-level leadership quarterly through fact sheets on the status of the National Partnership and success stories involving their agency.

   b. NPO will initiate support through the USDA undersecretary for small community and rural development by preparing a letter and supporting materials for the vice president on policy-level members in NRDC.

   c. NPO will initiate through the White House Economic and Domestic Policy Advisors a White House briefing that illustrates governmental collaboration in the National Partnership, with special emphasis on how NRDC exemplifies National Performance Review recommendations at the Washington level.

   d. The NRDC Steering Committee will draft additional actions and hold NRDC meetings to continue discussion toward agreement on strategy and actions.

   e. The NRDC Steering Committee will draft for NRDC members a brief description of what NRDC is, what it can do, and what it cannot do, following the decisions taken in the retreats.

Conclusions

State Rural Development Councils are mechanisms of intergovernmental policy development as well as vehicles for operationalizing new governance concepts. They clearly are dynamic entities that exhibit changing membership and leadership patterns. That this change is incremental is also clear, and makes it no less significant.

The SRDCs represent experiments in new governance that cross traditional boundaries (both horizontally and vertically) and serve to bring together seemingly diverse interests in a search for common ground in the quest to improve the quality of life in rural America. Building and maintaining networks serves to facilitate collaborative problem solving. Doing so also serves to make all those who choose to actively participate equal partners in the endeavor.

The SRDCs also represent experiments in intergovernmental management. As noted, states allowed SRDCs to take on aspects of a managerial role in the intergovernmental arena; facets of management involving interagency coordination and information sharing, for example. While limited by each participant's willingness to share power, these experiments nonetheless resulted in some reshaping of intergovernmental relationships.

At the same time, the SRDCs play a supplemental role to core state policy efforts. This marginal role aside, the partnership has effectively highlighted the breadth of the rural policy arena. Given the types of organizations involved in the effort, it would be difficult for any of them to ever again conceive of rural policy meaning farm or agriculture policy. Certainly, it involves those arenas, and it also involves community and economic development, health and human services, transportation, housing, environmental protection, land-use planning, and education, to name just a few.

SRDC leadership and membership patterns are to some extent moving targets. That leadership is issue-specific in most SRDCs is testimony to the fact that change is not only a constant, but in the world of new governance and collaborative problem solving, it is essential.

References

Agranoff, Robert. 1986. *Intergovernmental Management: Human Services Problem-solving in Six Metropolitan Areas.* Albany: State University of New York Press.

Agranoff, Robert. 1991. "Human Services Integration: Past and Present Challenges in Public Administration." *Public Administration Review* 51, 533–42.

Agranoff, Robert, and Michael McGuire. 1993. "Theoretical and Empirical Concerns for Intergovernmental Management and Policy Design: Examples from State Economic Development Policy." Paper presented at the 89th Annual Meeting of the American Political Science Association, Washington, D.C. (September).

Alter, C., and Jerald Hage. 1993. *Organizations Working Together.* Newbury Park, Calif.: Sage Publications.

Barzelay, Michael. 1992. *Breaking through Bureaucracy.* Berkeley: University of California Press.

Benson, J. Kenneth. 1975. "The Interorganizational Network as a Political Economy." *Administrative Science Quarterly* 20, 229–49.

Benson, J. Kenneth. 1982. "A framework for policy analysis." In David L. Rogers and David A. Whetten, eds., *Interorganizational Coordination: Theory, Research, and Implementation.* Ames: Iowa State University Press, 137–76.

Davis, Stanley M., and Paul R. Lawrence. 1977. *Matrix.* Reading, Mass: Addison-Wesley.

Elmore, Richard T. 1987. "Instruments of Strategy in Public Policy." *Policy Studies Review* 7 (1), 174–86.

Fosler, R. Scott. 1988. *The New Economic Role of American States*. New York: Oxford University Press

Franz, Hans Jurgen. 1985. "Interorganizational Relations and Coordination at the Policy Level." In Franz-Xaver Kaufman, Giandomenico Majone, and Vincent Ostrom (eds.), *Guidance, Control, and Evaluation in the Public Sector*. Berlin: Walter de Gruyter, 479–94.

Gray, Barbara. 1989. *Collaborating: Finding Common Ground for Multiparty Problems*. San Francisco: Jossey-Bass.

Hanf, Kenneth, Benny Hjern, and David O. Porter. 1978. "Local Networks of Manpower Training in the Federal Republic of Germany and Sweden." In Kenneth Hanf and Fritz W. Scharpf, eds., *Interorganizational Policy-Making*. London: Sage Publications, 303–41.

Hjern, Benny, and David O. Porter. 1981. "Implementation Structures: A New Unit of Administrative Analysis." *Organization Studies* 2, 220–33.

Jones, Virginia H., and Ellen Hutchins. 1993. *Finding Common Ground: A Call for Collaboration*. Arlington, Va.: National Center for Education in Maternal and Child Health.

Lindblom, Charles E. 1977. *Politics and Markets*. New York: Basic Books.

Lowi, Theodore. 1969. *The End of Liberalism*. New York: Norton.

McGregor, Eugene B. 1981. "Administration's Many Instruments." *Administration and Society* 13, 347–75.

Majone, Giandomenico. 1989. *Evidence, Argument, and Persuasion in the Policy Process*. New Haven: Yale University Press.

Mandell, Myrna P. 1988. "Intergovernmental Management in Interorganizational Networks: A Revised Perspective." *International Journal of Public Administration* 11, 393–416.

Mandell, Myrna P. 1991. Program structures: A revised paradigm for understanding the implementation of public programs. Unpublished manuscript, Workshop for Political Theory and Policy Analysis, Indiana University, Bloomington, Ind.

Meier, Kenneth J. 1987. *Politics and the Bureaucracy: Policymaking in the Fourth Branch of Government*, 2nd ed. Monterey, Calif: Brooks / Cole.

Metcalfe, Les. 1978. "Policy-making in Turbulent Environments." In Kenneth Hanf and Fritz W. Scharpf, eds., *Interorganizational Policy-Making*. London: Sage Publications, 37–56.

Morgan, Gareth. 1986. *Images of Organization*. Newbury Park, Calif.: Sage Publications.

National Rural Development Partnership. 1994.

Osborne, David, and Ted Gaebler. 1992. *Reinventing Government*. Reading, Mass.: Addison-Wesley.

Provan, Kenneth G., and H. Brinton Milward. 1991. "Institutional-level Norms and Organizational Involvement in a Service-Implementation Network." *Journal of Public Administration Research and Theory* 1, 391–418.

Radin, Beryl A. 1992. "Rural Development Councils: An Intergovernmental Coordination Experiment." *Publius* 22 (3), 111–28.

Radin, Beryl A. Forthcoming. "Managing Across Boundaries: The National Rural Development Council of the National Rural Development Partnership." In Donald F. Kettl and H. Brinton Milward, eds., *The State of Public Management.* Baltimore: Johns Hopkins Press.

Rogers, David L., and Charles L. Mulford. 1982. "The Historical Development." In David L. Rogers and David A. Whetten, eds., *Interorganizational Coordination: Theory, Research, and Implementation.* Ames: Iowa State University Press, 32–53.

Salamon, Lester M. 1981. "Rethinking Public Management: Third-Party Government and the Changing Forms of Government Action." *Public Policy* 29 (3), 255–75.

Sanderson, David R. 1993. Adjusting the course: Redefining the National Council's mission and roles. Prepared for the National Council and Partnership Office, Ellsworth, Me.

Additional Readings

Harker, J. 1992. "Wetlands Permitting for Introduction of Cranberry as a New Crop, and Cranberry Demonstration Farm Project." Maine Department of Agriculture and Maine Rural Development Council.

Mulford, Charles L., and David L. Rogers. 1982. "Definitions and Models." In David L. Rogers and David A. Whetten, eds., *Interorganizational Coordination: Theory, Research, and Implementation.* Ames: Iowa State University Press, 9–31.

6 | Intergovernmental Partnership Activities

THE STATE RURAL DEVELOPMENT COUNCILS not only seek to foster greater *cooperation* between federal and state agencies, but also engaging *collaborative* projects among their members. These connections reflect another variant of the new governance, as governmental organizations decentralize authority, flatten hierarchies, and get closer to the users of government services. Governments are engaging in lively new "partnerships," Osborne and Gaebler (1992, p. 12) maintain, between business and education, for-profits and nonprofits, between the public and private sector. They maintain that many institutions are adapting, becoming more flexible, innovative, and entrepreneurial.

Entrepreneurial government is not without its critics, particularly those who argue that it can lead to less accountable government where private parties and their values can replace governmental institutions and their values (Moe, 1994). Also, experiences with high risk-taking government has led to fiscal disasters, for example where governments have partnered in ventures with private entities which have then withdrawn or gone bankrupt, leaving government responsible (Gurwitt, 1994).

Despite the potential risk of such ventures, SRDCs represent new partnerships among federal, state, and local governments, associations of governmental officials, the private nonprofit sector, and the for-profit private sector. Their role includes use of these new partnerships to solve problems that relate to programs that cut across governmental lines.

These new partnerships are designed to play a central role in the operation of intergovernmental programs. For some years, there has been interest in experimental programs designed to change the way federal-state programs impact communities (e.g., Radin et al., 1981). In many ways the councils stand in this long stream of experiments devoted to improvement of managing federal-state programs. In keeping with the new governance, the council effort not only includes experiments but routine managerial activity, or intergovernmental management (Agranoff, 1989). In dealing with these programs, councils extend their scope beyond governments to include a broader set of actors that have become governing "partners" with public agency managers. Thus while intergovernmental management has been traditionally thought of as highlighting and emphasizing the role of managers (e.g., Rosenthal 1984; Wright 1984), the resolution of many issues often requires the joint efforts of key agencies, managers, and leaders inside and outside of governments, engendering such partnerships (Agranoff 1986; Agranoff 1990; Gage and Mandell 1990).

The activities and networks undertaken by the SRDCs reflect the range of actions taken as well as the partnerships forged in accomplishing these activities. While the specific activities may vary, each council is meeting the challenge of partnering to handle the complexity of intergovernmental programs. This chapter discusses this range of activities, particularly the partnering approaches utilized by the councils. It also provides a synthesis of the state project experiences of the councils studied.

The Partnership Approach

The need to engage in such intergovernmental problem resolution through partnerships has emerged from the growth, complexity, and growing interdependency of policy systems that rely on multiple governments for policy determination and execution. As national grant and regulatory programs have grown in number and size (for example, joining national enablement/funding/oversight with state and local planning and execution through a variety of public and private sector auspices), officials and managers find that they have to "make legislative enactments work." These implementation activities, then, constitute the core of the new partnerships. In the literature of public administration, these activities have been identified as intergovernmental management, which can be defined as "daily, purposive, transactional relationships between managers acting on behalf of component governments in a system of governments" (Agranoff, 1989), to which one would add, "and nongovernmental organizations."

As numerous illustrations in this book indicate, this approach has some special qualities that are consistent with the partnership activities of the SRDCs. They include a problem-solving focus, that is "an action-oriented process that allows administrators (and other network partners) at all levels the wherewithal to do something constructive" (Mandell, 1979, pp. 2, 6); a means of understanding and coping with the system as it is; and an emphasis on contacts and the development of communication networks (Wright, 1984, p. 431). These qualities operate within a context of understanding within which managers work, as the interacting partners jointly develop solutions, while confronting and making any necessary political, legal, or technical adjustments (Agranoff, 1986). In this regard, the approach has been clearly defined as a different kind of management for, as Rosenthal (1984) has maintained, responsibilities for producing a service or seeking compliance usually must be met through one or more organizations not under the program administrator's direct control. This in turn leads to conditions such as partial accountability, considerably different program objectives on the part of the managers (or partners) representing different governments (or organizations), ongoing cross-organizational linkages, and mechanisms or devices specified for the exchange of resources and information across formal organizational boundaries. Such actions often involve partners, such as those comprising the SRDCs, having to jointly resolve issues.

Why the SRDC Partnerships Focus on Intergovernmental Barriers to Rural Development

Growth, complexity, and interdependence have been identified as the real stimulators of the need to create intergovernmental partnerships. As is the case with most modern welfare states, the U.S. national government has generated this activity through the large number of grant programs (close to 600 in 1993) that involve assistance to state governments, local governments, special purpose governments, nonprofit organizations, private sector organizations, and individuals. Hundreds of regulatory programs have also been enacted, through such means as direct federal orders, conditions of federal financial assistance, and total or partial preemption of state regulatory machinery. Again, regulatory impacts not only affect other governments, but impact nonprofit and for-profit organizations and individuals. The state governments are also in the intergovernmental act. They are usually the pass-through agents for federal grants to local governments and nongovernmental organizations, are responsible for federal grants they operate within state government, and are responsible for federal regulatory programs within the states. Moreover, states have their own state-local grant and regulatory intergovernmental programs. Indeed, in the regulatory arena they are considerably more active with more programs than that of the national government. While less visible than federal programs, state-local control is legally more direct and many regulations or mandates are placed on local governments (Zimmerman, 1992). States also have their own programs of grants-in-aid, loans, credit assistance, tax relief, bonding authority, and many other means of assisting communities. With literally thousands of programs that involve multiple sectors, it is obvious that a need to organize and manage across such sectors has become important.

In a sense, what has happened is that the various elements of the system, ranging from small private organizations to the national government, have become potential or actual partners in a national system of governance (Rose, 1985). These interdependent systems are characterized by: linkages that arise from functional imperatives of program coordination, multiple institutions (public and private) that are used in the same programs, national (and state) government statutory authority and financial responsibility that needs to be blended with local delivery concern, and involvement of subnational governments in national (and state) programs encouraged because of the desire to allow communities to share in decision making and adaptation. Regardless of the formal-legal division of power, program-driven multiple institutional connections involves territorial authority and functional responsibilities. "Policy unites what constitutions divide," suggests Rose (1985, p. 22). Intergovernmental partnerships can contribute in an operational sense to this complex and interdependent approach to governance.

The NRDP effort itself is a clear recognition of the importance of partnering as an activity in managing complexity and interdependence. SRDCs were established to bring together the actors at various levels as a forum to better understand and approach the problems of multisector operations. With a specialized focus on rural development, actors from national, state, local government and the private sector have been brought together in a formal body to "identify, resolve, or eliminate intergovernmental and interagency impediments, bureaucratic red tape, turf issues, language problems and other barriers that hinder effective rural development efforts" (National Initiative, 1992, p. 2).

Some SRDC representatives have been working with each other to resolve intergovernmental problems for some time, on a more limited, project-by-project basis. The SRDCs are a recognition that rural development involves important linkages among many actors who must come to the table to formally engage in the resolution of intergovernmental issues.

From a rural community perspective, it is clear that no local government can "go it alone," but must depend on a set of important linkages for economic and community development. One set involves horizontal linkages, mobilizing different groups and interests within the community in order to support any effort to make changes. A city government, for example, would have to bring along the local development corporation, if there is one, and work with county government and any relevant commissions. Another set of linkages would be vertical, with regional planning bodies, state government, and federal officials, particularly to obtain the type of assistance available at these levels. Research on communities that have been successful in development has indicated that vertical networking or IGM activity is as important as is mobilization within the community (Flora and Flora, 1990).

Partnering Approaches

A full catalog of intergovernmental partnership approaches would fill many pages. Moreover, use is almost always developed within a particular policy or program context (Agranoff and McGuire, 1993). The most useful way to become familiar with the various approaches is by example. The councils as partnerships will be featured later in this chapter through a series of short cases that demonstrate SRDC partnership development. This section will identify those generic partnering approaches or techniques that have characterized the SRDCs in their early years.

Strategic planning, leadership development, and visioning. This not only includes the exercise of matching internal capabilities/options with external threats/opportunities but the skill elements of creating better leaders (group skills, conflict management techniques, learning about the content of programs, how to make intergovernmental contacts) and organizing around a stated vision. A number of SRDCs began their efforts by engaging in one of several forms of strategic planning. Others adapted activities that were closely related to strategic planning, or relied on the strategic plans of related groups in order to guide future action. For example, the Iowa SRDC updated the strategic plan for Rural Development Policy conducted by a panel of public and private sector leaders under the Rural Policy Academy sponsored by the Council of Governors' Policy Advisors. It is clear that possession of such a sense of where intergovernmental partners "are going" can help councils in dealings with state and federal governments. This process always begins with understanding where a jurisdiction or set of partners happen to be at a particular time within the intergovernmental system.

Direct and indirect contacts with other government officials. While the least visible approach, this is perhaps the most prevalent activity of all. It includes seeking information and guidance, and sometimes interpretations of standards and regulations in order to move a program along, for example, securing a grantor loan for community development purposes. The SRDCs engaged in many such cases of informal contacts, both with members of their council from other governments, and with non-SRDC member state and federal officials. Many of the councils also engaged in contacts with Washington, D.C.–based members of the NRDC over issues of regulatory relief. In some cases it involved a form of formal bargaining or negotiating.

Grantsmanship. Acquisition and administration of grants is increasingly important as the number of nonformula discretionary grant activities has increased. This is particularly important for individual communities in development because programs have proliferated. Councils thus became involved in helping communities with grant problems. Moreover, each SRDC received a very small grant for its existence. Other councils have sought various types of demonstration grants from public or private sources for modeling new approaches, establishing new information bases, or for planning large projects. Nevertheless, a great deal of the grantsmanship activity of the SRDCs was more in "smoothing" the way for communities to become involved in grants, such as in attempting to remove impediments in grants administration, creating resource directories, and in creating combined grant applications.

Regulation management. This actually involves a variety of activities, ranging from learning how to apply a regulatory program within a jurisdiction, to making adjustments to regulations, and sometimes assessing the costs/benefits and potential penalties of noncompliance (Wright, 1984). A number of the SRDCs were involved in studying regulatory impacts on rural development, particularly in terms of costs and benefits, and also in helping particular communities make changes in the impact of regulations in order to facilitate particular development projects.

Waivers, model program efforts, special programming. There are occasions where program purpose is impeded by program rules, standards, and regulations, and seeking "asymmetrical" treatment may help a jurisdiction. Thus, a demonstration or special effort is sought to sidestep a regulation or set of regulations, as do many of the state enterprise zone laws, for example. Some SRDCs were active in looking at where program rules constituted an impediment, such as grant rules that imposed heavy administrative burdens, and they tried to change them. One example is the efforts in changing wetlands regulations in Maine, in order to facilitate the growing of cranberries (described later). These were usually undertaken at the request of specific communities.

Joint or collaborative policy-making. This involves the representatives of different jurisdictions participating in shared investigation, strategy development, and decision making to enhance intergovernmental programming. In certain jurisdictions, having the various affected parties (e.g., private sector, tribal, local government, and state government) become involved as partners in the design of a program makes it work easier at the implementation stage, because some of the basic differences have been worked out and common understandings have been reached. A number of the SRDCs initially contemplated this type of joint policy-making but found state government officials conscious of their prerogatives and many of the federal officials who operate within the states did not have the authority to speak for their agencies. Nevertheless, some councils did engage in attempts to redefine some *aspects* of rural policy within their states.

Scale and efficiency approaches. A final approach to be identified is the use of organizational or innovative approaches to generate intergovernmental cooperation. Dozens of examples in practice include: service consolidations (schools, hospitals, detention facilities), decentralization of services (use of fiber-optic communications, mutual services agreements, purchase of services), compacts/cooperative agreements among governments, and governmental consolidation (city-county, counties)/reorganization.

These cooperative approaches often involve some form of agreement between jurisdictions or between the jurisdiction(s) and the nongovernment sector. Several varieties exist. At the most basic level are various avenues of informal cooperation and unwritten agreements by officials to engage in some activity. The contract involves the delivery of service by one unit of government or a private agency for another on a payment basis. Joint service agreements (or parallel actions) are agreements between two or more governments or between governments and private agencies for the joint planning, financing, and delivery of services. The compact or cooperative agreement is a formal agreement under which two or more governments or agencies undertake certain mutual obligations.

Scale and efficiency approaches are most familiar through the mutual contract for service between local governments. Contracting is very common across the country (Shanahan, 1991). The federal government engages in a number of cooperative agreements with states, such as the interstate Cooperative Health Statistics System, in which vital records are maintained by states but are part of a national network operated by the federal government. Joint purchases, pooled liability, and group employee benefit packages are other examples of scale and efficiency management across jurisdictions. Governments have also voluntarily engaged in tax-sharing agreements, such as the one employed by communities in Montgomery County (Dayton), Ohio, which is jointly managed by the various jurisdictional representatives for economic development purposes (Pammer and Dustin, 1993).

Given the nature of the rural sector, scale and efficiency approaches have proved to be important areas of investigation for a number of the SRDCs, inasmuch as small rural governments are often faced with relative inefficiency as a result of low-density-related problems.

There are many other approaches to managing within such partnerships (Agranoff, 1989, 1993; Anderson, 1983; Buntz and Radin, 1983; Henderson, 1984; Honadle, 1981) that communities themselves undertake when engaged in development. For example, communities often leverage their resources, e.g., land, buildings, personnel, or matching money to encourage other organizations to become involved in projects (Eisinger, 1988). But the seven approaches identified above appear to be the most related to the councils as intergovernmental managers and partnership brokers.

SRDCs: Roles as Managers in Intergovernmental Partnerships

The SRDCs have a special role as intergovernmental bodies, or organizations *specifically designed* to analyze and develop solutions for problems that cut across jurisdictions. Perhaps the most familiar intergovernmental bodies are councils of governments (COGs), voluntary groups of local government elected and appointed officials from different jurisdictions who deal with regional issues (Wikstrom, 1977). Many other intergovernmental bodies have been extensively studied (e.g., Agranoff, 1990; Gage and Mandell, 1990). They have emerged around specific problem arenas such as human services or emergency services, adding to those that are jurisdiction-based. The SRDCs, of course, are more "vertical" than "horizontal" intergovernmental bodies, in that they include representatives of all three levels of government and the private sector. Their focus is problem-oriented, in that they have the charge of dealing with rural development, although one would have to say that their potential scope is broad, since the policy focus of the SRDCs involves so many programs. Clearly, their primary domain includes those of an intergovernmental nature, making their activities not only managerial in the sense described earlier, but also in the realm of demonstrating how certain problems can be cooperatively solved and impediments can be removed, and potentially that of making real impacts on rural policies.

Most essential of the SRDC roles as intergovernmental partners is that of convening the actors. Anyone who has had experience with multilayered programs knows well that an initial and often essential task or step has been to get the right persons involved in a problem arena or course of action to meet. In rural development, clearly there are multiple stakeholders: the community/communities impacted, local governments, and the private sector; statewide nonprofits and interest groups; and state and federal governments. The SRDC has been a forum for bringing these actors together. This is particularly true in the case of bringing federal and state officials together, who often are called upon to make critical program adjustments. It is also the case of bringing local officials and the private sector together with state and federal officials to explore problems of rural development.

Pre-SRDC contact between officials tended to be limited in scope and effort. Prior to the formation of the councils a number of these officials, particularly small groups of federal and state officials, had worked together on specific projects. Examples would be work on grants, loans, regulatory relief, special demonstrations, and, in a few cases, support for a scale/efficiency approach, such as a consolidated service delivery program. The council brought a new dynamic, a large number of officials dealing with intergovernmental programs from all the major sectors. Their SRDC task orientation became potentially much broader than any earlier two-party or three-party focus. Thus, bringing these officials from different jurisdictions and program domains together had this important convening effect. In the case of the federal officials, representing so many different agencies and departments, and in some states scattered in many different locations, it brought a number of them together for the first time. For example, in one state when the SRDC was being formed the convening agency (FmHA) requested a list of all federal agencies and officials located within that state and none could be produced. In another state, the career representatives of the various units of the U.S. Department of Agriculture were said to have met for the first time at the initial SRDC meeting. State officials and local government and private sector representatives were reported to have had more knowledge of one another and experience in working together, but in many states the SRDC was the initial *systematic* attempt to undertake such partnering, that is, where there was a focus beyond the resolution of a specific issue.

This convening of the actors also has had important spin-off effects. As people on the councils came to know one another they felt more comfortable approaching new officials to solve noncouncil related problems. Also, officials who had worked together before were able to use the SRDC meetings as a convenient place to conduct additional project-oriented intergovernmental business. In addition, occasionally an individual issue would be "generalized" in the sense that the major actors involved felt that a specific issue could really be generalized to a large group of communities, and thus it would "bubble up" to the council agenda. This was the case in regard to regulation management. For example, individual community problems of wastewater treatment in a number of states led to broader council attention and attempts to solve the problem generically. This in turn was elevated to consideration by the NRDC for a more generic resolution of this problem.

Another partnering role of the state SRDCs was use of the council effort to support other strategies, particularly state rural development policy. As mentioned, Iowa had wrapped their rural efforts around a strategic planning process through their version of the Policy Academy on Rural Development of the Council of Governors' Policy Advisors. One of their five main planks involved intergovernmental cooperation and improved local government performance, a strategic element that is a part of the scale/efficiency approaches mentioned above. The early work of the SRDC has included exploration of clusters of community efforts in grants acquisition and in regulation management. One such result was the demonstration of the problems of small cities meeting OSHA compliance. This led to a pilot project for OSHA training by a consortium of organizations. Now a cluster of state-level organizations—Iowa League of Municipalities, Iowa Department of Labor, and Iowa State University Extension—provide training for small municipalities. A cluster rural housing demonstration is in the planning stages for 1994. Likewise the North Carolina SRDC is a partner in the North Carolina Rural Initiative, an economic development project that will invest $85 million in rural communities. The council has determined it will work most closely in housing, infrastructure, and business development, assisting with technical and financial resources in the area of federal and state funding, information, and technical services. Other actors will be directly involved in new project efforts such as promoting new business starts, job training and education programs, infrastructure, and housing improvements. The Maine wetlands permitting project, to be illustrated below, is part of a broader state agricultural promotion strategy, which in turn is part of the state's economic development effort. These SRDC supportive strategies can be essential links in the effort to create broader partnerships for rural development, inasmuch as so many developmental programs involve programs and resources of an intergovernmental nature.

Illustrative Partnership Efforts

In order to explain how SRDCs actually created new partnerships a number of illustrative situations will be highlighted. These examples focus on problem resolution as part of intergovernmental partnerships and demonstrate the generic approaches illustrated earlier. Each will be presented in capsulized form.

South Dakota: Federal Audits in Small Jurisdictions

This pilot SRDC spent its first two years focusing on the removal of federal impediments to rural development for its small communities, particularly in the area of regulatory management. This process has involved deliberation and action on some fifteen issues. Among these was the effort, stimulated by one small town, as well as the Northeast Council of Governments and the state Legislative Audit Department, to get FmHA to change their requirement that all loans for infrastructure or other community improvements be annually audited. These audits were costing small towns from $2,000 to $4,000 per year. On a $350,000 loan over a twenty-year period, this accumulates to a considerable expense, in many cases exceeding the amount originally borrowed. An appeal was made to the SRDC, which accepted it as an "impediments issue."

As is the case with many instances of federal government requirements the details are highly complicated and technical but the impact is difficult on small communities. The South Dakota SRDC presented the issue in the following way:

> The South Dakota Department of Legislative Audit has indicated that this requirement was specific to just FmHA, and not required by other federal agencies. South Dakota state law requires only those communities with over $600,000 in annual revenues to perform an audit. In the year the loan is made, FmHA requires an audit in accordance with OMB Circular A-128. In subsequent years, FmHA imposes different audit requirements which cause confusion, especially when other federal programs are operating in those years. In Instruction 1942-A 7CFR 1942.17 (q)(4)(i)(A)(2), the FmHA indicates that "audits required by this subpart should not be separate and apart from audits required by state and local laws." This seems to meet the spirit of the Single Audit Act of 1984. In applying the Single Audit Act requirements, however, it seems FmHA has lost that spirit by adding it's own requirements which result in confusion and lead to higher audit costs than would otherwise by the case. FmHA regulations require the unit to follow the requirements of 7CFR 1942.17 (q)(4)(i)(B). This regulation requires:
>
> 1. Audits shall be in accordance with OMB Circular A-110.
> 2. Audits shall be conducted annually unless otherwise prohibited.
> 3. Annual audits shall be completed and supplied to FmHA as soon as possible, but in no case later than 90 days following the period covered by the audit.

OMB Circular A-110 was not intended to apply to units of local government. It applies to "Grants and Agreements with Institutions of Higher Education, Hospitals, and other Non-profit Organizations." State and Local government units are covered by OMB circular A-128 (and formerly by OMB Circular A-102, Attachment P). To further confuse the issue, OMB Circular A-110, Attachment F (which is superseded by OMB Circular A-133) contains the audit requirement provisions for that circular. It does NOT mandate, but suggests that audits be performed on an annual basis. It does, however, require audits every two years. It does NOT require an audit to be completed within 90 days of the end of the fiscal period. While FmHA has required Circular A-110 to be followed, they have changed the audit frequency, scope, and have added a completion deadline that causes confusion and likely higher audit costs. Municipalities are told they must follow the requirements of Circular A-110 (not meant to include communities), but then not really, because even tougher regulations are imposed.

The council claimed that this audit requirement was expensive, excessive, and unnecessary and should be removed when a loan was made to a municipality. Furthermore, they claimed that OMB Circular A128, recognized by all other agencies, already covered the audit situation.

The concern was forwarded to the NRDC impediments task force which forwarded it to the FmHA. After some time delay the agency agreed that a change could be made. The additional audit was eliminated for small communities and loans. They announced that for loans under $500,000 or communities under 5,000 population, audits would only be required at the end of the loan period. This new procedure has been announced in the *Federal Register* and is operating under temporary rules. As of late 1993, it was awaiting publication in CFR.

Kansas: Joint Federal Loan Application

Facing myriad loan application forms from public and private agencies is a formidable challenge. All government lenders require the same basic information but all use different formats. Through a state-federal cooperative effort federal aid processing has been streamlined because of the impetus of SRDC. The Small Business Administration (SBA), FmHA, HUD, and the Kansas Department of Commerce and Housing, along with the Kansas Electrical Power Cooperative, the Rural Electrification Administration, and the Kansas Association of Certified Development Companies developed a single loan application using SBA's 7(a) form as a baseline. This standard application form is making credit access less burdensome for private business applicants.

The joint process simplifies loan processing by using the single form that is based on the SBA 7(a) guaranty loan application. The involved process of creating this common loan form included a block-by-block analysis of each additional form with 7(a) and creating a 7(a) supplement form. Minor differences were resolved as each interaction developed. The process began with SBA-HUD interaction, then SBA-FmHA, then SBA-Kansas Department of Commerce and Housing. The most formidable hurdle was sharing of credit analysis, due to potential liability if any errors were made by an analyst representing one agency processing a loan application for another agency. Ultimately a solution was reached to agree upon common benchmarks and a common time frame (past three years) for credit analysis. A specialized software program, FISCAL, was used for standardized credit analysis.

Several benefits are claimed from this process. The Kansas SRDC highlights four particular advantages:

1. Ease of accessibility to multiple funding opportunities by the borrower and its lender.
2. Promotion of joint funding by participating federal and state agencies. To date, these programs tend to be somewhat mutually exclusive of each other. It is anticipated that more joint funding in projects will result.
3. Through more standardized evaluation of credit and standardized information of credit criteria, it is anticipated that more prudent investment of public funds will result as well as a low incidence of failed loans by borrowers.
4. Reduced paperwork and filing and more standardized closing and servicing of loans, again with the idea in mind that a standardized approach would provide for greater prudence in loan making closing and servicing activities. This would also carry forward to the standardization of compliance issues such as appraisals, environmental assessments and etc.

The South Central Kansas Economic Development District (SCKEDD) is field-testing the application form. SRDC deems it important to use businesses to test the product that meet the criteria of using as many public lending sources as possible. An option suggested by the U.S. Department of the Treasury was to transfer the technology being adopted by the Texas Federal Rural Development Council on an electronic loan application process (ELAP) to the Kansas project. After close scrutiny of three vendors offering loan packaging programs one was selected to develop and deliver software that could handle the single loan application form. This gives the single loan application form not only a paperless companion, but offers an excellent tool for tracking all entities involved in the lending process. Currently a vendor has been retained by SCKEDD in order to expand the ELAP program available for testing.

During the process of securing the single application, the SRDC sought the assistance of NRDC, which worked with the agencies to get national agreement among the affected agencies. It was reported as not easy, inasmuch as officials in one agency perceived the single application as "breaking regulations." NRDC was able to exert top-down leverage to move this agency along. Interestingly, the Department of the Treasury had been given this task five years earlier by Congress. Members of NRDC saw this as an opportunity to fulfill that mandate. The U.S. Department of Treasury will now be compiling a cross-tabulation database showing all credit application differences.

Maine: Wetlands Permitting

One focal activity of the SRDC in Maine was a project in joint development of regulatory relief. The SRDC role was to facilitate meetings among federal regulators and state economic development interests for state efforts to revive the cranberry industry, particularly in Maine's 6.5 million acres of wetlands, which comprise 50 percent of the total land area. A committee began to study impediments after the state legislature enacted legislation to establish a state permitting process for cranberry growing in certain wetlands. Federal wetlands regulations, however, required individual permits for proposed land alterations. It was estimated that data needed to file for a Federal Clean Water Act permit for one acre of wetland fill would cost between $25,000 and $100,000. Permitting would also have required mitigation to compensate for the altered wetlands. Moreover, the Environmental Protection Agency (EPA) was routinely denying permits for new cranberry enterprises in wetlands. Meanwhile, banks were unwilling to consider crop loans to farmers until all permits were granted.

In 1992 the Maine SRDC held a meeting of the regional directors of EPA, Army Corps of Engineers, and Interior Department, as well as state agencies and private interests to discuss the regulatory constraints to cranberry development in Maine. At the meeting federal agencies felt that the state was not respecting federal mandates. Potential cranberry growers felt that the federal permit process was too costly and detailed for small family farms, and that Maine's unique situation demanded a special approach to permit application and review of wetland fills. State environmental and agriculture agencies also felt that the federal permit processes for wetland development often duplicated state efforts.

The meeting resulted in the Army Corps of Engineers agreeing to take the lead in establishment of a working committee with the express purpose of: establishing a permit process for wetland fills under Section 404 of the Clean Water Act to allow for less costly application requirements for small farmers; protecting federal agencies (EPA and Fish and Wildlife) permit review oversight for potential wetland impacts; and potentially reducing duplication of permit application processes between the state and federal wetland regulations for cranberry developments. In addition, EPA agreed to review possible sources of grants for development of demonstration projects to ascertain whether upland cranberry farming was a feasible alternative to wetland development. Potential cranberry farmers were concerned about delays in development of new projects, so a timetable of three to six months was established for the negotiation process to conclude.

The Maine Department of Agriculture, Development Division, was chosen to coordinate the state negotiating team and the U.S. Army Corps of Engineers was chosen to be the lead facilitator for the meetings. At the first meeting, the interagency committee discussed the specific concerns of the various agencies and private individuals. The corps decided that a general permit would be most applicable and solicited input on the major information necessary to meet each agency's needs. At the second meeting the committee toured potential sites and current cranberry farms in the state to ascertain the projected impacts on wetlands. Acreage thresholds and performance standards to be covered under the permit were discussed. The committee, with the assistance of the Maine Cranberry Development Committee and Grower's Association, sent out a survey in June to determine the extent of future cranberry development. A draft general permit was presented for review to all the agencies. The draft consisted of procedures to file a permit, type of wetlands that could be converted, threshold acreages which would be covered under the permit without triggering individual permit review, and other information, most of which would reduce and complement the state permitting process. A public notice with the draft permit was then issued to gather public comment and the corps has made some modifications based on comments received.

Potential cranberry growers were concerned that, even with the permits, many sites would require growing cranberries on soil types new to cranberries. In addition, EPA insisted that uplands be used as an alternative to wetlands based on limited Massachusetts trials. Research and the need for additional data would be required. The Cranberry Development Committee and the Rural Development Council held meetings with University of Maine, USDA Soil Conservation Service, and Cooperative Extension to develop research priorities. A proposal is being put together by the committee. EPA has also agreed to assist in providing funds and the Department of Agriculture is in the process of developing a proposal to submit to EPA's Wetland Protection Program.

The process of bringing federal and state agencies together to meet economic development and environmental conservation needs has met with success. The Rural Development Council's effort raised awareness of the issues to high-level officials. The commitment of federal and state agency technical personnel to address issues through consensus building meetings led by good facilitation resulted in a workable product. According to the participants, of critical importance to success of this process is the commitment of agencies and the private sector to continue to work together and to review the improvements with commitment from all agencies to renegotiate if necessary.

Oregon: Rural INFO

This project demonstrates how collaboration and commitment can advance program aims. It includes teleconferencing and an interactive data base of public and private resources for rural development. Citizens throughout the state can access this network. The Oregon SRDC (ORDC) spearheaded this effort through cooperation with an operating arm, Eastern Oregon State College (EOSC). Small rural governments lack expertise and funding to address local development problems. Rural Oregonians, as a whole, lack knowledge of available sources of expertise and funding, and lack knowledge about how to access these resources. Through a partnership process involving experts, amateurs, and potential users, the ORDC has designed an on-line information network called Rural INFO (Information Network for Oregon) which will make information about resources for rural development more accessible to rural communities. The network will feature an on-line database including the Catalog of Federal Domestic Assistance, a guide to Oregon's state programs, information on foundation and corporate resources, and an interactive capability to link communities working on similar problems. Additionally, communities working on similar problems will be identified with each other so they can share ideas and progress. EOSC has put funding together which includes the resources of its own library, $25,000 from EPA, and $15,000 from GTE. NASA has invited EOSC to apply for $25,000.

Subcontractors have been hired to develop a revised teleconferencing reference manual and training program for people who will participate in Rural INFO and to develop the database for electronic searching of state agency grant and loan program opportunities. Discussions are also under way to determine the costs for adding additional local dial-up access points in rural Oregon. Presently there are fourteen local dial-up access points where individuals can participate in the Oregon ED-NET telecommunications system without incurring long-distance charges. Oregon ED-NET has agreed to upgrade existing telecommunications equipment at its 14 local access dial-up points. Second, local telephone lines will be installed at each site to expand access for Rural INFO users, and capacity will be developed to remotely access the equipment if malfunctions occur.

As a support mechanism, the first group of Rural INFO "conferencers" has been trained. This group and those to be trained will be practicing teleconferencing skills in preparation for leading specialized conferences for solving problems identified by rural Oregon community leaders. Several agencies and organizations will be involved in order to test Rural INFO. Also the ORDC calendar, meeting notices and minutes, community issues, and a host of other topics will be found on Rural INFO. The Oregon State System of Higher Education has agreed to install local telephone access numbers for teleconferencing. These numbers will be available to the public, and serve the communities where campuses are based. Finally, a bulletin board has been created on the COMPASS network. The topic deals with the Northwest Economic Adjustment Program (Forest Conference Response). Additional bulletin boards scheduled for implementation are grantsmanship opportunities and water/wastewater issues.

Texas: Resource Team Pilot Project

As a pilot project, the Texas Rural Development Council (TRDC) is currently in the process of assisting the city of Hearne in evaluating Hearne's assets and liabilities and in developing a plan to improve the economic future of the city. The TRDC met twice with Hearne officials, once in Austin and once in Hearne, to lay out the perimeters of the process to be undertaken and to gain commitment from both TRDC and the city of Hearne to see the process through to fruition. After the second meeting, an eight-person resource team was selected to visit Hearne, interview citizens, business, and community leaders, and develop a plan of action for the city. In addition, others have been designated to assist the team in the management and evaluation of the effort.

The resource team toured the city in late 1993 and interviewed 103 individuals over a two-and-one-half-day period. The team interviewed representatives from the following segments of the Hearne community: agriculture, elderly, civic clubs, utilities, financial community, retail business, industrial business, youth, clergy, health professionals, Alamo Street merchants, government, and education. Each participant was asked to respond to three questions designed to begin communication and discussion and to serve as a basis for developing the action plan. At the end of the last day, each member of the resource team agreed to write up notes and forward them to the SRDC facilitator to write a draft summary and plan. Community challenges, opportunities, and objectives were presented in general community development and several other areas. A meeting was held in early 1994 in Hearne with all the participants, at which time the resource team presented its preliminary findings. Based upon the results of this pilot project, the TRDC will decide whether to continue this effort. The TRDC has been contacted by approximately twenty other communities interested in possibly availing themselves of this service.

South Carolina: Edgefield Wastewater Demonstration

The SRDC in South Carolina has received national attention for its demonstration project in combining efforts in infrastructure for economic development and increased efficiency. Three small towns were at capacity for sewage treatment. Two of these towns had expansion (or possible exit) plans. The other town was trying to service a school. All three wanted to apply for sewer funds from federal and state agencies. The SRDC effort emerged out of informal discussions at the meeting. A proposal was entertained to collect the sewage from the three towns and send it to neighboring Aiken County, where an existing facility contains excess capacity. A number of council members became involved in the project, representing their respective agencies.

The entire project is estimated to cost around $4.3 million. Of this total, $2 million is from EDA funds, $1 million in CDBG money through the governor's office, $456,000 from the state corrections department, $150,000 from state budget office, and $757,000 from FmHA. In the case of the EDA, it doubled its normal allocation because of the regional nature of the project and its potential value. The immediate benefits of the project are job retention and business expansion. Once the sewer lines are complete, the hope is that other firms will relocate in this area. The Edgefield project is considered to be the first phase in a planned four-county sewage treatment system.

Implementation of the regional model is proving to be more difficult than design. One key player involved in the process said, "The scope of this overall regional plan is enormous, with several conceivable bottlenecks along the way." Potential obstacles pointed out included permits, capacities, multijurisdictional agreements, and timetables. However, unless this is done, a section 208 water plan update, the plan may well unfold piece by piece and further design problems, timing problems, and even legal and financial problems may result. Thus, there is some risk of slippage between formulation and implementation.

Mississippi: Poultry Loan Eligibility

This low-visibility effort on the part of the council was initiated by the SBA representative on the council. Several small poultry producers wanted to expand production because of the rising demand for chicken. A group of representatives, including SBA, FmHA, and state agency representatives worked at broadening and expanding definitions of loan eligibility. Initially the group believed it required Washington approval, but they found it was not necessary. Federal officials said that the new approach to eligibility could be undertaken within existing authority. Thus, a change in dealing with federal programs was undertaken by seeking an interpretation of existing rules. The Mississippi poultry project demonstrates how partnerships among government officials at different levels can work with nongovernmental actors to solve problems through simple means.

Many programs are amenable to adjustment if the right contacts are made and the questions are asked. Agranoff's (1986) study of intergovernmental partnerships demonstrated that agents are able to solve many multijurisdictional issues by convening, identifying, and reaching agreement on the nature of the problems, searching for and forging joint solutions, and implementing decisions through joint action. Most solutions proved to be basic program accommodations, reciprocal tasks, or adjustments made to intergovernmental programs within requirements and standards, although they are shaped to local needs. In a similar fashion to the Mississippi Poultry Loan Project, they almost always turn out to involve very routine matters that rarely cause conflict once jurisdictional representatives had discussed them while focusing on specific problems.

Washington: Strategic Planning

The SRDC in this state has emphasized process and building an atmosphere for joint action among six constituency groups: tribal governments, local governments, private sector, nonprofits, state government, and the federal government. Together the parties are developing a strategic planning process. It began with a needs assessment that identified several critical issue areas: decline in timber harvesting and overall decline in the natural resource base of the economy, intergovernmental issues, health and human services, education, agriculture, environment, economic development, and job training/employment.

Council leaders began with the assumption that state and federal agencies were interested in modifying their rules to help small communities develop; that there are degrees of flexibility or even "permission that has not been explored." The strategy was followed by a work plan with eleven different activity areas, with goal statements, time frames, performance measures, tasks, participants, and cost allocations for each area. Strategic elements are focused on medium-term issues, such as rebuilding timber dependent economies.

Iowa: Regulation Management

This SRDC became fully active in 1993 and it began by examining the impact of regulations on small communities. Quarterly meetings during the first year were devoted to these concerns as their substantive agendas. It has conducted a series of consciousness-raising sessions in which federal impacts on rural communities are demonstrated. The sessions begin with presentations by communities affected by regulations. They are followed by an intergovernmental problem that is presented that requires creative resolution. Local presenters remain as resource persons and participants. Council members then divide up into local, state, and federal teams (usually involving role reversals), and engage in a measure of role playing, in order to understand how it feels at different process phases.

One such exercise has dealt with multicommunity small business and government compliance with OSHA regulations. Another focused on EPA standards for rural areas. In both cases multijurisdictional compliance with federal standards were explored. Proposed solutions were suggested for the involved communities, who are currently pursuing them. Moreover, the entire set of four sensitivity sessions led to the selection of Iowa's work areas: agriculture promotion, rural leadership/capacity-building, and governmental improvement/shared services. They have formed the basis of their current work groups. The IRDC effort has led to a new partnership to help communities meet OSHA regulations. Recognizing that worker safety and OSHA compliance are serious concerns for small cities and counties, the Council's Service Delivery Work Group brought together the efforts to improve occupational safety training. The new partnership includes the Iowa Department of Employment Services Division of Labor, the Iowa Association of Municipal Utilities, and the Iowa Association of Regional Councils as operating participants. These groups will work together to provide occupational safety training and consulting services to local governments around Iowa. The ability of each organization to provide services will be enhanced. Similar efforts are now under way to improve waste management training and consultative services to local governments through a consortium of organizations.

New Mexico: Community Response Teams

This SRDC relies heavily on the testimony of local residents in council meetings held around the state to define specific issues the intergovernmental body will address. Task forces of the council are addressing issues first raised at these community meetings in rural health, agriculture marketing, and solid waste. In its first year and a half of operation the SRDC received some sixty requests for assistance from small communities, although for many the needed actions were beyond the capacity of the council. In cases where the request is not within the scope of the SRDC, the executive director now makes the appropriate government agency referral.

One example of a successful effort by the New Mexico SRDC is the Santa Rosa–Guadalupe County Hospital project. In a community meeting in Santa Rosa, the Council was asked to help the community keep the hospital open. A sixteen-organization response team was established with representatives of the governor's office, state health department, county extension agent, FmHA, Rural Development Administration, state housing authority, state nonprofit organizations, and the private sector. While the county owned the building, it did not have the resources to run the hospital. The county and the response team sought and gained the involvement of the University of New Mexico Medical School, Presbyterian Hospital, and others. An emergency CDBG grant for equipment purchase was obtained and several other grant applications were submitted. The U.S. Department of Health and Human Services was asked to accelerate their permit process, which prevented the closing of the hospital as it changed hands. Personnel from surrounding county facilities have been loaned in order to keep the hospital operating.

A local community/county health council was formed. It will develop a pilot health services plan that can be replicated in other small communities. The council was also able to move forward stalled Medicaid payments that the hospital desperately needed. Guadalupe County citizens passed a mill levy to support operation of the hospital. While a long-term solution is yet to be found, the response team of the council has kept the hospital open, as it mobilized federal and state resources to solve the immediate problem. One long-term effect of the Santa Rosa–Guadalupe situation is that the University Medical School has adopted a stronger outreach program and has begun to rotate its students through rural hospitals.

This and other efforts to solve problems in solid waste, environmental management, and local infrastructure development indicates the seriousness of the New Mexico SRDC priority on local communities. The SRDC has held itself accountable by periodically reviewing the actions taken in response to the issues raised by the communities. To support this effort, the SRDC has received a HUD planning grant to offer technical assistance to small communities in preparing small cities' CDBG grant applications.

North Carolina: Local Partners Program

The council in this state is playing a role in a broader state initiative—the North Carolina Rural Initiative. This program, announced in late 1993, is a public-private partnership that will lead to investment of more than $85 million in rural communities throughout the state in order to "provide rural communities with the fundamental tools they need for building economic strength."

The council's role in the initiative is to assist with both financial and technical resources by streamlining the delivery of federal and state funds, and providing information and technical services to rural communities. The SRDC focus is on the efforts to increase local economic development through ongoing information and training programs to a network of locally designated partners—the Local Partners Program. Thus, in North Carolina one role of the council is to facilitate the interagency-intersector dimension of partnerships.

Vermont: Collaborative Communities and Other Networks

The SRDC in this state is one of several that is attempting to promote rural development through horizontal networking. The primary strategy here involves convening and organizing a group of public and private actors who explore a development problem, set a course of action, and seek support to promote the activity. Also, vertical networking is almost always bound up in these processes, particularly during the action stage.

Collaborative Communities, an offshoot of the Vermont SRDC, is a working group devoted to bringing communities together to share resources and use collaborative approaches, promote participation in local and national "information superhighway" access, and to enhance democracy through community self-development approaches. The activities proposed by this group include programs in: local leadership capacity building; electronic services linking local governments; electronic services linking the Vermont League of Cities and Towns to local government leadership; electronic services linking VRDC to grassroots leaders, and electronic services to link the towns and villages of Vermont to the United States and globally. Through affiliation with a foundation, the work group has fund-raising authority and will also explore federal grants to support these efforts.

Three additional Vermont networking efforts stand out. First, a rural arts partnership is being established to emphasize and enhance their economic and social impact on the state. These activities include a Tours and Detours project and a teleconference on Arts and the Economy. Second, in the area of small business financing, some twenty-five statewide groups are participating in strategies to provide working capital to new and small businesses. Third, a forestry and wood products coalition is being formed around marketing activities. It involves promoting the development of timber bridges, native wood retaining walls, and elements of industry modernization. These could prove to be important developmental projects in Vermont.

These examples highlight some of the exemplary means that the SRDCs have engaged in forging partnerships in order to face intergovernmental issues. As can be seen, many different approaches are used. In addition, those of a more routine basis, such as making direct contacts or grants writing, have not been illustrated here but are equally prevalent.

Synthesis of State Experiences

Scope of Projects

The variety of efforts has been assessed by the evaluation team in terms of the intergovernmental partnership focus of the various projects. Since the councils were given no specific charge or working mission other than to attempt to improve working relationships and to smooth out managerial impediments to rural development, the scope of efforts chosen by the SRDCs was necessarily broad. These efforts were organized into eleven different types of projects:

- Changing rural development policy. Alter the direction in which government at any level addressed some aspect of rural programming.
- Statutory relief. Achieve adjustment to a statutory impediment to development.
- Regulatory relief. Achieve adjustments to regulatory programs, such

as negotiating a different standard, waiver of program guideline, or finding an alternative means of compliance.

- Management improvement systems. Develop a new means of operating federal or state programs, such as a joint application form.
- Demonstrations/developmental projects. Create a rural development prototype or new program initiatives that have broader applicability, such as a new product from existing resources or a housing demonstration.
- Databases. Create new information systems of use to the rural development community.
- Communication/information. Broaden knowledge regarding rural problems and rural development.
- New funding. Bring different sources of funding into the SRDC itself, in order to create new programs for research and development.
- Cooperative ventures. Operate jointly projects by the SRDC and other entities, such as state government not-for-profit agencies.
- Outreach. Hold meetings in local communities to provide technical assistance, identify problems, gather information regarding rural problems, and to formulate future agendas.
- Leadership development. Strengthen the capacity of rural leaders by focused training projects.

Here is a typology of the SRDC project efforts:

Programmed policy changes
  Changing rural development policy
  Statutory relief
  Regulatory policy
Management and operational improvements
  Management information systems
  Databases
  Cooperative ventures
Intergovernmental innovations
  Demonstration/development projects
  Communication/information
  New funding
  Outreach
  Leadership development

An analysis of the projects undertaken in the councils suggested that overall, regulatory relief projects, databases, cooperative ventures, outreach activities, and demonstrations or development projects were the most common. Of lesser significance are projects relating to new funding initiatives (the least pursued innovation) and changing policy. Neither finding is surprising, inasmuch as these tend to be the domain of state governments agencies dealing with rural development. To make or change policy or to seek additional funds could easily be perceived as encroaching on the turf of these agencies. Helping these agencies to facilitate regulatory problems or with grant programs, or to provide information, or to demonstrate a new approach appears much less threatening. In terms of scope, the projects therefore steer clear of major state or state-federal efforts.

The variety of projects undertaken by the SRDCs no doubt reflects the broad charge given to the council program. Since each council has had the freedom to chart its course, choosing several or a few projects, and choosing the type of intergovernmental partnership effort they wish to engage, the variety is understandable. The range of the total number of project efforts was considerable, reflecting the age of the council and the tendency for some SRDCs to emphasize a particular type. Perhaps more important than numbers are the arenas or activities that councils approached.

Typology of Projects. SRDC activities in encouraging intergovernmental partnerships appear to fall into four different types that are identified as local community participation, technical assistance, information gathering, and council membership outreach. The variety of efforts explained in the previous section appear to fit within one of these four types.

Type of Project	*Definition*
Local Community Participation	Involving rural communities in bringing problems to the council
Technical Assistance	Discovering and filling information and knowledge gaps for the rural sector
Information Gathering	Examining the extent and depth of rural problems and bringing them to the attention of decisionmakers
Council Membership Outreach	Expanding the definition of the rural intergovernmental partnership to include a broader scope of membership.

204 | NEW GOVERNANCE FOR RURAL AMERICA

Local community participation involves council efforts at involving rural communities in bringing real-world problems to the council. This type has been manifested in different ways. Many councils rotate their meetings around the state and allow any local person or local officials to address problems and issues of their choice. The New Mexico council, for example, follows this model. They have also worked with communities to solve their problems, for example, the hospital project mentioned. Other councils are more specific in focus, allowing input on specific agenda topics, for example, environmental regulation. Iowa has followed this model. Councils that emphasize impediments removal, for example South Dakota, usually create some mechanism for communities to bring forth issues that they wished to address. Finally, the Texas council has experimented with sending SWOT teams into communities, helping them to identify problems and areas of action. Many of the twelve SRDCs studied were involved in this type of activity in some form or another.

Technical assistance refers to a variety of actions taken by the councils to fill knowledge gaps in rural development. The councils tried to ensure that communities or statewide rural development efforts received information or how-to demonstrations, due to gaps in technology or professional capacities often suffered in rural areas (Brown and Glasgow, 1991). Again, these barriers were overcome in many different ways. The Iowa SRDC used demonstrations of role-playing efforts, which then are expected to "bubble up" into demonstrations of new partnerships, as in the case of occupational health and safety. Other councils, such as Maine, have lent *process* assistance, such as the cranberry growers' demonstration effort. The South Carolina regional wastewater treatment effort would be another example of process assistance. The other councils simply made themselves available to solve problems or route them to the proper authorities. This was the least prevalent type of activity, with only six councils engaging in such technical assistance.

Information gathering refers to SRDC efforts to examine the extent and type of rural problems and to make them known to a variety of decision-makers. Many councils gathered initial information in the "environmental scan" part of their strategic plans. Others worked with university-based research bureaus to gather baseline information on the rural sector and on rural communities in their states. About half of the councils compiled economic and community development resource guides, providing readily accessible information for volunteers/nonpaid officials in small communities. Finally, a number of states focused on information gathering related to specific industries or problems such as timber (Washington) and cranberries (Maine), or gathered information related to compliance with environmental regulations. This was the single most prevalent activity.

Council membership outreach involves expanding the definition of the intergovernmental partnership to include a more extensive membership. Virtually every council in some way went through a process of discussing rural issues and problems, discovering a wider circle of potentially affected interests, and bringing in new members. Some councils, such as Texas, were originally restrictive, but later became more inclusive. South Dakota experienced minor conflict regarding the inclusion of some nominated new members, but in the end invited all entities that were nominated. However, some of those contacted showed no interest. Many councils sought to maintain a balance between the various sectors. A number of councils experienced difficulty in fulfilling some expected types of membership, such as tribal, which required extraordinary outreach efforts. Nevertheless, most of the councils saw expanding the partnership as an important activity in itself.

Characterization of Projects. In terms of managing, three different types of SRDC project efforts appeared to have emerged. The first type, which is called "fine-tuning," involves the council or affected jurisdictions to improve their coordination and/or cooperation at the margins of programs (Agranoff, 1989). Agencies represented in the council continue to carry out their normal activities. There are certainly many examples of this throughout the book. Kansas and Texas have been able to get the various agencies working together, and have fine-tuned their federal assistance through such means as single federal loan assistance applications and through electronic processing of project applications. The various resource guides in the different states would also appear to be a similar form of tuning up the way communities get information to access resources yet does not change the process. Iowa, South Dakota, South Carolina, and many other states have used the council both formally and informally to enhance contacts between federal and state officials. While very difficult to document unless there is a focused project effort, this type of activity may be among the most prevalent in the SRDCs.

A second approach is "project-oriented," where agencies represented on the SRDC convene to engage in a new effort, either for a particular program or for a community or region. There are many such case examples, such as Washington's strategic planning process, the Mississippi poultry loan application process for SBA, North Carolina's support for their Rural Initiative, New Mexico's community meetings, and Oregon's rural information system. In these and other situations the intergovernmental effort is to use the agency representatives on the council to manage a specific problem that has presented a barrier in development to resolution. The council sees that there is a need, the agency representatives feel it is legitimate, that it is within the scope of their agencies to solve, and they set out to work through the problem.

A final characterization of partnership efforts are projects that lead to a major "change of scope." That is, the SRDC itself develops a new function which is created in a dramatic new way, in design or implementing. Examples of these tend to be fewer, because the councils are new, but also because intergovernmental bodies by their nature are designed to engage in cooperative efforts or to take on specific problem-oriented projects. Nevertheless, a few examples exist. The new wetlands permitting process in Maine, the regional wastewater treatment effort in South Carolina, and the regional/multiagency approach to running the New Mexico hospital constitute new departures for implementation. Moreover, a number of SRDC efforts, such as Iowa's demonstration effort in developing a consortium of federal and state agencies and local nonprofit organizations, constitute major changes in the scope of programming. More of these types of demonstrators will no doubt occur in the future. The SRDCs are less likely to engage in this activity, however, because they represent partnerships that work more at the margin than at the core of development programs.

Conclusions

While the intention of the SRDC movement may have initially been to make a major impact on rural policy, core rural policy is driven by state governments. Some states, such as Iowa, Maine, North Carolina, and Utah, for example, nevertheless saw the SRDC as a way to support existing state rural program efforts by creating new partnerships. This has involved bringing the various agency representatives together to help smooth out intergovernmental programs and thus to make an indirect or "second level" impact on policy. In most of the other states, however, the SRDC took on a more independent role, that of dealing with specific issues as they were presented to them, choosing to work on those of an intersectoral nature. That is often the nature of partnerships such as the SRDCs (Alter and Hage, 1993). The activities of this latter group of SRDCs did not appear to be part of a broader strategy, but were more isolated attempts to use a partnership approach to deal with independent problems or to approach issues generated by the communities themselves. Remarkably, few of these issues were of an agricultural nature. The Maine Cranberry Project is a very significant exception, but even in this case the federal agency involved was not USDA, but EPA. Most problems the councils have dealt with have related to various facets of community and economic development, involving programming in the resource acquisition area, e.g., grants, loans, credit buy-downs, or in regulation management. Perhaps more important than any specific accomplishment, however, is the value of the contacts made within the councils. Since so much of this strategy involves contacts and communications, partnering as a regular form of this activity can enhance these efforts. Since there is such a large learning curve in building capability in order to solve intergovernmental problems, the SRDCs have also been most valuable in this regard. A component of capacity-building (i.e., the process building and using forged relationships) is of the most critical importance. Time will reap many additional benefits of the capabilities enhanced by partnership.

Rural development in the 1990s cannot proceed without the type of cooperative interagency/interorganizational efforts undertaken by the councils. Communities cannot do it on their own. Federal and state governments set the legal and program contexts, regulate activities, and possess the financial tools that must be accessed at other levels. Those who work at the community level need to network horizontally (to mobilize the community) and vertically (to engage in intergovernmental management) to make development successful. They can be helped by intergovernmental bodies such as SRDCs that can "smooth the way." In some cases the SRDCs can "fix" a specific problem, whereas in others they can be "process agents" by creating a new path. In others they can be "strategic planners" by forging new directions, and finally they can be "policy developers," creating new approaches. Given the nature of the intergovernmental field, all of these roles will be necessary for some time.

References

Agranoff, Robert. 1986. *Intergovernmental Management: Human Services Problem-Solving in Six Metropolitan Areas.* Albany: State University of New York Press.

Agranoff, Robert. 1989. "Managing Intergovernmental Processes." In James L. Perry, ed., *Handbook of Public Administration.* San Francisco: Jossey-Bass.

Agranoff, Robert. 1990. "Managing Federalism through Metropolitan Human Services Intergovernmental Bodies." *Publius* 20, 1–22.

Agranoff, Robert. 1993. "Intergovernmental Management for Community Economic Development." Paper prepared for Conference on Managing Municipal Change, Hong Kong / Guangzhou, P.R.C. (June).

Agranoff, Robert, and Michael McGuire. 1993. "Theoretical and Empirical Concerns for Intergovernmental Management and Policy Design: Examples from State Economic Development Policy." Paper presented at the 89th annual meeting of the American Political Science Association, Washington, D.C. (September).

Alter, C., and Jerald Hage. 1993. *Organizations Working Together.* Newbury Park, Calif.: Sage Publications.

Anderson, W. F. 1983. "Representing the Community with Other Governments." In W. F. Anderson, C.A. Newland, and R. J. Stillman, eds., *The Effective Local Government Manager.* Washington, D.C.: International City Management Association.

Brown, David L., and Nina L. Glasgow. 1991. "Capacity Building and Rural Government Adaptation to Population Change." In Cornelia B. Flora and James A. Christensen, eds., *Rural Policies for the 1990s.* Boulder, Colo.: Westview.

Buntz, C. Gregory, and Beryl A. Radin. 1983. "Managing Intergovernmental Conflict: The Case of Human Services." *Public Administration Review* 131 (5), 403–10.

Eisinger, P. K. 1988. *The Rise of the Entrepreneurial State: State and Local Economic Development Policy in the United States.* Madison: University of Wisconsin Press.

Flora, Cornelia B., and J. L. Flora. 1990. "Developing Entrepreneurial Rural Communities." *Sociological Practice* 8, 197–207.

Gage, R. W., and M. P. Mandell. 1990. *Strategies for Managing Intergovernmental Policies and Networks.* New York: Praeger.

Gurwitt, Rob. 1994. "The Entrepreneurial Gamble." *Governing* 7 (8), 34–40.

Henderson, L. M. 1984. "Intergovernmental Service Arrangements and the Transfer of Functions." *Baseline Data Report* 16 (6).

Honadle, Beth W. 1981. "A Capacity-Building Framework: A Search for Concept and Purpose." *Public Administration Review* 41 (5), 575–80.

Mandell, M. P. 1979. "Intergovernmental Management." *Public Administration Times* (Dec. 15), 2, 6.

Moe, Ronald C. 1994. "The 'Reinventing Government' Exercise: Misinterpreting the Problem, Misjudging the Consequences." *Public Administration Review* 54 (2), 111–22.

National Initiative on Rural America. 1992. "National Mission and Goal Statement." Washington, D.C.: National Initiatives on Rural America (December).

Osborne, David, and Ted Gaebler. 1992. *Reinventing Government*. Reading, Mass.: Addison-Wesley.

Pammer, William J., and Jack L. Dustin. 1993. "Fostering Economic Development Through County Tax Sharing." *State and Local Government Review* 25 (winter), 57–71.

Radin, Beryl A. et al. 1981. *Planning Reform Demonstration Project Evaluation*. Washington, D.C.: U.S. Department of Health and Human Services.

Rose, Richard. 1985. "From Government at the Centre to Nationwide Government." In Yves Mény and Vincent Wright, eds., *Center-Periphery Relations in Western Europe*. London: George Allen and Unwin.

Rosenthal, S. R. 1984. "New Directions in Evaluating Intergovernmental Programs." *Public Administration Review* 44 (6), 469–76.

Shanahan, Eileen. 1991. "Going it Jointly: Regional Solutions to Regional Problems." *Governing* 5 (8), 70–76.

Wikstrom, Nelson. 1977. *Councils of Governments: A Study of Political Incrementalism*. Chicago: Nelson-Hall.

Wright, Deil S. 1984. "Managing the Intergovernmental Scene: The Changing Dramas of Federalism, Intergovernmental Relations and Intergovernmental Management." In W. Eddy, ed., *The Handbook of Organization Management*. New York: Marcel Dekker.

Zimmerman, Joseph F. 1992. *Contemporary American Federalism*. New York: Praeger.

7 | Expectations and Outcomes

Changing Expectations

The rural initiative that emerged from the White House in 1990 went through a number of changes in the period from 1990 to 1994. Some of these changes are explained by shifts in personnel and the change in the presidency in January 1993. As important as these changes were, however, the transformation of the initiative also occurred as a result of an evolving and learning process at two levels: first, between the state councils and the Washington-based staff, and second, within the councils themselves.

As Chapter 4 indicates, in its early phase, the initiative was largely driven by the general ideology and substantive agenda of the Bush administration—questions of deregulation, reduced federal activity, emphasis on the private sector, devolution to the states, and a comprehensive rational approach to council activity. Within a year of the initial activity, a different approach took form, characterized by a process rather than substantive agenda. In this phase, the initiative focused on means rather than ends, attempted to broaden the range of actors involved in the councils, and tried to encourage initiative participants to focus on the complexity of the issues that were raised.

The 1992 publication of the Osborne and Gaebler volume, *Reinventing Government* gave participants in the process (particularly staff in the Washington-based aspects of the initiative) a language to use to describe their activity to others. That book allowed them to view their own concerns in a broader fashion, highlighting a modified role for the federal government (minimizing the traditional control aspects), diminishing the boundaries between levels of government and the public and private sectors, and emphasizing a collaborative approach to decision making. It also provided a bridge to the change of administration that took place in January 1993.

The Clinton administration, largely through the National Performance Review and its definition of new governance, embraced many of these principles. At the same time, however, there was also a substantive agenda that was imposed by the new appointees, particularly those within USDA. This new agenda provided a way for the Clinton appointees to make modifications in what was viewed as a Republican initiative. Concern about the membership composition of the councils (particularly the representation of racial and ethnic minorities) was articulated. In addition, the new officials searched for ways to mesh the councils and the initiative with other Clinton administration policies (such as the empowerment and enterprise communities). In this sense, the balance of the initiative tilted to a focus on substantive outcomes, looking to the process approach as a means to support substantive ends.

Expectations also changed within the councils themselves as the process unfolded. These shifts occurred as a result of the interplay between a broadened set of actors, experience with the complexity of the rural development policy field, and shifts in the state-level political and economic environment. In addition, councils began to learn from one another and to understand the similarities and differences between states.

The relationships between the councils and the Washington-based initiative staff also changed over the four years. Few councils continued to have a blanket negative characterization of "the feds" after operating for a few years. In some cases, the councils reduced their antagonism to Washington, D.C. In other cases, councils developed a less compliant approach, minimizing their perception that the effort "belonged" to the federal government and instead embracing it as an activity within the state. But whichever direction the shifts moved, there continued to be some tension between D.C. expectations and those of the states.

Initiative Outcomes

The seeming intractability of rural problems and the complexity that surrounds possible solutions make it difficult to evaluate the contribution of a single intervention in terms that focus only on a single measure. Although the real goal of this effort is to change the life conditions of rural Americans (particularly those who live in isolated and poverty-stricken areas), it is unrealistic to expect an initiative that focuses on changes in resource allocation, organizational and policy shifts, and is only four years old to be assessed in terms of its ability to provide new opportunities or services to rural residents. In addition, given the shifts in expectations that characterize the life of the initiative, there has not been a focused strategy for change that has emerged over these years. At the same time, however, it is possible to assess this initiative in terms of incremental changes that move states (and perhaps the country) toward these eventual goals.

Within the states themselves, as Chapter 6 has indicated, the councils vary in terms of the processes used to make strategic choices of programs (e.g., goals, objectives, their plan of action, their definition of mission). Some of these variations are explained by factors (e.g., political shifts) that are beyond the control of the councils themselves. Some choices are dictated by the type of rural setting within a state; others are a function of personalities and past relationships between council participants.

Given these constraints, this assessment of the outcomes of the initiative attempts to identify a number of indicators or actions that represent significant areas of possible change and reflect a movement toward increased attention to the problems of rural residents. This discussion focuses on six different types of outcomes that can be discerned from this initiative to this point: networking, developing strategies, allocation or reallocation of resources, visibility and awareness of rural development issues, redefinition of rural policy, and levels of institutionalization.

Networking

As is discussed in Chapter 5, the emergence of a variety of networks was one of the major results of the strategies behind the initiative. The relationships that developed through the activities within the councils became more complex and differentiated as the effort progressed. The multiple partnership configuration became a way of dealing with difficult or undeveloped relationships between a number of institutional actors. The council format became a way for some state-level actors to reach out to local levels, establishing connections that had been difficult to develop earlier. In some cases, federal officials had little contact with state officials, even when they operated in the same programmatic areas. Some councils provided a setting for new relationships between public sector and private sector actors (both for-profit and nonprofit groups).

While varied, many of the networks that emerged from the process had a number of common attributes. They were able to provide brokering and mediation functions; they were able to defuse past antagonisms, unfreeze some policy logjams, and smooth out conflicts as they created opportunities for participants to deal with one another in face-to-face, personal terms. They were also able to broaden the issue beyond traditional actors (although some actors, such as agriculture agencies and interests, continued to be important in a number of states) and sensitize some participants to the potential breadth of expertise that might be utilized to solve rural development problems.

The relationships that emerged from a number of the councils were possible only because of a concerted effort to depoliticize the rural development issue; that is, to acknowledge that concern about and ability to address these issues were not monopolies held by one political party or one institution (such as the legislature or the governor). The methods that were used to accomplish this were nontraditional in many states: meetings held in different geographical locations, shifting leadership responsibilities, and collegial relationships among participants. However, in several states the leadership was shared but shared only by the inner circle participants.

Networks of those concerned about rural development were not new in a number of states and the councils in those jurisdictions were able to pick up on investments that had already been made either within the state itself or as a result of activities such as the CGPA Academy. But even though networks may have existed in the past, the council activity was frequently able to expand their composition or, in a number of states, to create the momentum for the development of specialized networks around specific policy issues or focused on specific institutional actors. In a few states, the creation of the council provided the first opportunity for network development; no natural institution existing inside the state facilitated these types of relationships.

As might be expected, councils were not always able to deal with problems that had plagued the state in the past. Some councils were largely composed of the "same old players"; others existed as parallel institutions to the real power in the state. Political feuds between the governor and legislature or between the governor and lieutenant governor continued to be a part of the council's environment. Politics, race, and value conflicts could not be ignored in states with those policy battles.

It should be noted that networks also developed within the initiative between states. A number of councils developed relationships with other councils in their geographic areas, often around specific policy issues (such as the activity around the timber summit). Other councils were able to use the opportunities for meetings between executive directors to establish relationships and to share program and strategy ideas.

Developing Strategies for the Council

The councils have defined themselves, in terms of missions and goals, in quite diverse ways, as discussed in Chapter 3. Most states have adopted a strategic planning process to operationalize their activities, but the way in which the states use the process falls into three categories. Some states have developed plans that allow for significant flexibility in implementation. For example, a strategic plan may embody missions and goals but council activities are not necessarily specified. The specific activities to be undertaken may emerge through interactions with local communities or from working groups; The strategic plan incorporates a flexible, decentralized approach to implementing council activities. In a second group of states, the strategic plan is more detailed and used more formally in determining council activities. A council may even derive work plans directly from the strategic plan or assess proposed activities in terms of consistency with the strategic plan. A number of states use an annual review of the strategic plan as the reference point for internal accountability. In a third group of states, the strategic planning process is either perfunctory, for compliance purposes, or nonexistent. Some councils believe it is not their charge to determine strategic direction but rather look to other agencies (usually state executive agencies or the legislature) for direction.

Several states that became involved in the strategic planning process at a relatively late date have used the process to address or correct earlier shortcomings. Many states have addressed tensions between those advocating action-oriented, problem-solving approaches and those advocating a long-term policy development agenda by including both approaches in their plans. Elements for the strategic plans were often derived from the Rural Academy for those states participating in that activity.

Allocation or Reallocation of Resources

One means to measure the effect of councils is through changes in the allocation or reallocation of resources in the agencies and organizations that participate on the councils. Although councils themselves have very limited resources, they may be able to mobilize or affect the use of resources by others in their attempt to improve rural areas. To date, the councils have had quite modest effects on the actual use of resources. When such effects occur, they appear to be correlated with age of the council and the degree to which the council is project-oriented. The first-generation councils have had more time to develop relations with agencies and thus greater opportunity to affect resource allocation decisions. In addition, the councils that are action-oriented are more likely to affect resource allocation decisions as a result of projects undertaken or promoted by the council.

Councils can affect resource allocation in a variety of ways. Many councils assume the role of broker while working with agencies in council activities. This role is frequently seen in council-sponsored projects but can occur indirectly through spin-offs of council activities. A number of councils have been asked to review grant proposals in programs run by other agencies and thus affect resource allocation decisions of those agencies. In one case, a council actually administers a grant program for another agency (New Mexico). In another case, an agency created a new pilot program as result of learning about a particular problem in a council meeting (Texas).

The councils affect resource allocation in other, more subtle ways. A substantial number of examples have been found where agencies have started cooperating, opening the possibility of some reallocation of resources, after being brought together through the council. In these instances, the role of the council is not that of a broker, but rather the council provides a forum for agencies to interact. In addition, there are a significant number of examples where agencies assume responsibility for council functions, such as maintaining databases. These functions may coincide with ongoing agency functions, but nevertheless represent instances of their own resources for council activities. Finally, many agencies use councils as a means to discuss and promote their programs.

Most councils adopted a needs assessment exercise as they were formed. This step, recommended by federal officials, appears to have been a useful confidence building activity for councils. There was little evidence that the first round of needs assessment/inventories produced any notable results on subsequent council activities or on agencies. However, councils that display an ongoing concern with gaps/needs have produced some interesting results, particularly in those councils that place a high priority on local communities. Meetings in local communities have been useful for informing state officials and agencies about problems of rural communities. Problems of local communities have helped establish work agendas for several councils (for example, in Washington, Oregon, New Mexico, and North Carolina).

Visibility and Awareness of Rural Development Issues

Another potential outcome of councils is raising the visibility and awareness of rural issues in a state. On this measure, the councils have had very limited independent effect. In several states, visibility of the issues had already been established, as a result of the nature of the economy of the state (as in the plains states). A number of councils depend on state agencies or gubernatorial leadership for generating visibility about the issue. A few councils have adopted a low profile in their endeavors so as not to impinge on leadership roles of other agencies. The nonpartisanship posture taken by several councils may reinforce a low-profile orientation. It may also be the case that increasing the visibility and awareness of rural issues in a state will become a priority for councils once they have consolidated their institutional base; for the present, however, this is a low priority.

Redefinition of Rural Policy

The state rural development councils have, for the most part, not yet attempted to become involved in rural policy development in their states, much less attempted to redefine rural policy. The constraints on becoming active in policy development range from the prohibition against lobbying activities by federal employees to not wanting to infringe on the prerogatives of agencies or government officials. These constraints are substantial and councils may never become effective in this role.

The question of redefining rural policy, in the sense of broadening the definition beyond concerns of agriculture development, has been moot for most of the councils. It appears in virtually all states; the transition from the traditional agriculture-oriented policy to a broader definition has been made without much assistance from the councils. Even in the Plains states, where agriculture development is central to rural development, a sophisticated understanding of policy issues exists independent of council efforts. Nevertheless, many individuals participating in council activities report that they have a broader perception on rural issues as a result of their participation.

Level of Institutionalization of the Councils

Most of the council states that were studied had past experiences with initiatives that originated in Washington, D.C., and were skeptical of what they saw as a common pattern around these efforts: the tendency for initiatives to be short-lived, lasting only as long as a particular official or administration was in office. Indeed, several of the states were reluctant to invest in the organization of a council until they had fairly clear signals that the Bush initiative would be embraced (at least in some form) by the Clinton administration.

Despite this, several states were able to organize councils around existing state activity. In at least one case (North Carolina), the council was effectively grafted onto the governor's program. The experience in other states suggested that, even if federal monies would disappear, the institution would become a part of the state apparatus. Efforts have been made in the state of Washington to codify the council through state legislation. States have varied in the extent to which they have acted on an assumption that the councils will be permanent bodies. Some have behaved as temporary organizations, chosen to assume a low visibility posture within the state, to presume that the federal funds are likely to be time limited, and have tended to spin off activities to other groups (some of which may have been created through the council).

Perhaps the most important aspect of the federal funding occurs through the support for staff and administrative support. Given the tight budget crunch in a number of the states, it is not at all clear whether funds would be made available to pay for the support of a coordinating function. Such support would likely depend on the ability of the council to increase the visibility of the rural development issue within the state.

Variables and Outcomes: Patterns or Randomness?

Looking at this range of outcomes, a clear set of attributes does not emerge that seems to be associated with particular outcomes. This is not surprising, given the variability within the states. What appears to have

facilitated the activity of the council in one state can surface as a block-
ing attribute in another. In addition, the sixteen states that have been
studied represent three different generations of activity in the initiative.

This discussion includes attention to a number of variables that have
emerged during this study: the impact of past and ongoing efforts in the
state, generation differences between councils, membership strategies,
relationships with the local level, leadership patterns, agenda development, determinations of degree of visibility, and demographic characteristics of the state.

The Impact of Past and Ongoing Efforts in the State. States that had a heritage of efforts related to rural development prior to the establishment of
the council clearly had some head start on the activity. This was particularly true of the second generation of states studied. The issues were
known, people may have already been identified for participation, and
some level of conversations may have already taken place that facilitated
the process. A number of the states studied had participated in one of
the CGPA Rural Academies and were able to use much of the work done
for that effort in the early stages of the council process. However, the
past efforts may not have always been a positive force. In some cases,
these prior activities meant that turf was already established regarding
rural development, and actors had staked out specific areas. If the council believed that changes should be made, it was difficult to unfreeze
those expectations and begin with a new start.

Similarly, a close relationship between the council activity and that
which was ongoing in the state had both positive and negative consequences. Close proximity to ongoing efforts (either through the council
agenda or its physical location) usually meant that the council activity
would be taken seriously by other actors. In those states where rural was
already defined to include issues beyond those of farming and agriculture, the council did not have to invest in the education that was required to achieve that redefinition.

However, if the council was very close to the governor (or the lieutenant government or the legislature), then it was difficult to differentiate the activity of the council from those efforts. While this closeness was
productive in some states, such proximity might be viewed as a skewing
of the council's agenda (for example, in several states the councils chose
to ignore certain issues because they were effectively told to stay away
from them). Councils that were close to ongoing activity also were vul-

nerable to secondary effects from changes such as elections, budget issues, and state level reorganization.

Generation Differences between Councils. The three generations of councils studied clearly exhibited different characteristics as they engaged in the process. The first generation—the eight pilot states—largely had a trial-and-error approach to the effort both in terms of state level activities and in relationships with Washington, D.C.–based staff. These included Kansas, Maine, Mississippi, Oregon, South Carolina, South Dakota, Texas, and Washington. The pilots indicate a mixed record in terms of outcomes and, as well, most had a pattern of ups and downs during the course of the four years they were in operation.

By contrast, the second generation of states studied (Iowa, New Mexico, North Carolina, and Vermont) appeared to have two attributes that distinguish them from the pilots. First, as a group they were much closer to their governor (or other state officials) than the earlier generation. As such, their agenda was more closely meshed with activity within the state and the membership of the council (and the executive committee) was more likely to include top officials than the first generation. One result of this was an early focus on substantive projects and the development of processes that would facilitate the projects. Second, this group of councils appears to have consciously learned from the experience of the pilots in terms of relationships with Washington, D.C., officials and, as a result, was able to "work the system" quite effectively. These states did not go through the protracted learning process experienced by the pilot states.

The third generation of states studied (New York, North Dakota, Utah, and Wyoming) had some difficulty getting started. Each had somewhat different reasons for these delays; some involved state-level political issues while others involved the adoption of a wait-and-see attitude toward the Clinton administration. As of mid-1994, none of these states had hired an executive director.

Membership Strategies. By definition, the concept of the five partners to be engaged in the council activity suggested that the groups would reach toward an inclusive membership strategy. A number of the councils further defined the partnership categories to include others as well (adding the education sector, and differentiating between for-profit and non-profit private sectors, and including state legislators). A few of the councils, however, attempted to define the membership in more exclusive terms. (The contrast of approaches is found between Texas, with 1,552 members, and South Carolina, with 53 hand-picked members.) Some of the Councils defined membership in terms of position within an agency or organization, others opened it up to individual interests.

The inclusive membership approach provides a way for the council to identify the breadth of issues involved in rural development and to involve relevant actors in the process. At the same time, the open-door policy of the council may mean that the agenda of the group is not stable; when new people come into the group, significant time is required to socialize them to the effort and also to give them an opportunity to reinvent the activity.

Relationships with the Local Level. During the first stages of the initiative, few of the original pilot councils emphasized the involvement of local officials or others who could serve as surrogates for local concerns. By 1993, however, both the original and new councils developed methods for reaching beyond state-level concerns to focus on rural communities. The challenge for the councils was to find ways to bridge state and local relationships without devolving authority to them or involving all the localities within the state. Most councils wanted to reach beyond the state capitol but to do so in a way that did not raise local expectations that the council could "solve" their immediate problems.

Three approaches were used to create these bridges: through membership on the council, through contacts with local groups (such as COGs, or RC&Ds who might be involved in the delivery of activities that were identified by the council), and through meetings held around the state that could help state and federal representatives understand the problems experienced by rural citizens. Representatives of local government, substate entities, community-based organizations, and statewide organizations representing local government (such as leagues of cities and associations of county officials) became members of many of the councils.

Leadership Patterns. Although the initial responsibility for the organization of the pilot councils was given to the Farmers Home Administration representative in the state, few of these officials remained in leadership roles in the councils. In part this occurred because of the depoliticization of the activities (the Farmers Home representative is a political appointee). But it also was a part of a broader pattern of the absence of leadership by "traditional" rural actors, particularly those from USDA. Leadership in the councils rarely stayed with the same individuals; officer positions were rotated and new individuals were often brought into the organization to play leadership roles. Many councils appeared to search for individuals in leadership roles who could play a neutral broker role. In several instances, this meant that leadership came from representatives from the private sector or other groups that were not viewed as traditional rural actors.

Agenda Development. Councils frequently struggled to determine the dimensions of their agenda. By the end of the second year of the project, several of the pilot states focused on process issues to the exclusion of projects. Because the creation and development of a council required attention to process concerns (e.g., methods of communication, internal decision making protocols), this was not surprising. However, once past the developmental stage, there was pressure from members to reach toward project and substantive outcomes. Economic problems within states and political scrutiny made many members conscious of the need to justify their existence in project terms. The second-generation states were more conscious of the need to balance process and substance.

Councils also struggled with the time dimensions of their agenda. Some councils devised activities with very short time frames, concerned that they needed some "victories" to justify their operation. Other councils defined a longer-term agenda, focusing on more systemic problems of rural citizens. Still other councils decided that both dimensions were important and attempted to include both approaches in their strategies.

Determinations of Degree of Visibility. Councils differed in their determination of the degree of visibility that they would take within the state. Some councils sought a low profile approach, seeing their role as adviser or facilitator to others. These councils were not likely to receive much newspaper publicity but provided assistance to state and federal agencies (for example, some councils assisted the REA and the NEA in the establishment of project priorities). Other councils chose a more high-profile strategy, playing an active role in policy discussions, taking positions on state legislation, and vying with other actors for public attention.

Demographic Characteristics of the State. While geographical proximity does not explain many of the similarities or differences between states, there does appear to be a difference between the councils in small, rural states and all other states. The councils were more important and visible in small, homogeneous, and essentially rural states. Larger states with more diversity in population (including tension between urban and rural sectors) were less likely to invest heavily in council activity.

Impact on the Policy System

Change. This effort has operated in an environment characterized by turbulence and constant change. Participants in the process cannot assume that what works today will be effective tomorrow. Change comes from multiple levels: the churning that occurs through the political environment at both the national and state levels, the economy and (occasionally) natural disasters and other unpleasant surprises (e.g., the Midwest flood). It emerges from the idiosyncrasies of the individuals who participate in such an effort. It requires policy designers to be modest in their efforts.

Diversity. The Partnership provides evidence that it is possible to create a policy design that acknowledges that "one size doesn't fit all" and yet at the same time provides the structure for a learning system where participants can learn from one another. The construct of the effort has allowed states to respond differently, in ways that reflected the unique characteristics of their state populations, institutions, and processes. Many of the specific activities that took form in councils were developed as a result of state-specific opportunities to share information, develop common norms, and to create a sense of a collective enterprise.

Flexibility. Unlike most federal initiatives, the Partnership has worked to institutionalize itself in nonrigid, nonbureaucratic ways. It has been adaptable, has provided opportunities for participants to think in new ways, and stimulated their receptivity to engage in new behaviors. While a feature of the effort, flexibility is difficult to protect in traditional governmental systems. As such, flexibility hangs as a slender thread in the Partnership.

New Modes of Intergovernmental Relationships. The design of the Partnership has provided an unusual opportunity to combine both bottom-up and top-down strategies. Unlike most intergovernmental forms (which choose between one or the other), this effort provided for legitimate vertical (federal, state, local) as well as horizontal (interagency, interorganizational) involvement.

Collaboration. The creation of an ethic of collaboration has been pervasive throughout the Partnership and has involved a wide array of constituent groups. It took several forms—it created forums that provided venues for communication between players and it moved into the creation of arenas that provided a setting for collaborative policy-making and implementation. Collaborative environments were found in the SRDCs as well as in Washington, D.C. While conflicts and disagreements continued in those settings, the Partnership provided a way for participants to manage their points of tension and to appreciate—if not always agree with—the perspectives of other players. Care was taken to avoid turf battles both in the states and in Washington.

Process and Product. The experience with the Partnership indicates that there is a close relationship between investment in process issues and the ability to move toward product outcomes. The complex environment that surrounds the effort makes it difficult to move into a simple task orientation. SRDCs, for example, provided a way for participants to change attitudes and identify problems that crossed traditional agency or organizational lines. Without investing in the development of the organizations, councils would not be able to reach toward specific product outcomes. At the same time, however, the focus on process issues sometimes made the creation of a product seem remote.

Energy. Despite the ups and downs of relationships and uncertainties surrounding the Partnership, participants in all aspects of the effort were willing to spend one of their scarcest resources—time and energy—on Partnership activities. The Partnership evokes unusually sustained and high levels of time and commitment from the participants. SRDC members and others invested heavily in the effort and were willing to fight for its continuation.

Conclusions

The National Rural Development Partnership is a very different initiative in 1994 than was envisioned at its inception four years earlier. The road that was traveled over this period by a wide range of participants in the states, as well as in Washington, D.C., was not the path that they expected to traverse. During these four years, the participants learned many things. Most of all they learned that there was no consensus on what could be accomplished through these efforts and that expectations about uniform and consistent performance were unrealistic.

This "learning" posed special challenges for this study. It required the researchers to acknowledge that there are multiple criteria and diverse points of view throughout the process. What is clear and obvious for one set of participants—whether in Washington, D.C., or within the SRDCs—is controversial and murky for another. As this discussion has indicated, performance throughout the Partnership has not been uniform. Some SRDCs have been more effective in achieving their own goals than have others. Yet, overall, the process has been useful and has made some significant or noticeable contributions throughout.

While most rural development efforts are ultimately aimed at improving the economy of rural areas (and, as a result, indirectly aimed at improving the living conditions of rural residents), councils cannot be assessed in terms of their immediate effect on jobs and income. This is true for at least two reasons. First, councils are not involved in activities that directly affect the economy of rural areas but, rather, are aimed at having an impact on institutions that are engaged in the rural development arena. Second, councils are too new to expect such an impact.

At the same time, there are a number of indicators of success involving the Partnership. A relatively small and lean budget produced visible and often useful activity. Participants were willing to spend time and energy on the effort. The Partnership was able to deal with a broad range of issues related to rural development, working with a definition of the field that include both the traditional aspects (e.g., agriculture) as well as less traditional areas, such as human services and environmental concerns. The Partnership produced a number of demonstrations and projects that provided examples of new ways of doing things. Overall, the costs of the effort were outweighed by the benefits gleaned from it.

Mechanisms were developed to identify rural issues and utilize community input in the process. The networks that were created through SRDCs allowed opportunities to share information, to devise spin-offs, to develop new or improved personal relationships, and to provide the setting for collaboration. For the most part, the process was inclusive and developed ways to bring relevant actors to the table. The Partnership provided the venue for attitude change involving multiple players, particularly in terms of federal-state relationships. Evidence of an attitude change comes from the willingness of participants to talk about new ways of carrying out their work, even if they are not actually yet doing so. The shared leadership model that emerged in most SRDCs provided evidence that more than the paid staff member cared about the process.

However, one must acknowledge the limitations of the effort. The changes in the external environment over the four years of the effort meant it was difficult to define the Partnership's overall purpose. SRDCs generally adopted a low visibility posture and were not designed to be major policy actors. As a result, they operated in a way that was tangential to the core state and federal rural policy system. Relationships that were developed were often at the individual, not the institutional, level. Although traditional accountability relationships did not appear to be appropriate for the effort, it was difficult to define and measure accountability expectations for the various segments of the Partnership. Most of all, the experience of the Partnership indicates that efforts at shared leadership and new modes of behavior are extremely fragile and vulnerable.

What Does it All Mean?

There are two perspectives that help one understand the National Rural Development Partnership: the intergovernmental perspective and the rural development policy perspective. It is useful to return to these perspectives in an assessment of the NRDC experience.

The Intergovernmental Perspective

This effort took place in a policy environment characterized by constant conflict about the appropriate roles of federal, state, and local governments. American history—particuarly in the twentieth century—has been puncuated by accusations of too little or too much national government interference. Pendulum swings from one perspective to another have been frequent, vacillating between strategies that rely on bottom-up approaches and those that accentuate top-down methods.

The NRDP is a departure from this pattern. It showed that it is possible to create a setting that recognizes multiple perspectives and combines top-down and bottom-up approaches. It indicated that collaborative efforts between levels of government are possible. Despite the diversity (and often conflict) between actors, one can develop techniques that respect the perspectives of participants with very different goals, interests, and organizational realities.

Although much of what was accomplished within the Partnership was described as a part of "the new governance" approach, this experience suggests that it is somewhat misleading to view this effort simply as an example of the Osborne and Gaebler remedies for governmental change. The changes that took place through effort were both more lasting and stronger and yet, at the same time, more modest in outcome reach than the promises of the reinvention movement. While not achieving the sorts of headlines commanded by the reinvention gurus, one might expect the efforts undertaken through the Partnership to be sustained over the years.

The experience of the Partnership also stands as strong evidence of the breadth of policy actors in the late twentieth century. Boundaries between public and private groups are often very permeable. In this case, representatives from federal, state, local, and tribal governments were joined by individuals from both the for-profit and nonprofit private sector. This experience reinforces the views of those who have argued that intergovernmental dialogue crosses traditional boundaries of governmental action.

The effort also provided participants with modified views about the behavior of federal bureaucrats, particularly those found in the nation's capitol. The NRDC—the Washington-based element within the Partnership—provided a mechanism for intergovernmental learning; federal staff were able to "hear" state-level concerns and perspectives. They were amenable to change, willing to reach out, and responsive to suggestions for changes in their behavior. Involvement in the NRDC gave career bureaucrats who may not have formal job descriptions as boundary spanners an opportunity to view themselves as innovators or entrepreneurs.

The NRDC activities suggest that interagency efforts can be designed to minimize turf battles by working at the margins of agendas and missions of participating agencies and smoothing out organizational or policy problems in this way. It suggests that boundary-spanning organizations—not simply boundary-spanning activities—are both possible and productive in the federal government.

As has been noted, however, one should not expect these types of intergovernmental activities to yield dramatic changes or outcomes that rationalize a policy system in a comprehensive way. It appears that this is particularly true when the participating group is composed of individuals with very different perspectives. And while the specific outcomes of the Partnership were often modest (or, to some, even trivial), new relationships and understandings were created and spun off at both the national and state level. These have the promise of leading to more significant change in the future.

The Partnership was also able to wrap itself in a nonpartisan cloak, largely through the active involvement of the National Governors' Association. It is quite likely that the effort would not have been sustained in the transition from the Bush to the Clinton administration without the NGA's support.

The Rural Development Policy Issue

The Partnership also produced useful experience related to the rural development policy field. In many ways, one can see the effort as an extension of past programs and initiatives undertaken by earlier presidents and administrations. Yet at the same time, the collaborative intergovernmental frame around the rural policy issue appeared to move it into different directions than had taken place in the past.

It was somewhat surprising that the initiative was able to avoid a direct confrontation with the traditional agricultural interest groups and congressional committees. The low visibility and nonpolitical posture that was assumed by the effort clearly protected it from such a clash and the effort seemed to dance around the traditionally powerful farm constituency. During the Bush administration, disinterest in rural development by top political appointees and support from middle-level political appointees allowed the Partnership to develop in a protected environment. By the time the Clinton administration took office, there was broader interest in many of the rural development concerns that undergirded the Partnership but preoccupation during the first two years of the Clinton era with the reorganization of the U.S. Department of Agriculture.

As has been noted, the Partnership was able to move into states about the same time that governors acknowledged that the rural issue was of concern to them. This confluence of interest had several positive dimensions. First, it commanded some level of support from governors (at least enough to express interest in forming a council). Second, because the rural concern was new for many governors, there was a policy vacuum within governors' offices around this issue and only a few of them had to "undo" their own activities (or modify them significantly) to create the space for an SRDC.

Perhaps one of the most surprising aspects of the Partnership was its ability to deal with the extraordinary diversity found within rural America. Many efforts at national change tend to be crafted as "one size fits all" designs. The Partnership, by contrast, was designed in a way that created a national effort that was flexible enough to be molded to individual state needs. The range of structures as well as substantive experiences of SRDCs provides evidence of this flexibility. The eclectic approach to rural development, embracing both economic and community development aspects of the area, gave states enough discretion and autonomy to shape the program in their own image. Yet at the same time, the initiative was clearly a national effort with an identity that transcended the individual activities within the states. In addition, states were able to learn from one another—despite the acknowledged differences in their populations, geographic realities, and political cultures.

What Comes Next?

How generalizable is the NRDC experience? There are aspects of this activity that may be idiosyncratic to the rural development issue. It is a relatively low visibility policy issue that rarely commands newspaper headlines. It was possible for the partnership activity to develop in a protected, depoliticized environment without the attention of either interest groups or congressional players.

However, much of what has occurred in the National Rural Development Partnership is generalizable to other policy areas. The effort was able to assist in broadening or redefining the rural policy issue. Other issues that are undergoing redefinition may be amenable to the networking, boundary-spanning strategy. Perhaps most encouraging, however, is the evidence that the baggage of the past in intergovernmental relations can be lightened and that it is possible for individuals with very different perspectives to work together for the benefit of a group of Americans.

APPENDIX A. Nonmetropolitan Population—Size and Location, 1980–1900

| State | Population Size | | Population Change | Share Of Total (%) | | Population Share by Size (%) | | | | | | | | |
| | | | | | | Over 20,000 | | 2,500–19,999 | | Under 2,500 | | Adjacent to Metro | |
	1980	1990	1980–1990	1980	1990	1980	1990	1980	1990	1980	1990	1980	1990
Vermont	391,309	425,679	34,370	76.51	75.64	0.00	0.00	88.29	87.72	11.71	12.28	34.08	34.67
Maine	672,199	732,933	60,734	59.77	59.69	50.71	50.13	45.47	45.73	3.82	4.14	59.58	61.03
New York	1,688,788	1,746,558	57,770	9.62	9.71	65.34	65.22	33.31	33.41	1.35	1.37	70.35	69.44
Iowa	1,690,762	1,554,044	-136,718	58.03	55.97	25.76	26.22	63.01	62.85	11.24	10.92	41.26	42.10
Kansas	1,210,779	1,175,674	-35,105	51.22	47.45	32.27	32.72	49.02	49.52	18.71	17.76	22.43	22.82
North Dakota	418,382	381,412	-36,970	64.10	59.71	13.96	15.19	40.17	40.94	45.87	43.88	10.89	10.73
South Dakota	581,333	572,195	-9,138	84.16	82.21	18.46	20.43	45.47	46.12	36.06	33.45	9.98	9.95
Mississippi	1,804,453	1,797,542	-6,911	71.59	69.86	33.58	32.98	51.04	51.81	15.38	15.21	17.57	17.88
North Carolina	2,677,643	2,871,048	193,405	45.52	43.31	34.01	33.97	52.10	52.24	13.89	13.80	53.88	54.53
South Carolina	1,256,461	1,373,659	117,198	40.25	39.40	35.61	38.99	61.65	58.31	2.75	2.70	67.94	65.82
New Mexico	786,854	898,982	112,128	60.39	59.34	65.68	61.49	31.57	35.78	2.85	2.73	30.38	32.01
Texas	2,921,723	3,119,455	197,732	20.53	18.36	19.08	19.07	73.06	73.08	7.86	7.85	55.80	57.71
Oregon	869,829	895,154	25,325	33.03	31.49	0.00	63.85	0.00	31.56	4.64	4.59	33.25	33.59
Washington	809,888	890,506	80,618	19.60	18.30	61.59	60.18	32.73	34.43	5.69	5.39	51.82	52.71
Utah	322,709	387,033	54,324	22.77	22.46	17.18	18.13	69.73	69.73	13.08	12.14	48.16	48.18
Wyoming	397,701	392,362	-5,339	84.70	86.50	35.06	36.39	58.74	57.71	6.20	5.90	5.22	4.40
Total	18,510,813	19,214,236	703,423										

Source: U.S. Census Summary Tape Files, U.S. Department of Commerce.

231

APPENDIX B. Nonmetropolitan Population: Age Structure and Education, 1980-1990

State	Over 65		Under 18		Over 25 High School		Non–High School		16-19 Dropout	
	1980	1990	1980	1990	1980	1990	1980	1990	1980	1990
Vermont	12.48	12.91	30.60	27.57	69.15	79.09	0.00	9.45	10.11	9.05
Maine	12.87	13.69	31.04	27.26	67.46	77.69	0.00	9.47	10.90	8.95
New York	12.66	13.46	30.53	27.07	65.48	75.09	0.00	8.72	8.83	8.40
Iowa	15.42	17.80	29.98	27.41	68.76	77.97	0.00	11.32	7.61	5.90
Kansas	15.92	16.87	28.83	27.97	69.57	77.84	0.00	10.36	10.64	8.39
North Dakota	14.20	17.06	31.89	29.61	61.76	72.04	0.00	18.53	8.22	5.07
South Dakota	13.66	15.41	32.04	30.32	66.46	75.74	0.00	14.53	11.39	7.85
Mississippi	12.62	13.38	34.57	31.27	50.21	60.01	0.00	18.09	18.19	12.62
North Carolina	11.42	13.95	30.97	26.48	48.43	63.66	0.00	16.38	17.50	13.44
South Carolina	10.23	12.65	33.73	29.07	47.78	63.26	0.00	16.56	14.37	12.48
New Mexico	9.50	11.14	35.61	32.58	64.98	71.75	0.00	13.04	19.34	12.27
Texas	15.34	15.89	31.36	29.51	50.03	62.80	0.00	18.32	19.22	13.59
Oregon	11.92	15.50	30.37	27.44	71.94	77.67	0.00	7.36	15.64	11.97
Washington	12.43	15.11	30.05	27.92	72.43	78.20	0.00	7.96	13.70	12.75
Utah	8.97	10.60	40.40	39.57	76.50	82.23	0.00	4.51	11.70	6.60
Wyoming	8.20	10.36	33.03	31.38	77.07	82.68	0.00	5.95	15.03	6.96

Source: U.S. Census Summary Tape Files, U.S. Department of Commerce.

APPENDIX C. Nonmetropolitan Population: Race and Ethnicity, 1980-1990

State	White		Black		Native American		Hispanic		Others	
	1980	1990	1980	1990	1980	1990	1980	1990	1980	1990
Vermont	99.29	98.80	0.20	0.27	0.22	0.43	0.62	0.60	0.29	0.50
Maine	99.00	98.53	0.27	0.36	0.42	0.57	0.46	0.55	0.31	0.54
New York	96.95	95.12	1.71	2.78	0.47	0.57	1.14	1.93	0.94	1.53
Iowa	98.81	98.36	0.42	0.53	0.17	0.22	0.66	0.75	0.69	0.89
Kansas	95.11	93.43	2.39	2.59	0.68	0.89	2.49	3.74	1.82	3.08
North Dakota	95.07	93.34	0.30	0.45	4.17	5.65	0.44	0.65	0.46	0.56
South Dakota	91.59	90.30	0.32	0.41	7.65	8.54	0.57	0.83	0.45	0.75
Mississippi	62.06	61.34	37.31	37.85	0.30	0.41	0.85	0.43	0.33	0.40
North Carolina	72.68	73.01	24.98	24.08	2.03	2.30	0.85	0.74	0.31	0.61
South Carolina	60.75	61.80	38.65	37.39	0.20	0.26	1.19	0.58	0.40	0.54
New Mexico	72.57	72.78	1.59	1.62	12.07	13.02	34.60	35.96	13.77	12.58
Texas	83.83	81.07	9.10	8.50	0.35	0.43	18.93	21.87	6.72	10.01
Oregon	96.07	94.52	0.23	0.30	1.68	2.18	2.58	3.87	2.02	3.00
Washington	94.71	92.33	0.46	0.60	2.34	2.61	2.84	5.11	2.49	4.46
Utah	94.40	93.61	0.21	0.20	3.50	3.65	3.02	3.60	1.89	2.54
Wyoming	94.84	93.71	0.73	0.75	1.83	2.41	5.53	5.82	2.61	3.13

Source: U.S. Census Summary Tape Files, U. S. Department of Commerce.

APPENDIX D. Nonmetropolitan Economy: Sectoral Distribution of Income, 1979–1989

State	Nonmetro Share of State Total		Farm Nonmetro		Transfer Payment		Manufacturing		Services		Government	
	1979	1989	1979	1989	1979	1989	1979	1989	1979	1989	1979	1989
Vermont	75.01	72.58	3.84	1.98	15.59	14.87	18.03	12.71	13.04	16.23	9.48	9.30
Maine	57.35	56.47	1.42	1.11	18.43	17.18	21.25	16.63	10.38	13.19	14.76	13.07
New York	6.33	6.15	2.47	1.57	18.65	19.16	20.44	14.36	10.97	13.61	12.20	14.65
Iowa	56.00	53.40	13.30	10.68	12.44	16.25	14.55	13.77	8.28	10.90	8.60	9.42
Kansas	46.10	41.07	10.49	6.78	13.71	17.63	10.80	9.32	9.29	11.45	11.24	12.83
North Dakota	62.55	59.00	17.14	11.25	13.26	19.85	3.65	3.75	8.97	11.14	11.05	12.22
South Dakota	71.00	67.43	19.55	15.07	13.78	17.72	5.35	5.95	8.66	11.05	11.50	11.61
Mississippi	67.30	65.20	6.74	9.75	18.20	22.18	19.57	18.77	9.57	11.43	12.00	11.87
North Carolina	40.33	37.82	4.27	3.51	15.88	17.41	25.48	21.14	8.19	9.55	11.61	11.25
South Carolina	36.61	35.25	2.81	1.79	16.36	18.26	28.25	21.50	8.31	10.80	12.51	12.24
New Mexico	49.07	43.49	5.13	3.76	15.28	20.24	4.35	4.52	9.44	11.98	15.55	16.23
Texas	17.52	15.68	8.32	7.43	15.33	19.64	10.77	8.50	8.06	9.22	9.11	10.55
Oregon	30.01	28.23	4.64	5.45	14.67	19.28	21.41	16.25	9.26	12.09	12.04	11.73
Washington	17.64	15.56	7.33	7.95	15.15	19.77	17.37	11.82	8.48	10.15	13.34	13.80
Utah	20.98	20.57	4.55	4.25	13.09	16.49	11.14	14.03	7.97	11.26	15.29	15.83
Wyoming	66.95	68.68	4.17	1.88	8.37	13.98	3.56	3.22	10.02	11.59	11.35	16.39

Source: Local Area Personal Income, Bureau of Economic Analysis, U.S. Department of Commerce.

APPENDIX E. Nonmetropolitan Economy: Sectoral Distribution of Employment, 1979 and 1989

State	1979 Total	1989 Total	1979 Agriculture/ Farming Mining	1989 Agriculture/ Farming Mining	1979 Manu- factur- ing	1989 Manu- factur- ing	1979 Finance Insurance/ Real Estate	1989 Finance Insurance/ Real Estate	1979 Govern- ment	1989 Govern- ment	1979 Services	1989 Services
Vermont	74.57	71.75	6.99	5.02	20.64	15.27	4.87	6.55	14.37	12.79	24.18	27.64
Maine	55.64	54.81	6.57	5.01	24.14	18.22	3.13	4.20	19.37	16.93	19.65	23.65
New York	7.29	7.50	7.01	5.53	21.44	15.94	4.14	4.40	19.46	19.50	21.72	25.11
Iowa	55.22	52.63	19.03	15.07	15.20	15.57	4.07	4.80	14.16	14.37	16.54	20.49
Kansas	48.64	43.82	17.85	15.69	11.90	11.06	4.44	4.89	18.55	20.89	16.45	19.34
North Dakota	60.72	55.73	25.53	21.17	4.29	4.51	3.53	4.44	17.26	18.45	16.53	21.42
South Dakota	68.94	64.20	20.84	17.98	6.96	8.34	4.18	4.95	18.76	18.46	17.51	21.29
Mississippi	68.54	66.11	11.87	8.32	24.33	25.10	3.21	3.96	18.35	17.93	15.52	16.82
North Carolina	40.69	37.07	11.40	6.08	30.06	27.38	3.31	4.12	15.56	15.68	13.72	16.05
South Carolina	37.17	34.57	7.37	5.15	31.48	26.07	3.14	4.73	18.48	17.30	14.14	17.02
New Mexico	47.27	41.05	17.48	11.21	5.13	5.51	4.37	4.69	22.83	23.44	17.44	22.89
Texas	17.52	15.08	23.31	18.33	12.27	10.77	3.92	4.78	15.21	17.55	15.55	19.01
Oregon	29.99	28.17	10.63	10.84	19.93	17.12	5.31	5.15	17.79	16.73	16.60	20.95
Washington	18.29	16.07	13.79	9.21	16.14	12.83	4.76	5.33	19.83	19.87	16.61	20.20
Utah	21.11	20.34	17.81	11.37	11.60	13.68	4.03	4.64	22.87	21.65	13.02	19.68
Wyoming	67.24	69.21	23.45	16.55	3.90	3.98	3.53	3.90	16.89	21.91	16.89	21.75

Source: Local Area Personal Income, Bureau of Economic Analysis, U.S. Department of Commerce.

234

About the Authors

Beryl A. Radin is the Chair and Professor of Public Administration and Policy in the Graduate School of Public Affairs at Rockefeller College of the State University of New York at Albany. Currently the president of the Association for Public Policy Analysis and Management, her work has focused on intergovernmental and federalism issues in a number of policy areas (including rural policy, education, and human services). In addition, she has been involved in studies of federal systems in India and Australia. Her publications include numerous articles, book chapters, and several books. Professor Radin has been a consultant to a wide range of government agencies, including the U.S. Department of Agriculture, the World Bank, the National Institute of Mental Health, the Department of Health and Human Services, and NASA. She has received research support from the Ford Foundation, the Aspen Institute, the Fulbright Foundation, the National Science Foundation, and a number of other organizations.

Robert Agranoff is Professor of Public Administration in the School of Public and Environmental Affairs at Indiana University, Bloomington. His work has focused on issues of intergovernmental management both in the United States and in other federal systems, particularly in Spain. Dr. Agranoff is an affiliate faculty member of the Fundacion Ortega y Gossett in Madrid, Spain. A prolific scholar, he has written extensively on intergovernmental questions involving economic development and human services. Professor Agranoff has received research support from several foundations (e.g., the Fulbright Foundation and the Eli Lilly Foundation) as well as a number of federal, state, and local agencies (including organizations in Indiana, U.S. AID, and the U.S. Department of Health and Human Services).

Ann O'M. Bowman is Professor of Government and International Studies at the University of South Carolina. For the past seven years, she has coedited the annual review issues of *Publius: The Journal of Federalism*. She

is the author of a number of articles and several books on state and local
government issues as well as economic development policy. She received
a grant from the Lincoln Institute of Land Policy to study local economic
development. Professor Bowman received a Fulbright grant to teach in
Denmark in 1995–1996. Prior to her academic career, she worked for
the state legislature in Florida.

C. Gregory Buntz is the executive director of the Iowa Peace Institute in
Grinnell, Iowa. The institute is a statewide dispute resolution organiza-
tion that provides mediation services as well as conflict resolution education and training programs. Prior to this position, he was Professor of
Public Policy and Management in the School of Business and Public
Administration at the University of the Pacific, Stockton, California. He
has published articles on conflict management, dispute resolution, rural
economic development policy, and intergovernmental management. Dr.
Buntz has undertaken consulting projects and research for the Aspen
Institute, the U.S. Department of Agriculture, and the U.S. Department
of Health and Human Services.

J. Steven Ott is Associate Professor of Political Science at the University of
Utah, where he is also Director of Public Administration Education in
the Center for Policy and Administration. He has published widely in the
organizational behavior and theory field, including several books and
readers. His current work has focused on health services in several states.
Dr. Ott has received funding from a number of state and local agencies.
Prior to joining the Utah faculty, he was at the University of Maine.

Barbara S. Romzek is Professor of Public Administration in the Department of Public Administration at the University of Kansas. Her research
and teaching interests include public management, accountability, and
employee commitment. Professor Romzek's publications are extensive
and include numerous articles, book chapters, an edited volume, and a
textbook. She consults in the area of public management and personnel
administration and has conducted numerous professional development
and management workshops for federal, state, and local governments as
well as professional management associations. She is currently working
on an evaluation of the implementation and integration of total quality
management principles into State of Kansas human resources management systems.

Robert H. Wilson is Director of the Urban Issues Program and Mike Hogg Professor of Urban Policy in the Lyndon B. Johnson School of Public Affairs at the University of Texas at Austin. His work has focused on state and local development strategies, community participation in state and local policy-making, telecommunications, and Brazilian public policy. He is the author or editor of a large number of articles, book chapters, and books. His research support has come from the Ford Foundation, the National Science Foundation, the Fulbright Commission, and other sources. He has served as a consultant to the United Nations Development Program, the Organization of American States, and the Urban Institute.

Index